Vagrant Virtual Development Environment Cookbook

Over 35 hands-on recipes to help you master Vagrant, and create and manage virtual computational environments

Chad Thompson

[PACKT] open source*
PUBLISHING   community experience distilled

BIRMINGHAM - MUMBAI

Vagrant Virtual Development Environment Cookbook

First published: February 2015

Production reference: 1210215

Published by Packt Publishing Ltd.
Livery Place
35 Livery Street
Birmingham B3 2PB, UK.

ISBN 978-1-78439-374-8

www.packtpub.com

Credits

Author

Chad Thompson

Reviewers

Emilien Kenler

Darius Krištapavičius

Marcelo Pinheiro

Commissioning Editor

Usha Iyer

Acquisition Editor

Richard Brookes-Bland

Content Development Editor

Arwa Manasawala

Technical Editors

Vijin Boricha

Humera Shaikh

Copy Editor

Relin Hedly

Project Coordinator

Danuta Jones

Proofreaders

Simran Bhogal

Bridget Braund

Indexer

Hemangini Bari

Production Coordinator

Aparna Bhagat

Cover Work

Aparna Bhagat

About the Author

Chad Thompson is a software developer, architect, and DevOps specialist in Central Iowa. He has 15 years of experience in creating and deploying applications for the Web. Chad began using Vagrant 3 years ago when he was trying to solve a tough problem in legacy application development. Since then, he has made use of Vagrant and configuration management tools to support the development and deployment of several web applications in data centers and cloud platforms. He holds certifications in Puppet and Oracle technologies and has enjoyed the pleasure of speaking before several technical conferences and camps. Chad holds two degrees in physics and can be found playing low brass instruments in ensembles around the state of Iowa.

Chad has written articles for O'Reilly web publications and the IOUG SELECT Journal (where he briefly worked as an executive editor). Recently, he reviewed the book *Creating Development Environments with Vagrant* for Packt Publishing, and recorded a set of video presentations titled *Learning Git* by Infinite Skills.

I owe a great measure of gratitude to many people for helping me with the production of this book. I would like to thank my colleagues at Dice Holdings Inc. for their support and feedback during the development of the book. I would like to thank Zach Arlen of FullContact in Denver, CO, for introducing me to Vagrant as a solution to a problem years ago. Mostly, I would like to thank my family for their continued love and support.

With the publication of this book, I would also like to offer my gratitude to Dr. Robert Merlino and the late Dr. Nicola D'Angelo of the University of Iowa. They both taught me a great deal about formulating ideas and teaching others, which I hope serves the readers of this book.

About the Reviewers

Emilien Kenler, after working on small web projects, began focusing on game development in 2008 while he was in high school. Until 2011, he worked for different groups and specialized in system administration.

In 2011, he founded a company that sold Minecraft servers while studying computer science engineering. Emilien created a lightweight IaaS (`https://github.com/HostYourCreeper/`) based on new technologies (such as Node.js and RabbitMQ).

Thereafter, he worked at TaDaweb as a system administrator, building its infrastructure and creating tools to manage deployments and monitoring.

In 2014, he began a new adventure at Wizcorp, Tokyo. In 2014, Emilien graduated from the University of Technology of Compiègne.

For Packt Publishing, Emilien has also contributed as a reviewer on other books:

- *Learning Nagios 4, Wojciech Kocjan* (`http://www.packtpub.com/learning-nagios-4/book`)
- *MariaDB High Performance, Pierre MAVRO* (`https://www.packtpub.com/big-data-and-business-intelligence/mariadb-high-performance`)
- *OpenVZ Essentials, Mark Furman,* (`https://www.packtpub.com/virtualization-and-cloud/openvz-essentials`)

Darius Krištapavičius attended Vilnius University and studied software engineering as his major subject. In 2009, Darius started working with web application development and since then, he gained considerable experience and particularly developed various e-commerce systems. While working in this field, he learned the PHP programming language and different frameworks (such as CodeIgniter and Symfony2). At present, Darius is working as a professional web developer and is actively engaged in DevOps method, process automation, principles of Agile, and other associated subjects of web development.

Marcelo Pinheiro is a software engineer from Porto Alegre, Brazil. In 2000, he started to work as a web designer and programmer with ASP and PHP. Marcelo is still in touch with Microsoft .NET Framework and Java to run their respective choice of databases for web applications. Since 2003, he has been using Linux- and Unix-related operational systems, from Slackware to GoboLinux, Arch Linux, CentOS, and Debian. At present, he uses OS X, and he also uses FreeBSD to some extent. Marcelo lost a few nights compiling and applying patches on the Linux kernel to make their desktop work. He is an open source enthusiast and acts as a problem solver, irrespective of the programming language, database, or platform.

After a few years, he moved to São Paulo to work with newer technologies (such as NoSQL, cloud computing, and Ruby), where he began to present tech talks with these technologies in Locaweb, and RS on Rails, the biggest Ruby conference in South Brazil. As an observer, he created some tools to standardize development using tools (such as Vagrant and Ruby gems), some of these in their GitHub, in Locaweb to ensure fast application packaging and reduce deployment rollbacks. In 2013, Marcelo shifted his career focus to become a full-stack developer and began to follow the DevOps movement. In 2014, he attended QConSP-International Software Development Conference as a speaker and spoke about Packer and its use in Locaweb. Currently, Marcelo works as a DevOps engineer at Moip Pagamentos, where he is responsible for creating continuous deployment solutions, which cover non-PCI or PCI compliance environments. He is currently using Go as a preferable programming language.

He loves playing the guitar and spending time with his beloved wife and his cats, apart from traveling and drinking beer. He can be found on his blog (http://salizzar.net), Twitter (https://twitter.com/salizzar), GitHub (https://github.com/salizzar), and Linkedin (https://www.linkedin.com/in/salizzar).

First, I want to thank my wife for her patience, especially on days when I came home from work, ate something quickly, and went straight to my office, returning only to sleep. Secondly, I want to thank my friends, who believed in my potential since the beginning and kept in touch with me despite the distance, and lastly, my mentors Gleicon Moraes and Roberto Gaiser for the incentive and tips that helped me become a better software engineer.

www.PacktPub.com

Support files, eBooks, discount offers, and more

For support files and downloads related to your book, please visit www.PacktPub.com.

Did you know that Packt offers eBook versions of every book published, with PDF and ePub files available? You can upgrade to the eBook version at www.PacktPub.com and as a print book customer, you are entitled to a discount on the eBook copy. Get in touch with us at service@packtpub.com for more details.

At www.PacktPub.com, you can also read a collection of free technical articles, sign up for a range of free newsletters and receive exclusive discounts and offers on Packt books and eBooks.

https://www2.packtpub.com/books/subscription/packtlib

Do you need instant solutions to your IT questions? PacktLib is Packt's online digital book library. Here, you can search, access, and read Packt's entire library of books.

Why Subscribe?

- ▸ Fully searchable across every book published by Packt
- ▸ Copy and paste, print, and bookmark content
- ▸ On demand and accessible via a web browser

Free Access for Packt account holders

If you have an account with Packt at www.PacktPub.com, you can use this to access PacktLib today and view 9 entirely free books. Simply use your login credentials for immediate access.

Table of Contents

Preface

If you have written software on a desktop computer and attempted to deploy your code to another computer (a server), you have already encountered the challenges presented when deploying software. Developers and administrators frequently struggle with errors and defects, when development environments are different from the eventual production machines. There can be a number of differences introduced when the environments are different at the operating system level. Development with desktop operating systems (such as Windows or OS X) can introduce many issues when deploying to production environments that run a Unix (or Linux) environment.

The introduction of desktop hypervisor software allowed developers to develop and test software using virtual machines. A virtual machine is essentially a system within a system, wherein developers working on a desktop operating system can develop and deploy with a copy of the operating system and environment that closely mimics the eventual production environment. When desktop hypervisors became available, development teams found that they could share development environments by sharing the files used by the hypervisors to store the state of virtual machines. In many cases, sharing a virtual machine involved passing around copies of files on a portable hard drive or a shared network folder.

A few years ago, I encountered this specific example when working on a project that involved adding new features to software that ran on an environment, which we could not support with our modern desktop hardware. As many projects reveal, technical debt was introduced to the application by using some very specific features of the Java Development Kit (version 1.5), an environment that was impossible to work on with a 64-bit OS X machine. This machine had dual problems of being a 64-bit machine and it also lacked native support for Java 1.5 XML libraries. The solution to this problem was the creation of a single virtual machine that was shared between developers, passing around a copy of the machine created by a team lead and using it locally to compile and test our modifications.

As time passed by, changes to the environment became an issue, as we began struggling with the differences between not only the development and production environments, but also between our individual development environments as changes were made, making sure that each developer was working on the *latest version* of the virtual machine on that portable hard drive, which soon had a few different versions itself.

Eventually, the problem of maintaining development environments was large enough to begin looking for new solutions. Configuration management approaches helped us to start defining our environment in code, but we still had issues with sharing and maintaining our *base* environment. We found immediate use of an open source project called *Vagrant,* which was gaining some traction.

Vagrant (`http://vagrantup.com`) is a tool that allows you to define a virtual environment with code. A single file allows you to define a basic environment for a virtual machine as well as a series of provisioning actions that prepare the environment for use. Vagrant works by running code (Vagrantfiles) on top of packaged operating system images called *boxes.* The Vagrant code and box files can be versioned and distributed using automated tooling. This allows you to share virtual machines, which is not much different than the process of software development that uses source control.

Using Vagrant boxes and provisioning controlled by Vagrantfiles not only simplified the process of distributing virtual machines (and updates to virtual machines), but it also made the virtual machines we were working with *inexpensive* in terms of effort to rebuild. The amazing thing that we found was that Vagrant not only made it simple to distribute virtual machines, but also gave developers more freedom to experiment and make deeper modifications to the code without losing time due to changes in the development environment that could not be rolled back. This flexibility and a simplified on-boarding process for new developers made it much simpler for the team to spend more time doing software development (and tackling that technical debt!), rather than attempting to fix and find problems due to environments.

I've found Vagrant to be an invaluable tool in my work. I hope that this book can be a valuable resource for you in getting started with Vagrant, or perhaps, using Vagrant in new and different ways.

What this book covers

Chapter 1, Setting Up Your Environment, covers a few basics about hypervisor technology, the installation of Vagrant and VirtualBox, and some simple recipes to get started with Vagrant machines.

Chapter 2, Single Machine Environments, contains recipes to get started with writing single machine Vagrantfiles, including booting machines, forwarding ports, and customizing the virtual machine environment.

Chapter 3, Provisioning a Vagrant Environment, introduces the concept of provisioning Vagrant machines, installing software, and customizing the environment to develop and deploy software. This chapter focuses on using shell (bash) scripting to modify the Vagrant environment.

Chapter 4, Provisioning With Configuration Management Tools, contains simple recipes to provision Vagrant machines with four common configuration management tools: Puppet, Chef, Ansible, and Salt. These tools allow easier configuration of machines that have more complex environments. They also allow Vagrant machines to share the same provisioning instructions as other environments.

Chapter 5, Networked Vagrant Environments, contains recipes focused on networking Vagrant machines with external hosts and with each other. We cover a few topics from the basics of assigning host entries to networking a cluster of Vagrant machines with Consul.

Chapter 6, Vagrant in the Cloud, contains recipes to use Vagrant with cloud providers (specifically, Amazon Web Services and DigitalOcean). It also contains the use of Hashicorp's Atlas tool to share Vagrant environments with remote users.

Chapter 7, Packaging Vagrant Boxes, introduces methods to package Vagrant boxes for others to use. Recipes include the packaging of boxes using manual and automated tools and tips to share your box with others on Atlas.

Appendix A, Vagrant Plugins, gives a short introduction on how to extend the capabilities of Vagrant by developing plugins.

Appendix B, A Puppet Development Environment, expands on the introduction in *Chapter 4, Provisioning With Configuration Management Tools*, to set up a more robust configuration environment to develop Puppet scripts. While the focus is on using Puppet to provision, similar environments can be created to support the configuration management environment of your choice.

Appendix C, Using Docker With Vagrant, is an introduction to use Vagrant to create, deploy, and test Docker (`http://docker.io`) containers. This appendix introduces techniques to launch Docker containers with Vagrant as well as build and test a complete Docker environment.

What you need for this book

To use the recipes in this book, you will need:

- A development machine capable of running virtual machines with hypervisor software, such as VirtualBox (`http://virtualbox.org`) or VMware desktop products (`http://vmware.com`). You would want to get started with the freely available VirtualBox product and later on purchase the plugin to support VMware desktop products. Keep in mind that you will need a machine that is capable of running both your host operating system and also the guest operating systems that you will be creating with Vagrant. You will also want to ensure that you have enough storage (disk space) for virtual machine files. The disks created by Vagrant machines will typically be approximately the size required to operate the guest operating systems (approximately, 5-20 GB of disk space).

- ▶ If you plan on running 64-bit guests, you will also want to ensure that your processor is capable of Intel hardware virtualization (VT-x). In most cases, processors that support 64-bit operating systems already have this support built-in (with some exceptions, such as older Intel Celeron processors). See `https://www.virtualbox.org/manual/ch10.html` for more background on the requirements for hardware virtualization.

- ▶ Using cloud recipes (particularly, recipes involving Amazon Web Services and DigitalOcean) will require accounts with cloud providers. Running the examples might incur charges to your account, so make sure that you understand the financial impacts of running the examples and how to ensure that all created instances have been stopped or terminated to avoid extra charges for the use of computational resources. The recipes in this book are not expensive to run, but they are also not free. Machines that are left running for a period of time could also end up costing more than you had planned on, so make sure that any instance created with Vagrant is eventually destroyed.

Who this book is for

This book is for developers and administrators of nearly all skill levels. Throughout the book, I make a general assumption that you are creating Vagrant machines to support the development of other software. Vagrant itself does not become interesting or useful until you use it to support the deployment and development of other software. Vagrant makes it simple to create local environments that mimic production environments and takes advantage of the same provisioning techniques used on production servers. If you have a mature and robust deployment pipeline, Vagrant allows you to reproduce this process on development machines. If you do not have a robust development pipeline, Vagrant can help you begin developing the scripts and processes, making your development and deployment environments more consistent. Consistent environments will help you to reduce the problems associated with the deployment process, which allows you to focus on producing better software.

Sections

In this book, you will find several headings that appear frequently (Getting ready, How to do it, How it works, There's more, and See also).

To give clear instructions on how to complete a recipe, we use these sections as follows:

Getting ready

This section tells you what to expect in the recipe, and describes how to set up any software or any preliminary settings required for the recipe.

How to do it...

This section contains the steps required to follow the recipe.

How it works...

This section usually consists of a detailed explanation of what happened in the previous section.

There's more...

This section consists of additional information about the recipe in order to make the reader more knowledgeable about the recipe.

See also

This section provides helpful links to other useful information for the recipe.

Conventions

In this book, you will find a number of text styles that distinguish between different kinds of information. Here are some examples of these styles and an explanation of their meaning.

Code words in text, database table names, folder names, filenames, file extensions, pathnames, dummy URLs, user input, and Twitter handles are shown as follows: "The Vagrant installer will extract, copy files, and add the `vagrant` command to the executable path."

A block of code is set as follows:

```
-rw-------  0 cothomps staff 1960775680 Jul 24 20:42 ./box-disk1.vmdk
-rw-------  0 cothomps staff      12368 Jul 24 20:38 ./box.ovf
-rw-r--r--  0 cothomps staff        505 Jul 24 20:42 ./Vagrantfile
```

When we wish to draw your attention to a particular part of a code block, the relevant lines or items are set in bold:

```
# -*- mode: ruby -*-
# vi: set ft=ruby :
VAGRANTFILE_API_VERSION = "2"
Vagrant.configure(VAGRANTFILE_API_VERSION) do |config|
config.vm.box = "chad-thompson/ubuntu-trusty64-gui" config.
vm.provider "virtualbox" do |vbox|
```

```
    vbox.gui = true
  end
end
```

Any command-line input or output is written as follows:

```
vagrant box add http://servername/boxes/environment.box
```

New terms and **important words** are shown in bold. Words that you see on the screen, for example, in menus or dialog boxes, appear in the text like this: "A new installation of VirtualBox will display a welcome message in a window titled **Oracle VM VirtualBox Manager**."

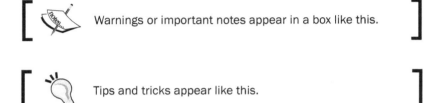

> Warnings or important notes appear in a box like this.

> Tips and tricks appear like this.

Reader feedback

Feedback from our readers is always welcome. Let us know what you think about this book—what you liked or disliked. Reader feedback is important for us as it helps us develop titles that you will really get the most out of.

To send us general feedback, simply e-mail feedback@packtpub.com, and mention the book's title in the subject of your message.

If there is a topic that you have expertise in and you are interested in either writing or contributing to a book, see our author guide at www.packtpub.com/authors.

Customer support

Now that you are the proud owner of a Packt book, we have a number of things to help you to get the most from your purchase.

Downloading the example code

You can download the example code files from your account at http://www.packtpub.com for all the Packt Publishing books you have purchased. If you purchased this book elsewhere, you can visit http://www.packtpub.com/support and register to have the files e-mailed directly to you.

Errata

Although we have taken every care to ensure the accuracy of our content, mistakes do happen. If you find a mistake in one of our books—maybe a mistake in the text or the code—we would be grateful if you could report this to us. By doing so, you can save other readers from frustration and help us improve subsequent versions of this book. If you find any errata, please report them by visiting http://www.packtpub.com/submit-errata, selecting your book, clicking on the **Errata Submission Form** link, and entering the details of your errata. Once your errata are verified, your submission will be accepted and the errata will be uploaded to our website or added to any list of existing errata under the Errata section of that title.

To view the previously submitted errata, go to https://www.packtpub.com/books/content/support and enter the name of the book in the search field. The required information will appear under the **Errata** section.

Piracy

Piracy of copyrighted material on the Internet is an ongoing problem across all media. At Packt, we take the protection of our copyright and licenses very seriously. If you come across any illegal copies of our works in any form on the Internet, please provide us with the location address or website name immediately so that we can pursue a remedy.

Please contact us at copyright@packtpub.com with a link to the suspected pirated material.

We appreciate your help in protecting our authors and our ability to bring you valuable content.

Questions

If you have a problem with any aspect of this book, you can contact us at questions@packtpub.com, and we will do our best to address the problem.

1
Setting Up Your Environment

In this chapter, we will cover:

- ▶ Installing Vagrant and VirtualBox
- ▶ Initializing your first environment
- ▶ Installing Vagrant providers
- ▶ Finding additional Vagrant boxes
- ▶ Using existing virtual machines with Vagrant

Introduction

Over the past decade, data centers and server architectures have been revolutionized with the practice of *virtualization*—the ability to host computational resources that once depended on hardware in specialized software containers. The ability to use flexible virtual environments on shared computational resources allowed system administrators to become more flexible on how software is configured and deployed. More recently, the advantages of virtualization got extended to the desktop. Software packages such as the VMware Desktop (Fusion for OS X, Workstation for Windows and Linux) along with Oracle VirtualBox make it possible to run different operating systems and environments in the context of the desktop operating systems. Web developers, for example, can run a Linux-based web server on their desktop without modifying the parent operating system or running entirely separate physical computers.

Vagrant was originally launched as an open source project by Mitchell Hashimoto with the core idea to make virtual machines simpler to manage. Virtual machines have been used for software development for some time. Some software development teams developed workflows around building virtual machines and shared them with others—often through the creation of a completely configured virtual machine (referred to as a "golden image") and shared by users. If you have worked with virtual environments for any length of time, you are likely to be familiar with the process of downloading a multigigabyte virtual machine or passing around a portable drive with virtual machine files. Vagrant makes it possible to share consistent and reproducible environments with code rather than binary files. In practical terms, this means that a virtual machine is often used by checking out the source definitions from version control and running a `vagrant up` command rather than finding ways to create, copy, and manage up-to-date versions of large binary files. More recently, Vagrant proved to be so useful and pervasive that Hashimoto founded HashiCorp to support the ongoing development and support of Vagrant. In addition to core Vagrant development, HashiCorp created add-on software that allows Vagrant to use other hypervisor software (plugins for VMware Fusion and Workstation) as well as other software projects. More recently, Vagrant has been extended with the provider framework in order to make development with containers (such as Docker available at `http://docker.io`) simpler. Developing with containers gives developers the option to create lightweight isolated Linux environments that can be easier and faster to work with these virtual machines.

In any case, the first step when using Vagrant is to set up a working environment in order to define and run Vagrant machines. With Vagrant, a virtual machine and the software that runs inside the machine can be defined in a special file called a **Vagrantfile**. A Vagrantfile defines a virtual machine, how this virtual machine interacts with the outside world, and how software is installed on the virtual machine.

Before we start with Vagrant, let's review some terminology that we will use in this chapter and throughout the book.

A **virtual machine** is a computing node that runs within a software process that mimics the behavior of a physical computer. The software process (often called a **hypervisor**) provides infrastructure to virtual machines such as computing power (CPU), memory (RAM), and interfaces to external resources (such as networking interfaces and physical (disk) storage).

A **host machine** is a computer that runs a hypervisor to host virtual machines. A host machine will, most likely, run one of two types of hypervisor:

> ▶ A *Type 1 hypervisor* that runs natively on host machine hardware. A Type 1 hypervisor does not require a separate operating system; the hypervisor itself controls access to physical resources and shares them between hosted virtual environments. Most modern shared virtual environments are Type 1 hypervisors (common examples include VMware ESX/ESXi, Oracle VM Server, and some versions of Microsoft Hyper-V). These environments are typically installed as shared resources that define server infrastructure or other shared resources.

- A *Type 2 hypervisor* is a software that runs on top of a traditional operating system. In this case, the hypervisor uses the underlying operating system to control (or define) resources and gain access to resources. Most use cases for Vagrant use Type 2 hypervisors as host environments for virtual machines and this will be the environment that will be used throughout this book. The two common Type 2 hypervisors are Oracle VirtualBox and the VMware Workstation / Fusion family of software. We'll take a look at these products later on in this chapter.

In both cases, the hypervisor is responsible for managing physical resources and sharing them with one or many virtual machines.

A **guest machine** is a virtual machine that runs within the hypervisor. The machines that we will define with Vagrant are guest machines that operate within the environment controlled by our hypervisor. Guest machines are often entirely different operating systems and environments from the host environment—something we can definitely use to our advantage when developing software to be executed on a different environment from our host. (For example, a developer can write software within a Linux environment that runs on a Windows host or vice versa.)

As we proceed with the recipes, you'll see that Vagrant is a useful tool to manage the complexities of hypervisors and virtual machines. Vagrant also allows a consistent API to operate virtual machines on different hypervisors—something that can make sharing virtual environments much simpler between teams and people working on different platforms.

Installing Vagrant and VirtualBox

Before we explore how to use Vagrant, we'll first need to install the software required to manage a virtual machine environment (a hypervisor) as well as the Vagrant software itself. In this recipe, we will install VirtualBox to use it with Vagrant. VirtualBox is an open source hypervisor that was initially the only hypervisor supported by Vagrant. As such, VirtualBox is broadly supported by the Vagrant community.

Getting ready

Before we install the VirtualBox and Vagrant software, we'll need to obtain its latest versions.

VirtualBox can be downloaded from the project website at `http://virtualbox.org`. You'll notice that while VirtualBox has a corporate sponsor (Oracle), the VirtualBox software is open source and freely available for use. VirtualBox is also supported on a wide variety of host platforms with a few limitations:

- VirtualBox is supported only on Intel or AMD hardware. The Intel/AMD platform constitutes the vast majority of personal computing platforms in use today, but there are always exceptions. Make sure to check the VirtualBox manual for supported operating systems.

▶ While the VirtualBox specifications note fairly minimal system requirements, keep in mind that your single workstation will be supporting two (or more) running operating systems at the same time. A rough guideline for system's RAM is to have minimal RAM to support your host operating system, plus the operating system requirements of the individual guests. This will vary depending on the guest operating system. For example, if you are running your Vagrant environments on a Windows machine with 8 GB of RAM, you'll want to limit your Vagrant machine to use 6 GB of RAM, leaving enough working memory for the host operating system. If the operating systems are using too much memory, you'll notice some significant performance issues as the host operating system begins paging to disk.

The packages downloaded from the VirtualBox site will be native to your particular operating system. Take particular care when downloading Linux packages; you'll want to ensure that the downloaded package is compatible with the operating system and system architecture. (Linux users might also find VirtualBox in repositories provided by your operating system provider. These packages are often outdated, but they may work with Vagrant. Be sure to check the minimum versions required in the Vagrant documentation.)

Vagrant packages are operating system-specific and can be downloaded from the Vagrant website at `http://vagrantup.com`. Download the version appropriate for your system.

Warning

Vagrant was initially available for download through the use of RubyGems and is still available through `gem install`. This version, however, is significantly outdated and unable to support most of the features that will be covered in this book. Due to the complexity of managing Ruby dependencies, the Vagrant maintainers decided to ship Vagrant as a standalone package with an embedded Ruby interpreter to avoid possible conflicts. It's recommended that you use the package distributions from `http://vagrantup.com`, wherever possible.

How to do it...

Installing Vagrant and VirtualBox is similar to other software installation for your particular operating system. The project sites include detailed instructions to install Vagrant or VirtualBox on the software platform of your choice. We'll go through the installation of Vagrant and VirtualBox on OS X. There are versions available for Windows and a wide variety of Linux distributions. In any case, the installers, all roughly, follow the same procedure for the OS X installation demonstrated here.

Installing VirtualBox

1. Download a copy of the installer from the VirtualBox website. In this example, we'll choose the version for OS X hosts.

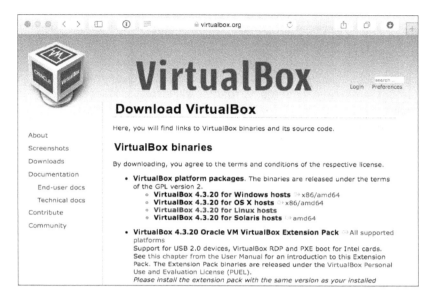

2. Start the VirtualBox installer by opening the downloaded (OS X disk image) file. The disk image will include an installer along with documentation for VirtualBox and, if necessary, an uninstall tool. Double-click on the installer package to begin the VirtualBox installation.

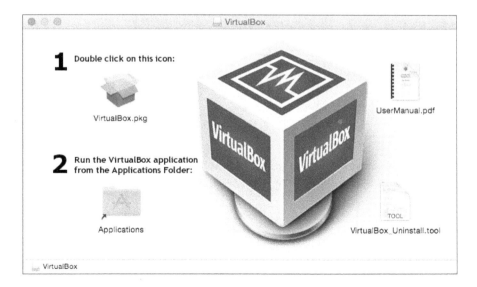

The VirtualBox installation will require administrator permissions to both install the package and to modify system network settings. The installation of the VirtualBox hypervisor requires the installer to create a set of new network interfaces, which will allow network communications between the host and guest operating systems.

3. Once the installation is complete, the installer will give you the option to open VirtualBox. A new installation of VirtualBox will display a welcome message in a window titled **Oracle VM VirtualBox Manager**. Once a few virtual machines are created, this dialog displays information about the machines created using VirtualBox (or the Vagrant VirtualBox provider).

After the installation is completed and we are presented with the **VirtualBox Manager** dialog box, we can proceed with the installation of Vagrant itself.

Installing Vagrant

1. Download a copy of the Vagrant installer from the Vagrant website (`http://vagrantup.com`). Select the appropriate version for your operating system. In this case, we will download the OS X universal installer that will download an installer that will work for both 32 and 64-bit machines. For the features discussed in this chapter (and for the majority of recipes in the book), you'll want to ensure that the Vagrant version is 1.5 or greater.

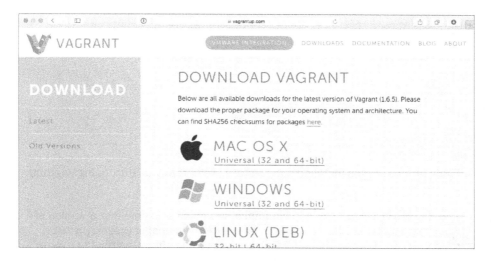

2. The OS X download contains an installation package and an uninstall tool. Double-click on the installer to begin the installation. The Vagrant package installer is a native OS X package that will run the OS X software installer. Installing Vagrant will not be much different than installing other OS X software.

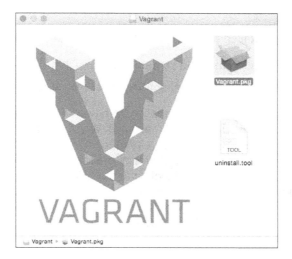

3. The Vagrant installer will extract, copy files, and add the `vagrant` command to the executable path. On OS X, this will install Vagrant to the default OS X `Applications/` directory. Vagrant is a command-line driven application, however, there are no programs accessed from the OS X Finder.

4. Verify that Vagrant is working by opening a terminal window and executing the `vagrant version` command.

```
1. cothomps@cthompson: ~ (zsh)
▶ vagrant version
Installed Version: 1.6.5
Latest Version: 1.6.5

You're running an up-to-date version of Vagrant!


▶ ▮
```

With both software packages installed successfully, we're ready to start using Vagrant!

If you are a Ruby user or programmer, you might also note that a version of Vagrant is available via the Ruby gem package manager (`gem install vagrant`). When Vagrant 2.0 was released, the official distributions were released as packages with an embedded Ruby runtime. As such, the versions installed with the gem installer are outdated and will not work with most of the examples in this book.

How it works...

What we've done here is installed a working Vagrant environment that consists of:

- ▶ A hypervisor application that can contain virtual machines
- ▶ Vagrant, a tool that makes managing these machines simpler and available in code

It's important here to note that Vagrant is simply a framework to manage virtual machines, not an application to create and host virtual machines. When using a Vagrant environment, you'll often encounter errors that are not only related to Vagrant itself, but also related to the hypervisor application. For this reason, the choice of hypervisor becomes important when working with Vagrant. Many users can find tools that make VMware Desktop applications (Fusion and Workstation) simpler to troubleshoot when working with many virtual machines, whereas some will find it simpler to use external hypervisors (such as Amazon EC2 or DigitalOcean). Some experimentation might find the right workflow for you—keep in mind that Vagrant is a layer on top of many choices.

See also

- VirtualBox: `http://virtualbox.org`. In particular, note the installation instructions for platforms other than OS X.

- Vagrant: `http://vagrantup.com`.

- Vagrant installation instructions: `https://docs.vagrantup.com/v2/installation/`.

Initializing your first environment

Once we have a working Vagrant environment with a hypervisor, we can initialize our first environment. There are two ways with which we can often work with Vagrant:

- In a new environment with a newly initialized Vagrantfile
- In an environment maintained in source control that has a Vagrantfile included in a project

Keeping Vagrantfiles and projects in a source control system (such as Git, SVN, and so on) is a powerful technique to manage and track changes in Vagrant environments. The use of source control systems allows developers and users to *check in* Vagrant projects, which makes modification of the project less risky and makes the sharing of Vagrant projects much simpler. The use of source code repositories reinforces the concept of *infrastructure as code*, giving administrators the ability to recreate environments in a consistent and repeatable way.

No matter how you use Vagrant, knowing how to initialize a new environment will aid you to effectively use Vagrant. In this example, we will initialize a new environment and look at the basic configuration of a Vagrantfile.

Getting ready

We've seen in the previous section that Vagrant itself is a command-line-driven application. There are some GUI tools available that can help start and stop environments, but in order to truly understand how Vagrant works, we'll use the command-line interface to initialize and interact with our environment.

For this example (and others in the book), you'll need to open a terminal window (a Unix terminal program in Mac OS X, or Linux, or the windows command application). Verify that Vagrant is installed by typing the command:

```
vagrant version
```

A full example of what the command-line session would look like is given in the following screenshot:

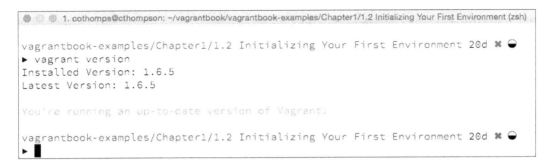

If you encounter errors or if the system cannot find Vagrant, you might either need to repeat the installation steps to install Vagrant in the previous recipe, or adjust your system path to include Vagrant. In most cases, the installer should complete this step for you.

Before proceeding with this first command, you might also want to make sure that your desktop machine is connected to the Internet with a fairly reliable and fast connection. In this example, you will be downloading a Vagrant *box* file that can be a few hundred megabytes in size. (Using a 12 MB/s download connection, I often note that Vagrant box downloads can take between 6 to 10 minutes on average.)

Once you've verified your command-line environment, we can proceed to initialize our first environment.

How to do it...

With a terminal window open and the command getting executed in a directory of your choice, run the command:

```
vagrant init puppetlabs/ubuntu-14.04-32-nocm
```

This command should return a brief text summary of your action, informing you that a new *Vagrantfile* has been created in the current directory. With this file in place, execute the command:

```
vagrant up
```

This command might output several results; we'll note a few important ones:

- A status message indicating that the default machine is being started with the VirtualBox provider.

- If you are running this command for the first time, a message will also be displayed noting that the box (in this case, `puppetlabs/ubuntu-14.04-32-no-cm`) cannot be found. Vagrant will automatically attempt to download a box file. This might take a while depending on the bandwidth available between you and the box provider. After starting a box for the first time, Vagrant will cache the *box* file itself so that subsequent uses of the box (even for different Vagrantfiles) will not trigger the download.

- After the box file is downloaded, you should see messages that note machine startup, port forwarding, shared folders, and networking.

After Vagrant returns to the command line, executing the `vagrant ssh` command will open a command-line interface in the newly initialized virtual machine. In this example, the operating system is Ubuntu 14.04, which is specified in the return prompt:

```
1. vagrant ssh (bash)
▶ vagrant ssh
Welcome to Ubuntu 14.04 LTS (GNU/Linux 3.13.0-24-generic i686)

 * Documentation:  https://help.ubuntu.com/
$ ▮
```

With the virtual machine running, feel free to modify the machine—create files, install programs, or make any modifications you wish. Once you are finished with this environment, log out of the virtual machine either with a `control-d` command, or by typing `exit`. At this point, we can either keep the machine active as a background process or we might wish to:

- Stop the machine, keeping the environment available for later use. This is accomplished with the `vagrant halt` command.

- Destroy the machine, discarding the entire working environment. This is accomplished with the `vagrant destroy` command.

In this example, we'll discard the virtual machine by typing `vagrant destroy`.

Vagrant will now prompt you to make sure that you want to destroy the environment; type `y` to proceed with destroying the environment and deleting the VM. The entire machine can be recreated in this directory again with the `vagrant up` command.

How it works...

What we've done in this example is use Vagrant to create and destroy a virtual machine—an instance of Ubuntu running within the VirtualBox hypervisor. The information that Vagrant requires to create the environment is stored in a special type of file called a Vagrantfile. While Vagrantfiles can grow to become quite complex, this Vagrantfile contains only a few basic items of configuration.

Let's open the Vagrantfile we've created to see what our basic configuration instructs Vagrant to do. The first thing you'll notice when opening this file is that the initial Vagrantfile contains quite a bit of instruction on how to use the file—from box definitions to provisioning instructions. The only parts of the initial file that are not commented are:

- A definition of the Vagrant environment itself
- A definition of the *box* that serves as the base template of the environment itself

The opening of the Vagrantfile looks like this:

```
# -*- mode: ruby -*-
# vi: set ft=ruby :

# Vagrantfile API/syntax version. Don't touch unless you know what
you're doing!
VAGRANTFILE_API_VERSION = "2"

Vagrant.configure(VAGRANTFILE_API_VERSION) do |config|
  # All Vagrant configuration is done here. The most common
configuration
  # options are documented and commented below. For a complete
reference,
  # please see the online documentation at vagrantup.com.

  # Every Vagrant virtual environment requires a box to build off of.
  config.vm.box = "puppetlabs/ubuntu-14.04-32-nocm"
...
```

You might notice a few features of the Vagrantfile itself:

- ▸ Take note that the Vagrantfile uses the syntax of the Ruby programming language (`http://ruby-lang.org`). In fact, the Vagrantfile itself is Ruby code—something we'll use later on when we create more complex Vagrantfiles.

- ▸ The Vagrantfile uses an API version. In this case, version 2: the most current version. Version 1 Vagrantfiles can still be found in use in a few projects as Vagrant itself can be backwards compatible. For most new projects, however, the latest revision of the API will be the one that is used.

- ▸ The sole line of uncommented code is the definition of the `config.vm.box` parameter. This parameter was initialized with our `init` command that used this box name as a parameter. If we wished to change the base box for our project, we could do that in the definition of the `config.vm.box` parameter.

This Vagrantfile can be expanded to include more complex requirements, which will be explored in later recipes.

Installing Vagrant providers

Vagrant and VirtualBox are a great environment to get started with. However, there might be instances where the use of other desktop hypervisors would be preferred, such as the VMware Desktop products (Fusion and Desktop). Recent versions of Vagrant (1.1 or higher) support VMware as a commercial addition. The VMware Fusion provider was the first commercial product released by HashiCorp and was quickly followed by VMware Desktop support. You can find more information about Vagrant and VMWare support at `http://www.vagrantup.com/vmware`.

Many users (including myself) immediately found the VMware provider to be tremendously useful for its improved speed and stability of the VMware platform. In this recipe, we'll look at installing the plugins for VMware Fusion, keeping in mind that the VMware Desktop products and the Vagrant provider for the VMware Desktop are commercial products. You'll need to have on hand a VMware Desktop license for your platform and need to purchase the Vagrant provider for VMware from HashiCorp. In this example, we'll look at the installation of the provider, but keep in mind that all the examples in this book should also work with the freely available VirtualBox or Vagrant environment.

Getting ready

Before we can start with this example, we'll have to assume that you have purchased and installed the VMware Desktop product for your platform: Fusion for OS X, Workstation for Windows or Linux. These products can be purchased from a number of retailers or directly from VMware (`http://www.vmware.com`).

With VMware installed, we'll have to obtain a copy of the Vagrant provider directly from HashiCorp. At the time of writing this book, the plugin is not available through third parties. You can purchase the VMware plugin at `http://vagrantup.com/vmware`.

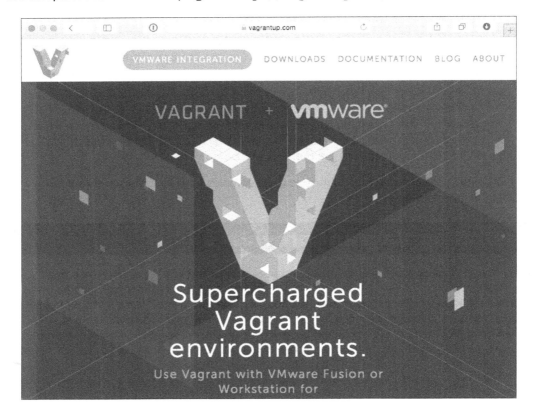

Once you have paid for the plugin, HashiCorp will send an e-mail with the download instructions and some basic instructions on how to install the provider. We'll walk through this installation in this recipe.

How to do it...

Vagrant providers rely on Vagrant's plugin capability—the ability to extend Vagrant through the Ruby environment. To install the plugin, open a command-line environment and execute Vagrant with the `plugin` command.

In this example, we'll install the VMware Fusion plugin, although the plugin installation will be similar for any number of providers. (See `https://github.com/mitchellh/vagrant/wiki/Available-Vagrant-Plugins` for a relatively up-to-date listing of maintained plugins.)

1. Install the VMware Fusion plugin with the `vagrant plugin install vagrant-vmware-fusion` command.

    This will download the plugin and add the code to your local Vagrant installation. With many plugins, this will be the final step—installation itself is pretty straightforward. In this case, however, we'll need to install the license for the plugin.

2. Install the plugin license using the `plugin license` command from the directory where the license file was placed:

    `vagrant plugin license vagrant-vmware-fusion-license.lic`

    This will install the plugin license and ready the plugin for use.

3. Verify the plugin installation with:

    `vagrant plugin list`

    A list of currently installed plugins is returned, including some that are packaged with the distribution, these are marked *system*.

4. Start a VMware environment by initializing a new environment. This will be identical to the steps in the prior recipe.

5. With a terminal window open and the command executing in a directory of your choice, execute the `vagrant init puppetlabs/ubuntu-14.04-32-nocm` command

    This will create a new Vagrantfile that is identical to the previous example. This time, we'll start the environment with the provider option:

    `vagrant up –provider=vmware_fusion`

    A boot sequence will be presented with the difference to the prior example being that a new environment (box file) will be downloaded and booted. This new machine will use the VMware Fusion hypervisor to manage the Vagrant virtual machine.

How it works...

This example installed a new bit of functionality within Vagrant; the expanded functionality of plugins allows Vagrant to manage different virtual environments with an identical API. In general, Vagrant plugins can be used to extend Vagrant in a number of different ways—providers are

You might have noticed that the only difference in starting the Vagrant environment from the previous recipe was the use of the provider option when starting the machine. If you want to ensure that a virtual machine always uses a specific provider when starting, set the `VAGRANT_DEFAULT_PROVIDER=vmware_fusion` environment variable.

Setting an environment variable depends on your system and terminal shell in a Unix- based system (OS X, Linux); you might set this variable in your login shell profile (either `.bash_profile` or `.bashrc`), and for Microsoft Windows, this variable is set in the **Environment Variables...** dialog. Consult the documentation for your platform on how to create system variables.

With a VMware Desktop plugin installed, you can use VMware to manage virtual environments, whereas with other plugins, we can also use Vagrant to manage virtual machines locally with other hypervisors (for example, Parallels on OS X) or even in remote hypervisors (for example, VMware ESXi environments, Amazon Web Services). We'll see examples on how to use Vagrant in these environments in later recipes in the book.

See also

> ▶ VMware: `http://vmware.com`. VMware provides a wide variety of hypervisor platforms from the desktop platforms used in this book to hypervisor infrastructures for data center management.

> ▶ A list of currently available Vagrant plugins: `https://github.com/mitchellh/vagrant/wiki/Available-Vagrant-Plugins`. The Vagrant project keeps a list of plugins that are available to extend the functionality of Vagrant. The VMware providers are only one example of a wide variety of plugins available.

Finding additional Vagrant boxes

Up to this point, we have provisioned Vagrant environments using a single *box*—a version of Ubuntu 14.04 LTS (Trusty Tahr) provided by PuppetLabs, a company that sponsors the open source Puppet configuration management software as well as commercial Puppet products. (We'll see how to use Puppet with Vagrant in later recipes.) There are two reasons why we used this box in the examples:

> ▶ PuppetLabs packaged Ubuntu 14.04 boxes for a few different hypervisors (VirtualBox and VMware).

> ▶ PuppetLabs, as a company, offered a relatively stable set of boxes to develop Puppet. These should be broadly available after the publication of this book.

Most users will likely want to use Vagrant boxes that reflect the eventual production deployment environment of the code being developed inside Vagrant boxes and not just the single distribution we've seen so far.

To use different operating systems and operating environments, we need to obtain (or create) different Vagrant *boxes*. A Vagrant box is a packaged virtual machine that consists of a virtual machine image (a set of VMDK files for VMware, OVF files for VirtualBox) and a metadata file that specifies (at minimum) the provider that the box file uses along with other information that box users might need. Several Vagrant workflows use a *base box* along with provisioning to create new development environments, where the base box is the operating system that is eventually used in a production environment. For example, if a production environment has standardized on CentOS 6.5 as an operating system to host a web application, developers can use a Cent OS 6.5 Vagrant box as a development environment, ensuring that the web server versions and configurations are identical between environments.

There are many cases where you will want to build an environment, but in this example, we'll take a look at finding Vagrant boxes on the Vagrant Cloud (`http://vagrantcloud.com`).

Getting ready

Vagrant Cloud is an offering from HashiCorp to use and share Vagrant environments. Vagrant Cloud allows box providers and other users the ability to publish and share Vagrant boxes with other users. In many cases, these shared boxes will have certain software preinstalled for your use, and in other cases, the boxes will be basic operating system installations for you to provision and configure.

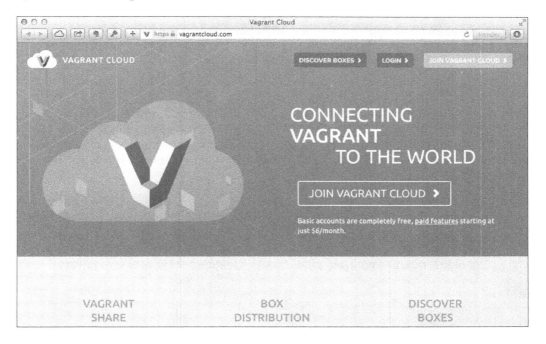

The navigation option **DISCOVER BOXES** on the top menu will take you to a repository (`https://vagrantcloud.com/discover`) for you to search for boxes and view information about box versions and what might be installed.

A note on types of boxes

In this example, we will be downloading and using 64-bit Vagrant boxes, which might cause problems with some environments. In particular, 64-bit guests require systems to have Intel processors that support **Intel Virtualization Technology** (**Intel VT**) and have Intel VT support enabled in the BIOS settings of the host operating system. If you are unsure of the support available for your platform, there is a useful article on the VMware Knowledge Base with some tools to test the ability of your desktop system to support 64-bit guests. The article can be found here:

`http://kb.vmware.com/selfservice/microsites/search.`
`do?language=en_US&cmd=displayKC&externalId=1003944`

How to do it...

HashiCorp provides a repository of box files that can be downloaded for use in the Vagrant Cloud repository. At the time of writing this book, HashiCorp is also migrating the Vagrant Cloud repository to the new Atlas platform. While Atlas might have additional features, HashiCorp has committed to keeping the Vagrant Cloud features free to the community, including the box repository.

Finding boxes

Within the Vagrant Cloud box repository, we can search for boxes based on providers, operating systems, or software packages installed. At the time of writing this book, the Ubuntu 14.04 LTS release (Trusty Tahr) is starting to come into more widespread use a few months after release. As an example, let's find a basic installation of Ubuntu 14.04 to use in our environment.

1. On the box repository page (`https://vagrantcloud.com/discover`), enter the search term `ubuntu 14.04`. You'll notice that by default, the discovery page displays a list of featured boxes—these are boxes that are popular or noted by the community as being of high quality or useful for a wide variety of environments. In our case, the Ubuntu release has not been published as a featured environment as of yet.

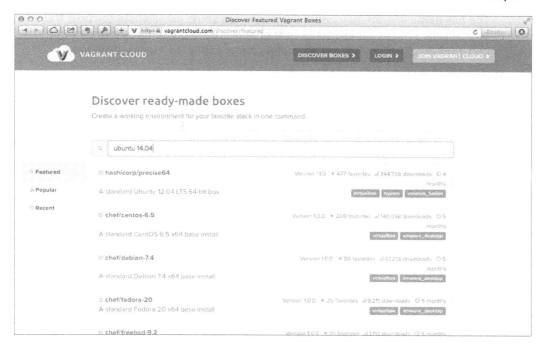

Once the search term has been entered, the repository allows you to filter search results; this is useful if you are looking for a specific desktop version (for example, VirtualBox or VMware).

Another item you might wish to note about the search results is that the repository also follows the naming convention for box naming of box creator or box name. Looking through the search results for ubuntu 14.04 and using the **virtualbox** filter, you'll find a box called ubuntu/trusty64. This box was created by the Ubuntu project itself and is fairly popular. At the time of writing this book, it has been downloaded over 200,000 times.

2. The box name is a link to a page, which displays some detail about the box. The box providers might publish some further information about the box and how it can be used. There is also a stanza that can be copied and used to initialize a new environment.

Now that we have found a box to use, there are a few ways that we can use this box in our environment.

Initializing an environment with a new box:

Initializing an environment with our new box is identical to how we initialized our first environment in the previous recipe. In this case, we can even copy the line presented in the detailed description of the box in the Vagrant Cloud repository. In this example, copy the `vagrant init ubuntu/trusty64` line into a new terminal window. This will generate a Vagrantfile with the `config.vm.box = "ubuntu/trusty64"` box definition.

As before, a simple `vagrant up` command will prompt Vagrant to download the box (if it has not been previously downloaded) and boot a new virtual machine instance. We now have an environment to begin provisioning and configuring.

Adding a new box without initializing an environment:

The other option to use a new box is to simply add the box to our local Vagrant cache for later use in Vagrantfile definitions.

Vagrant maintains a local cache of downloaded boxes for later use. New environments will simply copy the base image to boot new environments from the cache, rather than triggering downloads every time Vagrant is initialized. This is particularly handy when developing system configurations; destroying and rebuilding boxes will copy and provision *clean* images without requiring users to be concerned about maintaining snapshots, copies, or other artifacts of the virtual machine environment itself.

To cache a box for later use, execute this command in a terminal window:

```
vagrant box add ubuntu/trusty64
```

In this case, we're using the `vagrant box` command to manage our box cache. Using the `add` command will trigger the download of the box from the Vagrant Cloud repository to the local cache. With the box cached locally, we can use it later to initialize new environments without triggering a download. (As you might suspect, you can also clean up your cache by using the `vagrant box remove` command, or see a list of the boxes present in the cache along with the provider information about the box by using the `vagrant box list` command.)

There's more...

While there are several boxes to discover and use on the Vagrant Cloud, you might also encounter situations where there are different boxes or repositories used for Vagrant projects. In these cases, you can specify an HTTP URL to the `vagrant box` commands to cache boxes for later use. For example, a frequent case might be development teams sharing custom boxes on an internal server. In this case, adding the box would use the URL of the box file itself, as such:

```
vagrant box add http://servername/boxes/environment.box
```

Assuming the example here, `servername` represents a known web server address with a box called `environment.box` served from the `boxes` path on the web server. In this way, teams can share and use box files without requiring the use of the Vagrant Cloud service, or sharing Vagrant boxes using source control.

Using existing virtual machines with Vagrant

Using Vagrant to create new environments for use up to this point has been pretty simple so far. In the previous recipes, we have downloaded existing Vagrant boxes, created new Vagrantfiles, and booted entirely new environments. This is a pretty suitable use for new software (or configuration) projects, or to possibly create environments in order to migrate existing projects. This isn't such a good workflow if your team or you have existing virtual environments in use (such as the virtual machine on a network share or a flash drive that is passed around between team members).

Fortunately, we can repackage existing environments to use with Vagrant, replacing the shared disk with a new *box* file. While box files are still essentially virtual machines, boxes can be published (and updated) and even have additional configuration applied after booting. These box files can make managing virtual machines and different versions of these virtual machines vastly simpler, especially, if you don't want to build environments from base boxes every time.

Getting ready

In this example, we'll assume that we have an existing virtual machine environment built with Oracle VirtualBox.

Warning!

This example will use a VirtualBox-only feature to set up box packaging, as Vagrant has a built-in shortcut to package existing VirtualBox environments into box files. Creating Vagrant boxes for other platforms will be covered in later chapters.

In this example, I'll choose an existing environment based on the CentOS operating system that has been created as a VirtualBox machine. In this case, the virtual machine has a few properties we'll want to note:

▸ In this case, the virtual machine was created from an ISO installation of CentOS 6.5.

▸ There is a user account present on the machine that we want to reuse. The credentials are:

Username	`uaccount`
Password	`passw0rd`

▸ The machine is used as a development web server; we typically access the machine through terminal sessions (SSH).

WARNING!

We'll want to make sure that any machine that we will access using the `vagrant ssh` method has the SSH server daemon active and set to start on machine start. We'll also want to make one adjustment to the `sshd` configuration before packaging.

With the machine created and active on a development workstation, the listing appears in the **VirtualBox Manager** console:

If this machine boots locally and allows us to SSH into the machine *normally*, we can proceed to convert the virtual machine into a Vagrant box.

How to do it...

If we use an existing virtual machine with VirtualBox, we can use a few simple commands to export a new Vagrant box.

Packaging the VirtualBox machine

Before we can use the virtual machine with Vagrant, we need to package the machine into an appropriate box format.

1. Note the name that VirtualBox assigns to the machine. In this case, our virtual machine is named `CentOS` as displayed in the left-hand menu of the **VM VirtualBox Manager** console:

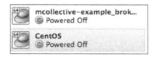

2. Create a temporary workspace to package the box. As with all Vagrant commands, you will do this on the command line. If you are working on a Unix machine (Linux or OS X), you can create a working directory with the `mkdir ~/box-workspace` command. This will create a folder in your home directory called `box-workspace`. Change directories to this workspace with `cd ~/box-workspace`.

3. Execute the packaging command. (Warning! This is for VirtualBox only.) This command is:

```
vagrant package --base=CentOS --output=centos64.box
```

We'll discuss a bit more about this in the following section. For now, Vagrant will return some text:

```
==> CentOS: Exporting VM...
```

This command might take some time to execute; Vagrant is copying the existing VirtualBox machine into a *box* file along with some metadata that allows Vagrant to recognize the box file itself. When this command is finished, you'll end up with a single file called `centos64.box` in the working directory.

4. Import the box file into your environment. In this case, we will directly add the box for use to our local Vagrant environment so that we can proceed to test the new box with a Vagrantfile. It is also possible at this stage to simply publish the box to a web server for use by others, but it is highly recommended to attempt to boot the box and access it with an example Vagrantfile. Your users will appreciate it. Add the box with the command:

```
vagrant box add centos64.box --name=centos64
```

This command will copy the box to your local Vagrant cache, so you are now ready to directly use the box!

Configuring a Vagrant environment

Now that the box is added to our local cache, we'll need to configure a new Vagrant environment to use the box.

1. Initialize a new Vagrant environment with our new box. Do this by executing the `vagrant init centos64` command. This will create a basic Vagrantfile that uses our new `centos64` box.

2. Configure the Vagrantfile to use the correct user to SSH into the machine. We'll use the supplied username and password given in the preceding table. Edit the Vagrantfile created in the previous step to include two new lines that specify parameters for the `config.ssh` parameters:

```
Vagrant.configure(VAGRANTFILE_API_VERSION) do |config|
  # All Vagrant configuration is done here. The most common
configuration
```

```
    # options are documented and commented below. For a complete
reference,
    # please see the online documentation at vagrantup.com.

    # Every Vagrant virtual environment requires a box to build off
of.
    config.vm.box = "centos64"
    config.ssh.username="uaccount"
    config.ssh.password="passw0rd"
```

By default, Vagrant relies on a common public key that is used by most box publishers that allows access to an account called `vagrant`. In this case, our environment will not have this key installed, we can instead configure the Vagrantfile to use a username and password. After the first login, Vagrant will place a key in the appropriate account; so, if desired, the password can be removed from the Vagrantfile after the first boot.

3. Boot the environment. You might need to specify the provider along with the `vagrant up` command:

```
vagrant up --provider=virtualbox
```

In this case, you will note quite a bit of output; the typical Vagrant boot messages along with some information about logging in with the password, replacing the password with the key, and so on. You might also (depending on how the box was packaged) see some information about `Guest Additions`. While Vagrant can use a virtual machine that has the guest additions disabled, some features (shared folders, port forwarding, and so on) rely on the VirtualBox guest additions to be installed. It's likely that your virtual machine has these already installed, especially if it has been used previously in a VirtualBox environment. Newly packaged boxes, however, will need to have the guest additions installed prior to packaging. (See the VirtualBox manual on the installation of guest additions at `https://www.virtualbox.org/manual/ch04.html`.)

Once the environment is booted, you can interact with the virtual machine, as you did previously, either through SSH or other services available on the machine.

How it works...

Using Vagrant with virtual machines is entirely dependent on the Vagrant *box* format. In this example, we used a built-in feature of Vagrant to export an existing VirtualBox environment into Vagrant. It's also possible to package box files for other environments, a topic we'll revisit later in the book. In this case, the `package` command generated a box file automatically.

The Vagrant box file is a file in a Unix **Tape ARchive** (**TAR**) format. If we untar the box file with the `tar xvf centos64.box` command, we can look at the contents of the box to see how it works. The following are the contents of the untarred file:

```
-rw-------   0 cothomps staff 1960775680 Jul 24 20:42 ./box-disk1.vmdk
-rw-------   0 cothomps staff      12368 Jul 24 20:38 ./box.ovf
-rw-r--r--   0 cothomps staff        505 Jul 24 20:42 ./Vagrantfile
```

So, the box file contains two files required to operate a VirtualBox virtual machine (the `vmdk` file that defines the virtual hard drive, and the `ovf` file that defines the properties of the virtual machine used by VirtualBox). The third file is a custom Vagrantfile that contains (primarily) the MAC address of the packaged virtual machine. There might also be custom files added to packaged boxes (such as metadata), describing the box or custom files required to operate the environment.

2
Single Machine Environments

In this chapter, we will cover:

- ▶ Defining a single machine Vagrant environment
- ▶ Forwarding ports from a Vagrant machine
- ▶ Starting a GUI with Vagrant
- ▶ Sharing Vagrant guest folders with the host
- ▶ Sharing folders using Network File Systems
- ▶ Sharing folders with rsync
- ▶ Customizing virtual machine settings (VirtualBox)
- ▶ Customizing virtual machine settings (VMware Desktop)
- ▶ Sharing environments with source control

Introduction

Creating simple Vagrant environments is rather straightforward. The recipes presented in the first chapter consisted of booting Vagrant box files with simple Vagrant environments. Vagrant is, of course, a much more powerful tool to customize and manage custom server environments. The Vagrant API (used in Vagrantfiles) contains a number of different options to customize virtual machines. This chapter will demonstrate:

- ▶ The definition of single virtual machines and how machines are defined in Vagrantfiles
- ▶ Sharing resources between virtual machines and the host operating system
- ▶ Customizing virtual machine settings for a specific hypervisor software

Defining a single machine Vagrant environment

The most basic mode of defining a Vagrant is the definition of a single machine environment. This type of environment defines a single virtual machine that is managed with a simple `vagrant up` command. In the first chapter, all of the Vagrant machines defined were single machine environments. In this recipe, we'll take a closer look at how these machines are defined.

How to do it...

There are two ways we can define single machine environments. A simple environment with global configurations can be used to create a single environment, or a defined environment can be used as the start of a multimachine environment. This chapter will focus on single environments, but you might find that defining virtual machines is a more flexible configuration.

Simple Vagrant environment

1. Initialize a Vagrant environment. This is very similar to how we initialized environments in *Chapter 1, Setting Up Your Environment*, in this case, start with an empty Vagrantfile by entering the `vagrant init` command.

   This will create a largely empty file with a single definition:

   ```
   config.vm.box = "base"
   ```

   There might be many other lines commented out, but for now, we are interested in the *box* definition.

2. Define the box for this single environment. Edit the `config.vm.box` definition to the following code:

   ```
   config.vm.box="puppetlabs/ubuntu-14.04-64-nocm"
   ```

   Save the Vagrantfile once this edit is made.

3. Start the box by issuing the `vagrant up` command. This will start the virtual environment, possibly downloading the box and booting a new machine. This is the mode in which we defined machines and environments in the first chapter. For many purposes, this type of definition is acceptable, particularly if the environment we want to create is a single machine environment or one that communicates with external resources. A good example of a single machine environment might be a development environment for a web application that communicates with an external database. In this case, the Vagrant box can be defined in a single environment with connection strings that connect to an external database, either a shared resource or even a database that is installed on the host machine.

A defined single machine environment

In some cases, we might wish to not have the environment to be defined by a default machine. Instead, we might choose to define a named environment that allows us to make the machine definition clearer or, perhaps, serve as a start to a multimachine environment. To create a named environment:

1. Initialize a new environment (you'll want to do this in a different location, rather than where we created the Vagrantfile in the first part of this recipe). Initialize a new environment by issuing the `vagrant init` command. This will again create a blank Vagrantfile for us to edit.

2. Define our new environment. Let's do this by removing the `config.vm.box="base"` line.

   While we're here, let's also remove all of the commented lines in the generated file; this will allow us to see the complete example. With the `config.vm.box` definition removed, the complete file looks like:

   ```
   # -*- mode: ruby -*-
   # vi: set ft=ruby :
   VAGRANTFILE_API_VERSION = "2"
   Vagrant.configure(VAGRANTFILE_API_VERSION) do |config|
   end
   ```

3. Create a definition for our new machine. We'll do this by adding a definition in the main configure block. The complete file now looks like:

   ```
   # -*- mode: ruby -*-
   # vi: set ft=ruby :
   VAGRANTFILE_API_VERSION = "2"
   Vagrant.configure(VAGRANTFILE_API_VERSION) do |config|
     config.vm.define "web" do |web|
       web.vm.box ="puppetlabs/ubuntu-14.04-32-nocm"
     end
   end
   ```

   In this case, we will define a single machine that we will refer to as web—perhaps because we will define this environment as a simple web server. Note here that the definition of the machine name is the first parameter "web" after `config.vm.define`. The |web| syntax is a Ruby syntax that defines a block; the code within this block and the definitions within the block are local to the block itself. Larger and more complicated environments can take advantage of these blocks to define variable scope, something that is of great utility in multi-machine environments.

At this point, we can execute a command to start the environment, this time also including our defined environment in the start command:

vagrant up web

In this command, the `web` tag tells Vagrant that we wish to start the defined box named `web`. When defining a machine in this manner, we also need to specify the machine name when we start the machine. In this case, `web` is the name of the machine we wish to start.

We can again shorten the command by passing a `primary` flag to the machine definition. When doing so, the complete Vagrantfile will look like:

```ruby
# -*- mode: ruby -*-
# vi: set ft=ruby :
VAGRANTFILE_API_VERSION = "2"
Vagrant.configure(VAGRANTFILE_API_VERSION) do |config|
  config.vm.define "web", primary: true do |web|
    web.vm.box ="puppetlabs/ubuntu-14.04-32-nocm"
  end
end
```

 Note the addition to the definition of web—`primary: true`. This ensures that we can once again start the environment by passing the `vagrant up` command.

How it works...

In this recipe, we've used two ways to define a single machine environment with Vagrant: one using a simple definition of a single environment using the `config` parameter, the second defining a separate configuration altogether. You'll want to note two things about these configurations:

▶ A configuration object is the basic unit of a Vagrantfile. Each Vagrantfile will require at least one configuration. The configuration object represents a virtual machine; operations added on to the configuration will define the operation of the machine and any operations that are executed against the machine.

▶ The configuration objects themselves (in fact, the Vagrantfile itself) are created using the syntax of the Ruby programming language. We can use Ruby to define other objects and how we define Vagrant machines.

Forwarding ports from a Vagrant machine

Although running a virtual machine in a completely standalone mode can be useful, we can also use Vagrant to extend the utility of local computing environments. For example, when developing web applications, Vagrant can be used to create a virtual machine for the runtime environment of the application. When testing the application, however, it might be simpler to refer to the application as running on the host machine: a *localhost* URL. Using localhost URLs allows for simpler configuration: a localhost configuration avoids the need to maintain configuration settings to use the application in the virtual machine. We can enable a Vagrant virtual machine to listen on localhost ports through a technique known as **port forwarding**. Port forwarding allows us to forward a port on the Vagrant machine to a port on the host machine. For example, forwarding port 80 (the standard HTTP port) on the Vagrant machine to port 8080 on the host machine allows us to access a web server on the virtual machine by accessing the http://localhost:8080/ URL. This can be helpful to manage and interact with a development environment on a Vagrant machine.

In this recipe, we will install a simple service (a web server) and forward the port of the virtual machine to a port on the host machine.

How to do it...

1. We'll start with a simple Vagrantfile that defines a single machine. (This is the same Vagrantfile that was created in the previous recipe.)

```
# -*- mode: ruby -*-
# vi: set ft=ruby :
VAGRANTFILE_API_VERSION = "2"
Vagrant.configure(VAGRANTFILE_API_VERSION) do |config|
  config.vm.define "web", primary: true do |web|
    web.vm.box ="puppetlabs/ubuntu-14.04-32-nocm"
  end
end
```

2. Configure the Vagrant machine to forward the port from the guest to the host. In the definition section of the web machine, assign a value to the web.vm.network parameter:

```
config.vm.define "web", primary: true do |web|
  web.vm.box ="puppetlabs/ubuntu-14.04-32-nocm"
  web.vm.network "forwarded_port", guest:80, host:8888
end
```

3. We'll need to install a service that will run on port 80 of the guest machine. To do this, we'll add a simple provisioning command. The complete Vagrantfile now looks like this:

```ruby
# -*- mode: ruby -*-
# vi: set ft=ruby :
VAGRANTFILE_API_VERSION = "2"
Vagrant.configure(VAGRANTFILE_API_VERSION) do |config|
  config.vm.define "web", primary: true do |web|
    web.vm.box ="puppetlabs/ubuntu-14.04-32-nocm"
    web.vm.network "forwarded_port", guest:80, host:8888
    web.vm.provision "shell", inline: "apt-get install -y  nginx"
  end
end
```

This Vagrantfile defines the machine, the forwarded port, and installs a web server (nginx) to listen on port 80 of the guest machine.

4. Start the machine with the `vagrant up` command. This will generate output on the forwarded port along with the output related to the installation of the nginx web server.

5. Once the virtual machine starts, open a web browser on your host machine at `http://localhost:8888`. This should present the nginx **Welcome** page:

How it works...

The configuration of the `forwarded_port` option instructs the hypervisor application to route a port that listens for requests on the guest machine to a port that will listen for requests on the host machine. The general technique is referred to as *port forwarding*. Port forwarding allows a single *host* machine to service requests on behalf of one (or more) virtual machine(s) running on the machine. Port forwarding is typically used in server applications to make network management simpler, something we will repeat on the desktop. With forwarded ports, the Vagrant machines running on your desktop can be referred to as *local* services rather than networked services.

There is also something else to be noted; in this example, we will instruct Vagrant to forward the HTTP port (port 80) on the Vagrant machine, specifically to port 8888 on the host machine with this configuration:

```
web.vm.network "forwarded_port", guest:80, host:8888
```

If port 8888 on the host machine is blocked by another process, the Vagrant startup will fail as the Vagrant machine will be unable to associate to port 8888. To avoid these types of scenarios, known as **port collisions**, we can instruct Vagrant to automatically reassign to a different port using the `auto_correct` option:

```
web.vm.network "forwarded_port", guest:80, host:8888, auto_correct:
true
```

With the `auto_correct` option, Vagrant will first attempt to connect to the specified port (in this example, 8888), then fail over to a different port if the one specified is being used by another process. You might have noticed this correction already when starting up virtual machines. Vagrant uses auto correction that allows the SSH port on the guest machines to forward different ports on the host. This allows Vagrant to maintain a list of both virtual machines and available ports so that each machine can be accessed with the `vagrant ssh` command.

Starting a GUI with Vagrant

So far, we've seen how to start Vagrant using virtual machines that run in a mode that is not running a graphical interface, which is most often referred to as *server* or *headless* mode. There are also cases where virtual machines that host a graphical environment must be shared (from experimentation or development of GUI software to sharing entire development environments).

The key to start a GUI with Vagrant is to use (or create) a box that has a windowing environment installed. In some cases, you can create an environment from scratch; in this case, we'll find a box with a windowing environment installed from the Vagrant Cloud.

Getting ready

Before we can start a machine and configure it for use with a graphical user interface, we will need to find a box that has the graphics libraries installed and active. These boxes can be somewhat large due to the extra software required by GUI environments, so there are typically not many of them published to public repositories.

Introducing Atlas

Before we can start a Vagrant box with an installed GUI, we first need to find a Vagrant box configured to run a graphical user interface. HashiCorp (the original authors and sponsors of Vagrant) provides such a tool with Atlas, which is a centralized portal and repository for nearly every HashiCorp product. Atlas (`https://atlas.hashicorp.com`) is accessible (at the time of writing this book) in a technical preview and will continue to support free features for the Vagrant community.

> **Note**
>
> While it is not strictly necessary to register for an Atlas account, it might be simpler to search for boxes and access other features with a registered account. In this case, we are going to use the box repository that is freely available, yet not listed on the public homepage. The URL for the Vagrant box repository is `https://atlas.hashicorp.com/boxes/search`.

After accessing the Vagrant box repository (`https://atlas.hashicorp.com/boxes/search`), we can search for boxes using the Atlas search feature. A simple search for GUI provides a few examples of Vagrant boxes configured with user interfaces; although, due to the sheer size of boxes with graphical user interfaces, there are not many that are shared through the Atlas repository.

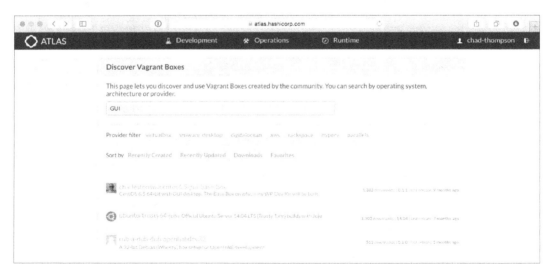

There are also many other boxes available with GUI environments and installed applications (one of them on the Atlas repository might meet your particular need). For this example, we'll use a box created specifically for this recipe at `https://atlas.hashicorp.com/chad-thompson/boxes/ubuntu-trusty64-gui`.

Starting GUI environments in Vagrant can also differ by provider; in this specific example, we will look at starting up a GUI, where the box provider is VirtualBox.

How to do it...

1. Initialize our new box environment. We'll do this with the `init` command:

    vagrant init chad-thompson/ubuntu-trusty64-gui

    This will create a new Vagrantfile. If we edit out the commented lines, our compact Vagrantfile will look like this:

    ```
    # -*- mode: ruby -*-
    # vi: set ft=ruby :
    VAGRANTFILE_API_VERSION = "2"
    Vagrant.configure(VAGRANTFILE_API_VERSION) do |config|
      config.vm.box = "chad-thompson/ubuntu-trusty64-gui"
    end
    ```

2. To enable the GUI, we will need to add a provider-specific block to the configuration. In this case, the provider is `"virtualbox"`. The Vagrantfile with the added code block is shown in the following code snippet:

    ```
    # -*- mode: ruby -*-
    # vi: set ft=ruby :
    VAGRANTFILE_API_VERSION = "2"
    Vagrant.configure(VAGRANTFILE_API_VERSION) do |config|
    config.vm.box = "chad-thompson/ubuntu-trusty64-gui" config.
    vm.provider "virtualbox" do |vbox|
        vbox.gui = true
      end
    end
    ```

3. Start the environment with the `vagrant up` command.

This will start the virtual machine; you should note that VirtualBox opens a new window that displays the Ubuntu startup screen and after boot, the box immediately logs in as the *vagrant* user. In this case, you might note that the boot takes a bit more time to start a headless server, and Vagrant might display an SSH timeout message or two. This is not a problem as Vagrant will continue retrying the SSH connection until the machine boot is complete.

How it works...

As Vagrant is simply an interface to other hypervisor software (in this case, VirtualBox), starting a GUI requires using specific functions of the hypervisor. In the Vagrantfile, we added a provider-specific block with a single configuration parameter: the `gui` parameter:

```
config.vm.provider"virtualbox" do |vbox|
  vbox.gui = true
end
```

This prompts Vagrant to initialize the environment with properties specific to the provider being used.

As the blocks are provider-specific, we can also make our Vagrantfiles a bit more generic. A Vagrantfile can include multiple provider blocks in the same file, provided that you have box files for each provider type. For example, if we have box files for VirtualBox and VMware Fusion, we can specify the blocks to execute for each one of these providers. For example, we can extend our Vagrantfile to boot a GUI for either VirtualBox or VMware Fusion:

```
config.vm.provider "virtualbox" do |vbox|
  vbox.gui = true
end
config.vm.provider "vmware_fusion" do |fusion|
  fusion.gui = true
end
```

Now, if we use our Vagrantfile with a VMware Fusion box file and provider, VMware Fusion will boot the GUI, whereas the VirtualBox provider block will be ignored.

There's more...

In the first part of this recipe, we modified a Vagrantfile created with the Vagrant `init` command, which created a Vagrantfile for us to modify. In the most recent versions of Vagrant (1.7 or greater), the `vagrant up` command also supports using a box name for an argument. For example, the entire initialization and boot process can occur with a single command:

vagrant up chad-thompson/ubuntu-trusty64-gui --provider virtualbox

This will initialize a default Vagrantfile and boot the machine, downloading the box file if necessary. Using the simple `vagrant up` command would not work for this specific example, as the Vagrantfile required modification for the user interface. When searching for boxes in the Atlas repository, you'll note that the `vagrant up` command is provided as a shortcut to download and test the box. Be aware that in most cases, the one line command will not start a Vagrant machine with the desired features.

Sharing Vagrant guest folders with the host

There are a number of cases where it is useful to share a folder between the host operating system and a Vagrant machine guest. When using Vagrant to develop software, shared folders can quickly become the primary advantage to use Vagrant. A shared folder allows us to execute code within a server environment, while having access to the full suite of development tools available for our host operating system.

Getting ready

Before setting up a shared folder scheme, it will be useful to plan how you would like to set up folder sharing. There are a few tips to keep in mind:

- Sharing a folder will only work for folders that exist on the host operating system before starting Vagrant. This will also ensure that the contents of these folders remain even if the Vagrant machine is destroyed.

- If you wish to share data generated by a Vagrant machine with the host, you will need to configure services to write to a previously existing shared folder.

- Plan ahead when thinking about folder sharing schemes. It can often be useful to share folders that map to system directories, such as a root directory for a web server.

- Keep in mind that Vagrant shares the working directory of the Vagrantfile in the root `vagrant` directory by default. Executing the `ls /vagrant/` command (on a Linux guest) should return at minimum a listing of the Vagrantfile and any files present in the working directory. This can be handy in provisioning machines. Shared folders are set up prior to executing provisioning; this will allow assets in the working directory of the Vagrantfile to be copied or executed within the guest.

How to do it...

Let's look at an example of using shared folders to set up a web server to develop HTML files. To do this, the host will need to share a source folder that contains HTML documents with the guest. Before starting the environment, let's create a sample HTML file to serve from the Vagrant machine.

1. In a working directory, create a new directory called `vagrantsite` that will hold our working HTML files.

2. In the `vagrantsite` directory, use your favorite text editor to create a file named `index.html`'. For this example, the contents of `index.html` are:

```
<html>
  <body>
```

```
      <div align="center">Vagrant Machine</div>
    </body>
  </html>
```

3. Create a new Vagrantfile in the directory where the `vagrantsite` directory created in step 1 is located. For this example, lets start with a Vagrantfile that was created in an earlier recipe to start a machine and provision a web server. Here is the complete Vagrantfile:

```
# -*- mode: ruby -*-
# vi: set ft=ruby :
VAGRANTFILE_API_VERSION = "2"
Vagrant.configure(VAGRANTFILE_API_VERSION) do |config|
  config.vm.define "web", primary: true do |web|
    web.vm.box ="puppetlabs/ubuntu-14.04-32-nocm"
    web.vm.network "forwarded_port", guest:80, host:8888
    web.vm.provision "shell", inline: "apt-get install -y  nginx"
  end
end
```

4. Add a `synced_folder` directive to the web server configuration. Immediately, after the definition of the box, add the line:

```
web.vm.synced_folder "vagrantsite/", "/opt/vagrantsite"
```

This will link the `vagrantsite` directory we created in step 1 to the `/opt/vagrantsite` directory on the guest machine.

5. Finally, add an additional command to the `web.vm.provision` line in the Vagrantfile to create a symbolic link from this directory to a directory in the nginx default `web` directory. The complete Vagrantfile (with the addition to the provisioning command) is:

```
# -*- mode: ruby -*-
# vi: set ft=ruby :
VAGRANTFILE_API_VERSION = "2"
Vagrant.configure(VAGRANTFILE_API_VERSION) do |config|
  config.vm.define "web", primary: true do |web|
    web.vm.box ="puppetlabs/ubuntu-14.04-32-nocm"
    web.vm.network "forwarded_port",
    guest:80, host:8888
    web.vm.synced_folder "vagrantsite/", "/opt/vagrantsite"
    web.vm.provision "shell", inline: "apt-get install -y  nginx;
ln -s /opt/vagrantsite /usr/share/nginx/html/vagrantsite"
  end
end
```

Note that we are executing the provisioning command as a single command that will be executed once on machine startup. Creating the symbolic link will ensure that the `index.html` page created in step 2 is ready to serve when the machine starts.

Now that the machine is defined, executing `vagrant up` will allow us to open the page by opening `http://localhost:8888/vagrantsite/` in a web browser:

This `index.html` file is the one we created in the working directory of the Vagrantfile. We can also edit `index.html` (and other HTML documents) on the host machine. Having access to tools on the host with code being executed on the server will allow us to modify `index.html` with design and development tools on the host machine while the pages are served (or executed) from the runtime of the virtual machine.

How it works...

Creating a shared folder with a Vagrant environment is similar to other Vagrant commands in which Vagrant does not implement any new functionality, but rather relies on the underlying functions of the hypervisor. In the case of VirtualBox and VMware Desktop, sharing a folder uses the `shared folders` functions of the hypervisor software.

Sharing folders will require that the proper tools to share folders with host operating systems are installed. For VirtualBox, this means having the *guest additions* installed in the packaged box file. For VMware Desktop, this means having the *VMware tools* installed. Most boxes you'll find on the Vagrant Cloud will have these tools installed. If you are packaging your own box, installing these additions will be important prior to packaging.

Shared folders can also be implemented in different ways. Sharing content between host and guest can also be accomplished by:

> ▶ Using networked file systems such as NFS (Linux, OS X, and other Unix hosts) and SMB (for Windows hosts). These options might offer better file-sharing performance than shared folder functionality of the hypervisor. Many VirtualBox users in particular have noted better I/O (input/output operations on disk) performance when using NFS sharing over using the *guest additions* method that is demonstrated here. See the next recipe, *Sharing folders using Networked File Systems*.

The use of NFS on systems that support the export of file shares such as NFS (OS X and Linux) can offer significant performance improvements with applications that require frequent disk access to shared folders. A significant example is the use of Java application servers within a Vagrant machine; the startup and bootstrapping processes can generate significant file I/O on start and stop procedures. Enabling NFS in these situations is almost a necessity when using the VirtualBox hypervisor. Mitchell Hashimoto compared the performance of shared folder implementations and file I/O (visit `http://mitchellh.com/comparing-filesystem-performance-in-virtual-machines` for more information.)

▶ A Vagrant machine executing on a remote hypervisor (such as a cloud service) will usually not have shared filesystems available. In this case, Vagrant provides methods to copy files from host to guest using the `rsync` protocol. We'll see examples of this type of sharing in later recipes.

See also

▶ Vagrant documentation on shared/synced folders: `http://docs.vagrantup.com/v2/synced-folders/index.html`

▶ *Comparing Filesystem Performance in Virtual Machines, Mitchell Hashimoto*: `http://mitchellh.com/comparing-filesystem-performance-in-virtual-machines`

Sharing folders using Network File Systems

The previous recipe showed us how to share folders between a host operating system and a virtual machine guest using the hypervisor tool. This typically works for the majority of cases, but there are some situations where virtual machines can take advantage of networked file systems for ease of use or better performance.

Vagrant supports two different networked file systems:

▶ The Unix **Networked File System** (**NFS**)

▶ The Windows **Server Message Block (SMB)** protocol

Keep in mind that the protocol that you will use depends on your host operating system as a shared volume will be presented to the guest virtual machine. In this example, we'll demonstrate using VirtualBox on Mac OS X to share a folder between the host (OS X) operating system to an Ubuntu guest.

Before we begin this recipe, we'll address a bit of the reasons behind using the NFS over shared folder mechanism. The primary use case to use NFS is due to performance, and primarily the performance of the VirtualBox shared folder implementation. In many cases, this performance difference is not noticeable, particularly in typical development cases where a developer is working on a few files at a time, whereas performance does become noticeable when many file operations are performed that require access to shared folders. A good example here is the use of automated test suites against a Vagrant machine; many operations in a short period of time can make the Vagrant machine sluggish if the system cannot complete read/write operations fast enough for the automated process. This performance difference is not as noticeable with the VMware providers, but if you note that Vagrant machines seem unusually slow or display a large *uptime* due to being I/O bound, consider using networked folders (or perhaps copying files with `rsync`) instead of native shared folder implementations.

Getting ready

Sharing directories from the host operating system will require the host system to export a directory for use by the guest machine. When using NFS, for example, this means that Vagrant will add an entry to the native `/etc/exports` file to define the rule to export the specified directory to the guest machine.

Note

You will need to ensure that you have administrative privileges on your computer before proceeding with this recipe.

You'll note after a while that Vagrant adds entries to `/etc/exports`, but does not remove them. This can be somewhat problematic if you have NFS settings already defined or if you create or destroy many Vagrant machines with NFS mounts. It can be a good practice to clean up unneeded exports from time to time.

Prior to starting, you will also need to ensure that **Network File Share Daemon (nfsd)** is installed on your OS X or Linux machine. This is installed by default on OS X, but might require a package installation on Linux.

How to do it...

Let's start with a sample Vagrantfile that has some basic setup (and folder sharing) completed. This Vagrantfile is the one developed for shared folders in the previous recipe:

```ruby
# -*- mode: ruby -*-
# vi: set ft=ruby :
VAGRANTFILE_API_VERSION = "2"
Vagrant.configure(VAGRANTFILE_API_VERSION) do |config|
  config.vm.define "web", primary: true do |web|
```

```
      web.vm.box ="puppetlabs/ubuntu-14.04-32-nocm"
      web.vm.network "forwarded_port", guest:80, host:8888
      web.vm.synced_folder "vagrantsite/", "/opt/vagrantsite"
      web.vm.provision "shell", inline: "apt-get install -y  nginx; ln
-s /opt/vagrantsite /usr/share/nginx/html/vagrantsite"
    end
  end
```

This example will start an NFS mount on a host OS X operating system

1. With the preceding Vagrantfile, modify the `synced_folder` line to include a type option. The complete file line is as follows:

   ```
   web.vm.synced_folder "vagrantsite/",
     "/opt/vagrantsite", type:"nfs"
   ```

   The only difference in the Vagrantfile in this recipe and the prior one is the definition of the `synced_folder` type.

2. Start the Vagrant environment (in this case, OS X or Linux) with `vagrant up`.

3. During startup, Vagrant notes the installation of the NFS client in the virtual machine and will prompt you for your administrator password. Vagrant requires this password in order to modify the `system/etc/exports` file that defines a filesystem to export to the virtual machine.

4. After entering your administrator password, Vagrant will complete the machine startup and provisioning of a web server on the system. In this case, the `vagrantsite` folder that is in our HTML document directory is shared from the host operating system to the guest with NFS. You can verify this by opening an SSH session to the Vagrant machine (`vagrant ssh`) and executing the `mount` command (assuming a Linux guest). The `mount` command should contain an entry that looks like this (in this case, the IP address is autogenerated):

   ```
   192.168.30.1:/Users/<<PATH TO FOLDER>>/vagrantsite on /opt/
   vagrantsite type nfs (rw,vers=3,udp,addr=192.168.30.1)
   ```

How it works...

Sharing folders from a host machine to Vagrant guests is similar to how you might configure a server to share volumes on a network. Vagrant automates the process of configuring the host exports and the guest mounts, making the use of a networked filesystem easy to manage.

There's more...

The main example in this recipe demonstrated the use of a Unix-based host operating system, which only supports the use of NFS filesystems. Windows hosts will be a little different. Instead of NFS, Windows hosts can export SMB shares to be used in the Vagrant guest. The Vagrantfile is simply modified by changing the `synced_folder` type. In the example, for this recipe, modify the `synced_folder` directive to:

```
web.vm.synced_folder "vagrantsite/", "/opt/vagrantsite", type:"smb"
```

However, before starting the Vagrant environment, keep in mind that similar to Unix and NFS mounts, the Vagrant command will need to be run as an administrative user. Running a shell with administrator privileges will allow Windows to export an SMB share to be mounted on the guest machine. One method for doing this is to start a command window (or a PowerShell window) with administrative privileges. For example, executing PowerShell as an administrator requires you to right-click on the PowerShell executable and select **Run as Administrator**:

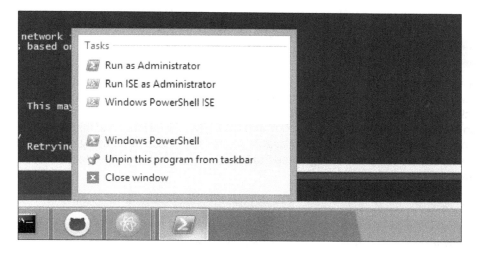

After executing the `vagrant up` command to start the environment, Vagrant will prompt for the username and password of the current administrative user to start the SMB share.

Sharing folders with rsync

Sharing files and folders with Vagrant machines is a typical use of Vagrant in a development environment. Files on a host machine can be shared with a running Vagrant machine, giving developers the advantage of being able to execute code in a *production-like* environment while having the ability to use desktop productivity tools (IDEs and text editors) to modify code. There are some cases where sharing folders between a host and a guest might not be possible, or might not perform well for the task at hand.

Two possible examples are:

> ▶ **Processes that generate significant disk activity (I/O) on shared folders**: Hypervisor folder sharing (particularly VirtualBox) can cause Vagrant processes to become I/O bound. Using NFS can help, but might not always be available. (Exporting NFS shares require root access to the host machine and in a few cases, it might not be available at all.)

> ▶ **Vagrant can be used to control virtual machines in remote locations (even in remote data centers accessed over the public Internet)**: In this case, sharing folders can introduce I/O issues in a Vagrant machine due to basic network latency.

In these cases (and others where shared folders won't work), a better solution would be to copy files and folders required by the Vagrant machine to the local disk of the Vagrant machine itself. Vagrant provides (in versions later than Vagrant 1.5) a feature to copy files and folders with the `rsync` utility. This feature allows Vagrant to copy files and folders to a remote machine on machine startup and also with the `vagrant rsync` command.

In this recipe, we'll take a look at setting up a simply synced folder with `rsync` and Vagrant.

Getting ready

Before we can start with copying files with `rsync`, we will need to ensure that our system has a working copy of `rsync` prior to creating the Vagrant machine. Most operating systems (or package repositories) have a version of `rsync` available (make sure that you have a version installed for Vagrant to use). Linux and OS X typically have `rsync` installed as part of the operating system installation (or available with a quick installation using native package management). Windows users might need to install `rsync` that uses Unix toolkits such as **Cygwin** to install `rsync`.

How to do it...

1. Start our project with a simple Vagrantfile. This Vagrantfile simply starts a new Vagrant machine:

    ```ruby
    # -*- mode: ruby -*-
    # vi: set ft=ruby :

    VAGRANTFILE_API_VERSION = "2"

    Vagrant.configure(VAGRANTFILE_API_VERSION) do |config|
      config.vm.box = "puppetlabs/ubuntu-14.04-32-nocm"
      config.vm.synced_folder "html", "/opt/html", type:"rsync"
    end
    ```

2. In the working directory, create a folder called `html` that will hold content that will be copied to the Vagrant machine.

3. Create a simple file to copy to the Vagrant machine. In this case, a simple `index.html` file will allow us to demonstrate *rsyncing* folders:

```
<html>
  <body>A synced folder</body>
</html>
```

When the setup is complete, our working directory will have the following structure:

```
.
├── Vagrantfile
└── html
      └── index.html
```

4. With the working `html` directory in place, create a synced folder definition for the folder using `rsync`. This definition is similar to other shared folders; the main difference is that we are defining the folder type to be `rsync`. Add the following line immediately below the `config.vm.box` definition:

```
config.vm.synced_folder "html", "/opt/html", type:"rsync"
```

This will sync our `html` directory on the host machine to the `/opt/html` folder on the guest.

 In this example, we will see that our working directory will also be shared with the Vagrant machine, using the default `/vagrant` directory in the Vagrant machine as well. While we might not want to use this in a *real* scenario, in this example, it will allow us to demonstrate the actions of the `vagrant rsync` command later on.

5. With the synced folder definition in place, start the Vagrant machine with the `vagrant up` command. Note that the output of the Vagrant startup will also include a notification of the folder synchronization.

```
4. cothomps@cthompson: ~/vagrantbook/vagrantbook-examples/Chapter2/2.10 Sharing Folders With RSync (zsh)
==> default: Machine booted and ready!
==> default: Forwarding ports...
    default: -- 22 => 2200
==> default: Configuring network adapters within the VM...
==> default: Rsyncing folder: /Volumes/WD HDD/vagrantbook/vagrantbook-examples/Chapter2/2.10 Sh
aring Folders With RSync/html/ => /opt/html
==> default: Waiting for HGFS kernel module to load...
==> default: Enabling and configuring shared folders...
    default: -- /Volumes/WD HDD/vagrantbook/vagrantbook-examples/Chapter2/2.10 Sharing Folders
With RSync: /vagrant

vagrantbook-examples/Chapter2/2.10 Sharing Folders With RSync   master ✗            34d ✖ ◦ ◯
▶ []
```

6. If we access the machine with the `vagrant ssh` command, we can also see that the `index.html` file, that we previously defined, is now in two locations in our Vagrant machine: `/vagrant/html/index.html` and `/opt/html/index.html`. By running the `diff` command, we can also see that there are no differences between them.

```
                                    4. vagrant@localhost: ~ (ssh)
▶ vagrant ssh
Welcome to Ubuntu 14.04 LTS (GNU/Linux 3.13.0-24-generic i686)

 * Documentation:  https://help.ubuntu.com/
Last login: Thu Dec 18 19:36:36 2014 from 192.168.30.1
vagrant@localhost:~$ diff /vagrant/html/index.html /opt/html/index.html
vagrant@localhost:~$ []
```

7. Make a change to the `index.html` file on the host machine. The change in this file will be immediately shared with the Vagrant machine in the shared folder at `/vagrant/html/index.html`:

```
<html>
    <body>A synced folder - modified to demonstrate the rsync
      process.</body>
</html>
```

8. Access the Vagrant machine again with the `vagrant ssh` command. If we execute the `diff` command on the `index.html` file in the `/vagrant/html` folder and the `/opt/html` folder, we can now see that the files are different.

```
                                    4. vagrant@localhost: ~ (bash)
▶ vagrant ssh
Welcome to Ubuntu 14.04 LTS (GNU/Linux 3.13.0-24-generic i686)

 * Documentation:  https://help.ubuntu.com/
Last login: Thu Dec 18 19:38:36 2014 from 192.168.30.1
vagrant@localhost:~$ diff /vagrant/html/index.html /opt/html/index.html
2c2
<     <body>A synced folder - modified to demonstrate the rsync process.</body>
---
>     <body>A synced folder</body>
vagrant@localhost:~$ █
```

9. Synchronize the /opt/html directory by executing the vagrant rsync command in the working directory on the host. Note that the command produces output from the rsync process.

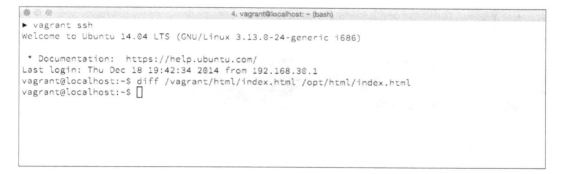

```
4. cothomps@cthompson: ~/vagrantbook/vagrantbook-examples/Chapter2/2.10 Sharing Folders With RSync (zsh)
▶ vagrant rsync
==> default: Rsyncing folder: /Volumes/WD HDD/vagrantbook/vagrantbook-examples/Chapter2/2.10 Sh
aring Folders With RSync/html/ => /opt/html

vagrantbook-examples/Chapter2/2.10 Sharing Folders With RSync   master ✗ ⋮        34d ✗ ⋆ ◕
▶ ▮
```

10. Access the machine again with the vagrant ssh command and compare the /vagrant/html/index.html and /opt/html/index.html files.

```
4. vagrant@localhost: ~ (bash)
▶ vagrant ssh
Welcome to Ubuntu 14.04 LTS (GNU/Linux 3.13.0-24-generic i686)

 * Documentation:  https://help.ubuntu.com/
Last login: Thu Dec 18 19:42:34 2014 from 192.168.30.1
vagrant@localhost:~$ diff /vagrant/html/index.html /opt/html/index.html
vagrant@localhost:~$ ▯
```

 Note that once again there is no difference in the shared folder (using hypervisor folder sharing) and the *rsynced* copy.

How it works...

The use of the rsync command creates a shared folder on the Vagrant machine that is updated on either system reload or repeated executions of the vagrant rsync command. This allows our Vagrant machine to access working files on the *local* disk that is not bound by I/O considerations of shared or remote folders.

Using rsynced folders is most useful in situations where file I/O or network constraints introduce bottlenecks in Vagrant system performance. We could also use an rsynced folder as part of a provisioning workflow within a Vagrant machine.

For example, a Java build process might generate an executable that we wish to deploy to an application server running on a Vagrant machine. Rsyncing build artifacts might allow us to more easily deploy compiled code to an app server; copying a WAR file allows you to build artifact in order to be deployed. Any compilation steps in the app server (such as a JSP compilation) would have the added benefit to generate compiled files without the overhead of shared or networked folder performance.

The other prominent example is the synchronization of files to remote servers. In fact, many Vagrant cloud providers (such as the AWS provider) use rsyncing by default to share folders between a local Vagrant process and a remote virtual machine.

In either case, synchronization of folders using `rsync` gives developers more flexibility to use Vagrant in order to meet specific performance or to test use cases.

See also

> ▸ The rsync project: `https://rsync.samba.org/`
> ▸ Cygwin Unix utilities for Windows: `https://www.cygwin.com`
> ▸ Vagrant rsync synced folders: `https://docs.vagrantup.com/v2/synced-folders/rsync.html`

Customizing virtual machine settings (VirtualBox)

Up to this point, we have seen the creation and execution of Vagrant environments largely as it is. Every environment started has been controlled either by the default settings or settings that have been provided in packaged boxes. This is sometimes okay, but it is often desirable to use the Vagrantfile to control settings on the virtual machine in order to allow the virtual machine to run as efficiently on the host as possible. The primary example is, of course, changing the settings of the virtual machine to use more (or less) system memory (RAM) and virtual processors.

Getting ready

Modifying the runtime settings of a virtual machine is dependent on the features of the hypervisor. Changing the runtime for VirtualBox will be slightly different for VMware Desktop and other hypervisors. Vagrant provides a few shortcuts to common items (RAM, CPU), but modifying these settings require the use of provider-specific blocks in the Vagrantfile.

How to do it...

To start the example, create a Vagrantfile that we have built in previous recipes. This file creates a single box named web and installs the nginx web server. Here is the complete Vagrantfile to start the example:

```ruby
# -*- mode: ruby -*-
# vi: set ft=ruby :
VAGRANTFILE_API_VERSION = "2"
Vagrant.configure(VAGRANTFILE_API_VERSION) do |config|
  config.vm.define "web", primary: true do |web|
    web.vm.box ="puppetlabs/ubuntu-14.04-32-nocm"
    web.vm.network "forwarded_port", guest:80, host:8888
    web.vm.provision "shell", inline: "apt-get install -y  nginx"
  end
end
```

In this recipe, we'll modify the runtime of the virtual machine to use 2 GB of RAM and 2 virtual CPUs to run our web server.

>
> **Note**
>
> When changing memory settings, make sure to note the settings of the box that you are using, in particular, check whether the box and OS install are 32-bit or 64-bit operating systems. If the box is an installation of a 32-bit operating system (as in this example), then the maximum RAM that the virtual machine can support is 4 GB.

1. Define a configuration block for the web server that is VirtualBox-specific. Add this (empty) block after the web.vm.provision line:

   ```ruby
   web.vm.provider "virtualbox" do |vbox|
   end
   ```

2. With the provider block defined, add two provider configurations: one defines an amount of memory (system RAM), the second defines a number of virtual CPUs. The block within the two parameters is as follows:

   ```ruby
   web.vm.provider "virtualbox" do |vbox|
     vbox.memory = 2048
     vbox.cpus = 2
   end
   ```

Note

The amount of system memory here is in megabytes. Take care to ensure that you are not assigning more RAM to your virtual machine than the host operating system can support. Keep in mind that the host operating system will also require resources to operate.

The complete Vagrantfile for this example is:

```ruby
# -*- mode: ruby -*-
# vi: set ft=ruby :
VAGRANTFILE_API_VERSION = "2"
Vagrant.configure(VAGRANTFILE_API_VERSION) do |config|
  config.vm.define "web", primary: true do |web|
    web.vm.box ="puppetlabs/ubuntu-14.04-32-nocm"
    web.vm.network "forwarded_port", guest:80, host:8888
    web.vm.provision "shell", inline: "apt-get install -y  nginx"
    web.vm.provider "virtualbox" do |vbox|
    vbox.memory = 2048
    vbox.cpus = 2
    end
  end
end
```

3. Start the virtual machine with the `vagrant up` command.

4. Verify that the system has the amount of memory allocated. On Ubuntu (and most Linux distributions in general), you can find this value in the `/proc/meminfo` file. Look at the first few lines of this file with the `head` command:

```
vagrant@localhost:~$ head /proc/meminfo
MemTotal:      2072440 kB
MemFree:       1893628 kB
...
```

Keep in mind that these RAM calculations will not be precise, but the system is reporting *approximately* 2 GB of RAM that we specified in the Vagrantfile.

How it works...

Provider-specific settings (such as memory and virtual CPU) rely heavily on the functionality (and API) of the underlying hypervisor. For VirtualBox in particular, this requires the use of the VBoxManage utility and the `modifyvm` command. Vagrant provides a shortcut for the common modifications of setting the amount of RAM and number of CPUs, but we can also access the VBoxManage commands directly.

For example, two lines can be added to the configuration block in order to start a GUI on the `vagrant up` command, but use the VBoxManage command to fade the *VirtualBox* startup logo immediately:

```
web.vm.provider "virtualbox" do |vbox|
  vbox.memory = 2056
  vbox.cpus = 2
  vbox.gui = true
  vbox.customize ["modifyvm", :id, "--bioslogofadein", "off"]
  end
```

A full listing of available options to modify the runtime is available in the VirtualBox documentation for the VBoxManage command. (At the time of writing this book, it is `https://www.virtualbox.org/manual/ch08.html`.)

The use cases to modify Vagrant environments beyond RAM and CPU are rare, but it is important to note that Vagrant allows you to use VirtualBox commands to modify the environment directly.

Customizing virtual machine settings (VMware Desktop)

The customization options that are available through the VMware Desktop (Fusion and Workstation) are somewhat limited in comparison to VirtualBox. VMware does not publish a documented API to control virtual machines in the desktop environment (the Vagrant documentation only provides a firm example to configure the amount of RAM and CPU).

This example will demonstrate configuring RAM and CPU using the VMware Fusion provider.

Getting ready

Modifying runtime parameters of a virtual machine are dependent on the commands exposed by the hypervisor application. In the case of VMware Desktop products, this takes the form of key/value pairs that the runtime maintains in a `vmx` file. Vagrant essentially modifies this file prior to booting the machine, as such, it is possible to overwrite parameters that Vagrant uses to manage the machine, or even parameter settings required for the virtual machine to operate.

As we proceed through this example, also note that there are two VMware products that will behave identically, yet have different provider names:

- For OS X, the hypervisor application is called **VMware Fusion**. This provider is specified in the Vagrantfile with the name `vmware_fusion`.
- For Windows and Linux, the hypervisor application is called **VMware Desktop**. This provider is specified in the Vagrantfile with the name `vmware_desktop`.

How to do it...

To start this example, create a Vagrantfile, which we have built in previous recipes. This file creates a single box named web and installs the nginx web server. Here is the complete Vagrantfile to start the example:

```ruby
# -*- mode: ruby -*-
# vi: set ft=ruby :
VAGRANTFILE_API_VERSION = "2"
Vagrant.configure(VAGRANTFILE_API_VERSION) do |config|
  config.vm.define "web", primary: true do |web|
    web.vm.box ="puppetlabs/ubuntu-14.04-32-nocm"
    web.vm.network "forwarded_port", guest:80, host:8888
    web.vm.provision "shell", inline: "apt-get install -y  nginx"
  end
end
```

In this recipe, we'll modify the runtime of the virtual machine to use 2 GB of RAM and 2 virtual CPUs to run our web server.

> **Note**
>
> When changing memory settings, make sure to note the settings of the box that you are using, in particular, check whether the box and OS install are 32-bit or 64-bit operating systems. If the box is an installation of a 32-bit operating system (as in this example), then the maximum RAM that the virtual machine can support is 4 GB.

1. Define a configuration block for the web server that is VirtualBox-specific. Add this (empty) block after the web.vm.provision line:

    ```
    web.vm.provider "vmware_fusion" do |vmware|
    end
    ```

    In this case (VMware Fusion on OS X), using vmware_fusion is the proper value for the provider; VMware Workstation users will use the vmware_workstation provider name.

2. With the provider block defined, add two provider configurations, one that defines the amount of memory (system RAM), the second that defines a number of virtual CPUs. The block with the two parameters is as follows:

    ```
    web.vm.provider "vmware_fusion" do |vmware|
      vmware.vmx["memsize"] = "2048"
      vmware.vmx["numvcpus"] = "2"
    end
    ```

Note

The amount of system memory here is in megabytes. Take care to ensure that you are not assigning more RAM to your virtual machine than the host operating system can support. Keep in mind that the host operating system will also require resources to operate.

The complete Vagrantfile for this example is:

```ruby
# -*- mode: ruby -*-
# vi: set ft=ruby :
VAGRANTFILE_API_VERSION = "2"
Vagrant.configure(VAGRANTFILE_API_VERSION) do |config|
  config.vm.define "web", primary: true do |web|
    web.vm.box ="puppetlabs/ubuntu-14.04-32-nocm"
    web.vm.network "forwarded_port", guest:80, host:8888
    web.vm.provision "shell", inline: "apt-get install -y  nginx"
      web.vm.provider "vmware_fusion" do |vmware|
      vmware.vmx["memsize"] = "1024"
      vmware.vmx["numvcpus"] = "2"
    end
  end
end
```

3. Start the virtual machine with the vagrant up command.

4. Verify that the system has the amount of RAM that we specified in the provider configuration block. On Ubuntu (and most Linux distributions in general), you can find this value in the /proc/meminfo file. Look at the first few lines of this file with the head command:

```
vagrant@localhost:~$ head /proc/meminfo

MemTotal:        2064268 kB

MemFree:         1942356 kB...
```

Keep in mind that these RAM calculations will not be precise, but the system reports *approximately* 2 GB of RAM that we specified in the Vagrantfile.

How it works...

Provider-specific settings (such as memory and virtual CPU) rely heavily on the functionality (and API) of the underlying hypervisor. VMware does not, unfortunately, publish documentation about all the options available to virtual machines in the desktop hypervisor products. These options are available to users using the key/value syntax that was used in the recipe to modify the RAM and CPU count. For example, the `vmware.vmx["key"] = "value"` line would set the `"key"` property in machine boot to `"value"`. It is rare that desktop users will modify these parameters directly, but Vagrant exposes these options for users that require them.

Sharing environments with source control

The biggest challenge that users (and development teams) typically face when working with virtual machines on the desktop is sharing and maintaining versions of virtual environments. Traditionally, this has meant placing virtual machine files (for either VirtualBox or VMware) in a shared network location or even on a USB thumb drive that is shared among the team to copy to a workstation. These methods also mean that each virtual machine has to be configured for each use. The combination of large file sizes and individual configurations makes shared virtual machines difficult to use in traditional file-sharing scenarios.

Vagrant, on the other hand, relies strictly on text files (namely the Vagrantfile) to define virtual environments. Text files are easy to modify, track, and share using traditional source control methods. Vagrantfiles can even be kept in the same repository that hosts source code, giving developers the opportunity to store both application source and server configurations in the same repository.

In this recipe, we'll take a look at using source control to keep (and share) a project with a source control system.

Getting ready

With this example, we'll use GitHub as a source repository to host our project using the Git source control system. You can find more information on GitHub (and Git in general) at `http://github.com`. While an account is not necessary to clone and use code published in a public repository, creating new repositories will require an account with GitHub.

How to do it...

In this example, we'll start from an existing Vagrant project—in particular, the web project created in the *Sharing folders with Network File Systems* recipe, a Vagrant environment that represents a simple HTML website with a Vagrantfile that defines a simple web server. The file listing for our beginning directory looks like this:

```
● ● ●   2. cothomps@cthompson: ~/vagrantbook/vagrantbook-examples/Chapter2/2.5 Sharing Folders With The Host (zsh)
▸ ls -la
total 8
drwxr-xr-x   4 cothomps   staff   136 Aug 13 14:31 .
drwxr-xr-x  10 cothomps   staff   340 Aug 12 22:09 ..
-rw-r--r--@  1 cothomps   staff   488 Aug  7 21:08 Vagrantfile
drwxr-xr-x   3 cothomps   staff   102 Aug  7 20:55 vagrantsite

vagrantbook-examples/Chapter2/2.5 Sharing Folders With The Host   ma25d ✖ ◐
▸ ▯
```

For this example, we wish to share our Vagrant environment using GitHub. The steps here will create a local repository and push it to a public repository. (This repository is available at `https://github.com/chad-thompson/vagrantbook-web`).

1. Initialize a local Git repository with the command-line client. Open the directory where our Vagrantfile resides and issues the `git init` command. This will initialize a repository on our local filesystem.

2. Create a file named `.gitignore`: a file instructing Git to not operate on certain files. In this case, we'll create a `.gitignore` file with only

3. Add our files to this repository using the `add` command. From the same directory as step 1, execute:

   ```
   git add -all
   ```

   Verify this command by executing:

   ```
   git status
   ```

This will display all files that we have selected to add to the repository.

```
2. cothomps@cthompson: ~/vagrantbook/vagrantbook-examples/Chapter2/2.5 Sharing Folders With The Host (zsh)
▶ git status
# On branch master
#
# Initial commit
#
# Changes to be committed:
#   (use "git rm --cached <file>..." to unstage)
#
#       new file:   Vagrantfile
#       new file:   vagrantsite/index.html
#

vagrantbook-examples/Chapter2/2.5 Sharing Folders With The Host    master   +
▶ []
```

4. Commit the added files to the local repository. From our directory location, execute:

   ```
   git commit -m "Initial Import of Vagrant Web Project"
   ```

   This will package a new commit to our local repository. Before we can share this repository, we will need to create a public *remote* endpoint that can be used by other developers. (Keep this terminal window open for later.)

5. Log in to GitHub (see the *Getting ready* section for information about GitHub accounts) and select the **New Repository** option. The new repository dialog will prompt for a repository name and description. Deselect (if selected) the option to **Initialize this repository with a README**.

Note

There are also options for public or private repositories. Private repositories are, however, a paid feature of GiHub.

Once the name, description and other options are correct, select **Create repository**.

6. Note the instructions for the new repository. An empty repository will display instructions along with some options that we will use to push our *local* repository to this new GitHub repository.

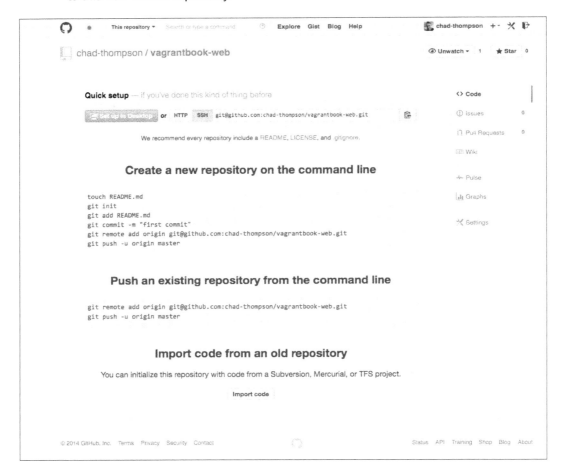

7. Add the GitHub repository as a remote to our local repository. In the command window we left open in step 3 (a command prompt open to the directory where our Vagrantfile is located), execute:

    ```
    git remote add origin git@github.com:chad-thompson/vagrantbook-
    web.git
    ```

    Make sure to substitute the name of the account or repository for your own account. This command is available in the documentation described in step 5.

8. With the remote defined, push the local repository and set upstream tracking with:

```
git push -u origin master
```

This will push our *local* repository to our public GitHub repository. With the repository available in GitHub, other developers can access the code (including the Vagrantfile) with a simple `git clone` operation.

Once these steps are complete, sharing the Vagrant environment is as simple as allowing other developers to access the source repository and cloning the repository. Once a new developer clones the repository, a new development environment can be started with the simple `vagrant up` command, provided that the other developer also has Vagrant and a hypervisor application installed. Modifications to both the source code and environment are managed through source control, and not through shared binary files.

How it works...

Unlike the traditional methods of sharing virtual machines with large binary files, Vagrant environments are largely managed with text files. Text files are both small and easy to manage with source control. In this case, we are managing source with a Git repository, but any form of source control (SVN, CVS, and so on) would work just as well. With Vagrant, it is also possible to include an operating environment with the source of the application that allows for joint development of code and server environments, particularly when configuration management tools are used to ensure consistency between development, testing, and production environments.

A few tips to keep in mind are:

 ► While Vagrantfiles and accompanying provisioning scripts are simple to maintain in source control, box files will require a different publishing mechanism if you have packaged custom boxes. There are options to publish boxes from web servers on a local network to publication in a box repository (such as the Vagrant Cloud).

 ► Environments and Vagrantfiles can be modified and shared, but it might require other developers to destroy and/or reprovision local Vagrant machines for those changes to take effect. Make sure that changes to server environments (including Vagrant environments) are accompanied with plenty of discussion and notification between anyone using the Vagrant environment.

See also

▶ *GitHub*: `http://github.org`, a popular open Git repository. There are also other options available to host Git such as BitBucket (`http://bitbucket.org`).

▶ *TryGit*: `http://try.github.io`, a resource to learn the basics of using Git and the command line.

▶ *Getting Git Right*: `https://www.atlassian.com/git/`, a set of tutorials published by Atlassian that are a good introduction to both using Git and development workflows for Git.

3
Provisioning a Vagrant Environment

In this chapter, we will cover:

▸ Running basic shell commands

▸ Executing shell scripts in a Vagrantfile

▸ Provisioning with external shell scripts

Introduction

Starting a basic operating system environment from a Vagrantfile can be useful, but the real power of Vagrant is the ability to not only define operating parameters, but also to provision environments in a repeatable way. Vagrant implements a number of methods to install and configure software wherein each different method is referred to as a **provisioner**.

This chapter introduces and expands on the basic concept of provisioning a Vagrant environment. In the previous chapters, we have seen how to launch and configure basic environments, some of which included basic provisioning such as installing a web server. In reality, simply installing software is only the beginning (the process of configuring software for use is where the real work begins). Automating this process through scripts and configuration management will give you the dual advantage of saving time and environment stability. Vagrant is an ideal tool to test configuration management—creating, provisioning, testing, destroying, and iterating on environment configuration becomes simple with Vagrant.

Running basic shell commands

The most basic method of provisioning is to run simple shell commands in the Vagrant machine. For Linux environments, this typically means executing basic shell commands with shells that are typically bundled with distributions (sh, bash, zsh, and so on). The provisioning process can also execute other command-line applications if runtime environments are installed (such as system provisioning with Ruby or Perl).

In this example, we'll use a shell command to install a basic Message of The Day command to output a greeting on login using the vagrant ssh command.

How to do it...

1. We'll start this example with a simple Vagrantfile that boots a basic Ubuntu environment. Here is the complete Vagrantfile:

    ```
    # -*- mode: ruby -*-
    # vi: set ft=ruby :

    VAGRANTFILE_API_VERSION = "2"

    Vagrant.configure(VAGRANTFILE_API_VERSION) do |config|
      config.vm.box = "puppetlabs/ubuntu-14.04-32-nocm"
    end
    ```

    Booting this environment with vagrant up will start a basic Ubuntu operating system. Before starting the system, let's add our provisioning command.

2. To display a message to users on login, we'll have to place this message in the /etc/motd file. We can write this file in a Unix shell, directing the output of the echo command into a file. The basic command is:

    ```
    echo 'Vagrant Cookbook Example Environment' > /etc/motd
    ```

    Vagrant can execute this command using a provision definition in the Vagrantfile. Adding a command to be executed using the provision definition looks like this:

    ```
    # -*- mode: ruby -*-
    # vi: set ft=ruby :

    VAGRANTFILE_API_VERSION = "2"

    Vagrant.configure(VAGRANTFILE_API_VERSION) do |config|
      config.vm.box = "puppetlabs/ubuntu-14.04-32-nocm"
      config.vm.provision "shell",
    ```

```
        inline: "echo 'Vagrant Cookbook Example Environment' > /etc/
motd"
end
```

3. Start the environment with the `vagrant up` command. When running this Vagrantfile, you'll note the output of the provisioner:

```
    1. cothomps@cthompson: ~/vagrantbook/vagrantbook-examples/Chapter3/3.1 Basic Shell Commands (zsh)
==> default: Waiting for HGFS kernel module to load...
==> default: Enabling and configuring shared folders...
    default: -- /Volumes/WD HDD/vagrantbook/vagrantbook-examples/Chapter3/3.1 Ba
sic Shell Commands: /vagrant
==> default: Running provisioner: shell...
    default: Running: inline script
==> default: stdin: is not a tty

vagrantbook-examples/Chapter3/3.1 Basic Shell Commands   master  X     29d  ✖  ⚑  ●
▶ █
```

4. Once the machine is booted, access the machine with the `vagrant ssh` command, the login shell will display the message created with the inline shell method along with the default Ubuntu messages. (In this example, 0029).

```
    1. vagrant ssh (bash)
▶ vagrant ssh
Welcome to Ubuntu 14.04 LTS (GNU/Linux 3.13.0-24-generic i686)

 * Documentation:  https://help.ubuntu.com/
Vagrant Cookbook Example Environment
$ █
```

How it works...

In this case, we have provisioned a single file (`/etc/motd`) with a simple Unix command. This was all accomplished with a single line:

```
config.vm.provision "shell",
    inline: "echo 'Vagrant Cookbook Example Environment' > /etc/motd"
```

The provisioning command here is executed with the Vagrant `provision` command. The command took two arguments:

 ▶ The type of provisioner being executed, in this case, the `shell` provisioner

 ▶ The command to be executed by the shell with the `inline` argument that contained the command that was executed

Now that a provisioner has been defined, Vagrant allows provisioners to be executed multiple times on an environment with the `vagrant provision` command.

Executing the `vagrant provision` command will only execute commands defined in provisioners. For example, if the Vagrantfile in the example was edited to contain a different message:

```
config.vm.provision "shell",
    inline: "echo 'Knock Knock!' > /etc/motd"
```

Then, executing the `vagrant provision` command will execute only the provisioning cycle:

```
1. cothomps@cthompson: ~/vagrantbook/vagrantbook-examples/Chapter3/3.1 Basic Shell Commands (zsh)
▶ vagrant provision
==> default: Running provisioner: shell...
    default: Running: inline script
==> default: stdin: is not a tty

vagrantbook-examples/Chapter3/3.1 Basic Shell Commands    master  ✗    29d  ✖  ⬤
▶ █
```

Accessing the machine with the `vagrant ssh` command will show our new message on login:

```
1. vagrant ssh (bash)
▶ vagrant ssh
Welcome to Ubuntu 14.04 LTS (GNU/Linux 3.13.0-24-generic i686)

 * Documentation:  https://help.ubuntu.com/
Knock Knock!
Last login: Sat Dec 13 18:48:04 2014 from 192.168.30.1
$ █
```

While this provisioning command will work well for our simple command that simply overwrites the `/etc/motd` file, in more complex examples, there might need to be a little work done to make sure that shell commands do not leave our system in a *broken* state (particularly when the commands are executed multiple times with provisioning commands). Commands that leave our system in the desired state without causing provisioning failures are referred to as **idempotent**, a concept that we will explore further in our next recipe and in *Chapter 4, Provisioning with Configuration Management Tools*, when we discuss provisioning Vagrant machines with configuration management software.

Executing shell scripts in a Vagrantfile

Provisioning a Vagrant machine with single inline string arguments can make simple provisioning tasks easy, but more complicated requirements can require more complicated scripts. Scripts can be defined within Vagrantfiles using the multiline string feature of Ruby. A multiline string will allow a definition of a set of commands that can be executed with the Vagrant `inline` command.

This example will also demonstrate how we can make a script idempotent, which is capable of being executed multiple times without changing the end state of the machine after every run.

Getting ready

In this example, we will provision a new Vagrant environment, install the nginx web server, and replace the default web directory with a directory in our working directory. The working directory that holds the Vagrantfile is shared, by default, with the guest operating system as the `/vagrant` folder.

Before we start our Vagrant environment, create a directory named `html` in the working directory. Most Vagrant boxes (including the box used in this recipe) automatically share the working directory with the virtual machine. On the virtual machine, this file is often mounted on the root filesystem as `/vagrant`. We can modify these files and see the changes immediately (if the synced folder is mounted with a shared folder, NFS or SMB mount) or after a `reload` or `rsync` command, if the folder is synced with rsync. By creating an `html` directory in the working directory, we can access this folder in the guest at the `/vagrant/html` location.

In the `html` directory (which we will link to become our web root), create a file named `index.html` that is a very simple HTML document. The entire file looks like this:

```
<html>
  <body>
    The index.html file in the Vagrant directory.
  </body>
</html>
```

This will be the file served as the default page by the web server running in our Vagrant environment.

How to do it...

1. To start, define a basic Vagrantfile that defines a simple box definition:

    ```
    # -*- mode: ruby -*-
    # vi: set ft=ruby :
    ```

```
VAGRANTFILE_API_VERSION = "2"

Vagrant.configure(VAGRANTFILE_API_VERSION) do |config|
  config.vm.box = "puppetlabs/ubuntu-14.04-32-nocm"
end
```

2. At the top of the Vagrantfile, define a variable that will hold the script named `nginx_install`. We'll start this variable with the syntax required for a Ruby multiline string:

```
# -*- mode: ruby -*-
# vi: set ft=ruby :

VAGRANTFILE_API_VERSION = "2"

$nginx_install = <<SCRIPT
SCRIPT

Vagrant.configure(VAGRANTFILE_API_VERSION) do |config|
  config.vm.box = "puppetlabs/ubuntu-14.04-32-nocm"
end
```

3. In this script, add the logic to install nginx. Note that we'll use an `if` command to determine whether or not to install the package.

 Note that the installation instructions here are specific to the installation on the Ubuntu operating system. The location of executables and configuration can vary based on the operating system and the specific installation package. For this recipe, we will simply be relying on the defaults provided in the `nginx` package in the Ubuntu 14.04 repositories. The script can easily be modified for different environments by changing the installation instructions (such as `yum install nginx` for Fedora or Red Hat variants).

The script block will then look like the following code:

```
$nginx_install = <<SCRIPT
  if [ ! -x /usr/sbin/nginx ]; then
    apt-get install -y nginx;
  fi
SCRIPT
```

4. With the `nginx install` command in place, add a section to the script following the `nginx install` to determine whether or not the default nginx root directory is a symbolic link. This section will do a simple test to see whether the directory is a static link (making the assumption here that only our script would create this static link) or a real directory. If the directory is not a static link, remove it and replace the nginx root directory with a symbolic link:

```
$nginx_install = <<SCRIPT
  if [ ! -x /usr/sbin/nginx ]; then
    apt-get install -y nginx;
  fi

  # Default NGINX directory: /usr/share/nginx/html
  # Replace this with symbolic link to vagrant directory.
  if [ ! -L /usr/share/nginx/html ]; then
    rm -rf /usr/share/nginx/html
    ln -s /vagrant/html /usr/share/nginx/html
  fi
SCRIPT
```

5. Now that the provisioning script has been written, add a `provision` property to the box definition that will use our script in a Ruby variable:

```
config.vm.provision "shell", inline: $nginx_install
```

With this line (and an addition of a networking setting to forward the port), the complete Vagrantfile is as follows:

```
# -*- mode: ruby -*-
# vi: set ft=ruby :

VAGRANTFILE_API_VERSION = "2"

$nginx_install = <<SCRIPT
  if [ ! -x /usr/sbin/nginx ]; then
    apt-get install -y nginx;
  fi

  # Default NGINX directory: /usr/share/nginx/html
  # Replace this with symbolic link to vagrant directory.
  if [ ! -L /usr/share/nginx/html ]; then
    rm -rf /usr/share/nginx/html
    ln -s /vagrant/html /usr/share/nginx/html
  fi
SCRIPT

Vagrant.configure(VAGRANTFILE_API_VERSION) do |config|
  config.vm.box = "puppetlabs/ubuntu-14.04-32-nocm"
```

```
        config.vm.provision "shell", inline: $nginx_install
        config.vm.network "forwarded_port", guest:80, host:8080
    end
```

6. With the Vagrantfile complete, execute the `vagrant up` command in the working directory. When the machine is booted, open `http://localhost:8080` in a local browser to see the HTML file in our working `html` directory:

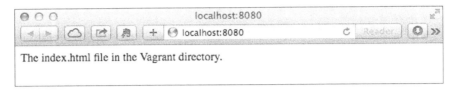

7. As a test of idempotency, execute the `vagrant provision` command in the current working directory. You should note that this command will exit rather quickly, as all conditions within the script should be satisfied.

How it works...

In this example, we will execute a shell script within the Vagrant machine. Configuration of Unix environments with shell scripts is a common task, but there are a few things to keep in mind when provisioning Vagrant machines.

Shell scripting in vagrant machines

We might have not noticed in prior examples where simple commands were executed, but in the case of larger scripts, it becomes important to know how to write Vagrant shell provisioning scripts. Vagrant will (by default) use the default shell for the box, which is typically the default shell for the operating system. In most Linux distributions, this is typically the **Bourne Again Shell** (**bash**), so many examples will use bash scripting or scripting for the **Bourne Shell** (**sh**). These two Unix shells might cover a vast majority of cases, although other scripting languages can be used when executing shell commands with external scripts. We'll investigate this a bit further in the next recipe.

Script idempotency

The definition of a script within a Vagrantfile relies on using Ruby syntax to define a multiline string. The ability to script also allows our scripts to be *idempotent* if we implement checks on actions or the existence of resources. In particular, the shell script checks for the existence of the `nginx` executable using the `-x` flag:

```
    if [ ! -x /usr/sbin/nginx ]; then
      apt-get install -y nginx;
    fi
```

The script also checks for the existence of a symbolic link using the `-L` flag:

```
if [ ! -L /usr/share/nginx/html ]; then
  rm -rf /usr/share/nginx/html
  ln -s /vagrant/html /usr/share/nginx/html
fi
```

When this script is executed twice in a row, this should yield in no action being taken in subsequent calls to `vagrant provision`. This allows you to not only avoid repeating actions, but also to allow for easy iteration on the environment. Subsequent provisioning operations should only apply changes, not the entire script.

See also

*   Vagrant documentation on the shell provisioner: `http://docs.vagrantup.com/v2/provisioning/shell.html`.
*   *ShellHacks* has a good overview of `bash` commands to verify file existence: `http://www.shellhacks.com/en/HowTo-Check-If-a-File-Exists`.
*   *Linux Shell Scripting Cookbook, Second Edition, Shantanu Tushar* and *Sarath Lakshman, Packt Publishing*. This is a good guide to get started with shell scripting with some recipes on more complex cases than what will be covered in this book.

Provisioning with external shell scripts

While inline scripts can be a useful tool to execute larger command blocks, some provisioning operations are so large and/or complex that it can be useful to create and maintain them separately from the Vagrantfile itself. Maintaining these scripts separately can also make maintaining provisioning scripts and Vagrantfiles much simpler.

Getting ready

In this recipe, we'll modify the `nginx-install` script, which was created in the previous recipe. In that example, a provisioning script was defined within a Ruby variable: a string embedded within the Vagrantfile itself. When provisioning scripts begin growing to involve multiple steps or different logic, it can be difficult to create and modify scripts within a Vagrantfile. In most cases, we will want to remove the scripting from the Vagrantfile and instead execute provisioning from standalone scripts.

Before we create new provisioning scripts, let's recreate our `html` directory configuration of the previous recipe. In a working directory, initialize a Vagrantfile and create a subdirectory named `html`. This `html` directory, in our working directory, will be shared with our guest machine, which is mounted from the root filesystem at `/vagrant/html`. This will become the document root for the web server running in the Vagrant machine.

In this `html` directory, create a file named `index.html` (this will be the default page for the web server). In this example, the full content of the `index.html` file will be:

```
<html>
  <body>
    The index.html file in the Vagrant external script directory.
  </body>
</html>
```

With this file in place, our working directory will look similar to the previous recipe:

```
├── Vagrantfile
├── html
│    └── index.html
```

In this recipe, we will add a provisioning script that will install the nginx web server and link the default document root to the shared `/vagrant/html` directory in the Vagrant machine.

How to do it...

1. In our working directory, create a script, which will hold provisioning instructions named `nginx-install.sh`. The contents of this file will hold a simple script that will install nginx and create a symbolic link from the default nginx root to `/vagrant/html`.

 This recipe assumes that we are using the Ubuntu 14.04 LTS distribution specified in the Vagrantfile. We will use the `nginx` package in the default Ubuntu 14.04 repositories (this assumes that the `nginx` binary will be installed at `/usr/bin/nginx` with the web server document root being at `/usr/share/nginx/html`). This recipe can be modified for other Linux operating systems (such as Fedora and Red Hat variants) by using the `yum` package (`yum install nginx`) and the configurations for the `yum` package.

The contents of the shell scripts will be similar to the string defined in the previous recipe:

```
#!/bin/bash

if [ ! -x /usr/sbin/nginx ]; then
  apt-get install -y nginx;
fi

# Default NGINX directory: /usr/share/nginx/html
# Replace this with symbolic link to vagrant directory.
```

```
if [ ! -L /usr/share/nginx/html ]; then
  rm -rf /usr/share/nginx/html
  ln -s /vagrant/html /usr/share/nginx/html
fi
```

2. With the shell script in place and the `html` directory as described in the preceding section, start with a simple Vagrantfile:

```
# -*- mode: ruby -*-
# vi: set ft=ruby :

VAGRANTFILE_API_VERSION = "2"

Vagrant.configure(VAGRANTFILE_API_VERSION) do |config|
  config.vm.box = "puppetlabs/ubuntu-14.04-32-nocm"
end
```

3. Add configuration directives to execute the shell script with a `path` command, and add a directive to forward web traffic on the guest (port `80`) to our host port (`8080`). The complete Vagrantfile is as follows:

```
# -*- mode: ruby -*-
# vi: set ft=ruby :

VAGRANTFILE_API_VERSION = "2"

Vagrant.configure(VAGRANTFILE_API_VERSION) do |config|
  config.vm.box = "puppetlabs/ubuntu-14.04-32-nocm"
  config.vm.provision "shell", path: "nginx-install.sh"
  config.vm.network "forwarded_port", guest:80, host:8080
end
```

4. Execute the `vagrant up` command. After the machine successfully starts, open `http://localhost:8080` in a web browser. The HTML file in the working directory is displayed as follows:

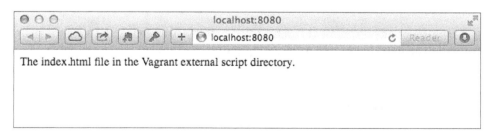

How it works...

Executing shell scripts outside of the Vagrantfile provides a few distinct advantages to inline scripting.

Shell provisioning

The use of external shell scripts enables us to create more complex scripts (perhaps testing and maintaining them outside the Vagrantfile itself). This is typically the case when executing more than one or two commands or perhaps using conditional logic when provisioning. Shell scripting can also be combined with other shell commands or even different provisioners. One example can be to use a shell script in order to bootstrap configuration management software before executing the appropriate provider. A Vagrantfile that bootstraps a working Puppet environment prior to executing the Puppet provisioner might look like the following code:

```
config.vm.provision "shell", path: "bootstrap.sh"
config.vm.provision "puppet" do |puppet|
  ...
end
```

Provisioning with different shell languages

The other ability that external shell scripts allows is the ability to define and use scripts written using languages other than the default shell scripting languages of the box. For example, we could write a Perl script to install our nginx web server:

```
#!/usr/bin/perl -w

unless(-e '/usr/sbin/nginx'){
  `apt-get install -y nginx`
}
```

If we save this script as `ngnix.pl`, we can execute this Perl script using the Vagrant shell provisioner. The definition of this provisioner in a Vagrantfile would be:

```
config.vm.provision "shell", path: "nginx.pl"
```

As long as the scripting environment (such as Perl or Ruby) is installed, the Vagrant shell provisioner can be used to execute provisioning scripts that are written in a number of scripting languages.

See also

▶ Vagrant shell provisioner documentation: `http://docs.vagrantup.com/v2/provisioning/shell.html`

4
Provisioning with Configuration Management Tools

In this chapter, we will cover:

- ▸ Configuring Vagrant environments with Puppet
- ▸ Configuring Vagrant environments with Chef
- ▸ Configuring Vagrant environments with Salt
- ▸ Configuring Vagrant environments with Ansible

Introduction

Vagrant environments can be provisioned using various scripting languages and the Vagrant shell provisioner, but in many cases, developers and administrators might find advantages in provisioning Vagrant environments using configuration management tools. The number of configuration management tools available to users is large (and growing). In these recipes, we will focus on four primary configuration management tools in Vagrant environments:

- ▸ Puppet
- ▸ Chef
- ▸ Salt
- ▸ Ansible

These four tools are (at the time of this writing) the most popular choices to manage not only Vagrant environments, but also large-scale systems' deployments. These tools can be used to manage Vagrant environments alone, but in many cases, the configuration scripts developed for Vagrant environments can be deployed across larger environments, allowing configurations used for development to ultimately be used in production websites. Vagrant is then the *glue* that helps systems administrators tie development environments into something that very closely mirrors configurations in production environments.

The choice of configuration management tools typically relies on development skills and the types of environment(s) that are being managed. This chapter cannot cover all the options and features of each environment, but will hopefully give a quick introduction to each of them. In all cases, the configuration management tools will enable administrators to create provisioning scripts that are:

- ▶ **Cross-platform**: Scripts written in a development environment on one platform can often be applied to other environments with less modification than shell scripting.

- ▶ **Reusable**: Most configuration management tools allow developers to create modular code that can be reused in different scenarios and use cases. For example, installing and configuring software packages from repositories is rarely a task that will be performed in specific environments. For example, the deployment and configuration of a web server such as the Apache web server is a task that is identical in different environments, making an *Apache module* an ideal case for a reusable package.

Configuration management and Vagrant boxes

The primary difference in approach between the various configuration management tools is the *agent* infrastructure. Some tools (such as Puppet or Chef) rely on software installed on the virtual machine (or node) itself to manage provisioning tasks. Other tools (such as Ansible) rely on software installed on a single machine (such as the host machine in a Vagrant setup) to perform remote commands on a target node (or virtual machine), requiring software installation on the host machine rather than the guest.

Due to this difference, tools that require agents often provide Vagrant boxes with the agent installed (Puppet Labs provides these machines through the Vagrant Cloud), or developers could write bootstrap scripts to prepare a virtual machine to configure management agents.

Configuring Vagrant environments with Puppet

Puppet Labs (http://puppetlabs.com) is a suite of configuration management tools to manage servers and desktops. Puppet comes in two flavors: open source versions that are the core functionality of the suite and the commercial Puppet Enterprise that combines and extends the open source core to be a complete product for data center management. Puppet is also a cross-platform configuration management tool; scripts can be written with Puppet that can configure most Unix (Linux, OS X) and Windows machines.

Vagrant machines use the Puppet agent infrastructure to perform provisioning operations on a machine. Puppet agents can function in one of two ways:

▶ By connecting to a **Puppetmaster** to retrieve configuration information. A Puppetmaster is a server (or cluster of servers) that is a centralized location for systems to retrieve system configurations.

▶ By executing a `puppet apply` command to interpret and apply configurations locally. This is often referred to as the *masterless Puppet* approach.

The use of Puppet will vary based on how Vagrant environments are managed. It might be desirable to manage stable environments from a centralized Puppetmaster, or it might be desirable to allow for local modification (or Puppet development) from configurations locally executed.

In this recipe, we will use the masterless approach to apply Puppet configurations locally with some reusable code (a Puppet module) that is obtained from the Puppet Forge repository.

Getting ready

Before we can start with configuring a machine with Puppet, we will need to note a few things about our environment:

▶ When we install software with Puppet, it is necessary to use a Vagrant box that either has the Puppet agent installed or creates a *bootstrapping* script that configures package repositories and installs the Puppet agent in the virtual machine. In this case, we can use a Vagrant box provided by Puppet Labs that can be found in the Vagrant Cloud repository. In this specific example, we will use an Ubuntu 14.04 box that contains the Puppet agent:

```
https://vagrantcloud.com/puppetlabs/ubuntu-14.04-64-puppet
```

▶ If the environment being created is for Puppet development, it might also be necessary to install the Puppet agent on the host machine. Having the agent installed on the host will allow for management of Puppet modules and resources by the host for Vagrant guests to be provisioned. A common example is to use the `puppet module` utility (or the `librarian-puppet` tool) to manage and use modules. For example, the `apache` module code used in this example can be downloaded directly from the Puppet Forge by executing the command (with `vagrant_directory` being the location of the Vagrantfile):

```
puppet module install puppetlabs-apache \
  --modulepath <<vagrant_directory>>/puppet/modules
```

How to do it...

To use Puppet (or any configuration management tool), there are typically two main items to manage: the Vagrant environment (Vagrantfile) and the configuration management code executed by a provisioner. This recipe will use Puppet to install and start the Apache web server in our Vagrant environment.

Setting up the Vagrant environment

1. Setting up the Vagrant environment starts with defining a basic Vagrantfile. In this example, we will use a Vagrant box provided by Puppetlabs that has the Puppet agent preinstalled. We will also define the default box as `web` and forward port `80` on the guest (the standard HTTP port) to port `8080` on the host machine:

```
# -*- mode: ruby -*-
# vi: set ft=ruby :
VAGRANTFILE_API_VERSION = "2"
Vagrant.configure(VAGRANTFILE_API_VERSION) do |config|
    config.vm.define "web", :primary => true do |web|
      web.vm.box = "puppetlabs/ubuntu-14.04-64-puppet"
      web.vm.hostname = "web"
      web.vm.network "forwarded_port", guest: 80, host: 8080
  end
end
```

2. Create a `puppet` directory to hold the Puppet code. While not strictly necessary, keeping provisioning code in a separate directory can make managing multiple provisioners simpler. Within this directory, create a `manifests` directory and a `modules` directory. With all directories in place, the structure (including the Vagrantfile) should look like this:

```
.
├── Vagrantfile
└── puppet
    ├── manifests
    └── modules
```

3. Configure the Puppet provisioner in the Vagrantfile. The Puppet provisioner requires parameters to be set that define paths to our `manifest` and `modules` directories that we created in the previous step, as well as a manifest filename. (In this case, `site.pp`.) We will create this file in the next section:

```
web.vm.provision "puppet" do |puppet|
  puppet.manifests_path = "puppet/manifests"
  puppet.manifest_file  = "site.pp"
  puppet.module_path = "puppet/modules"
end
```

 There is no requirement for a `modules` directory when running the Puppet provisioner or Puppet in general. It is a rare case where a project does not use modules, so we have included a `modules` directory and `module path` directory.

With the Puppet provisioner configured, we can start writing our Puppet code.

Configuring Puppet

With the Vagrant environment in place, we can start putting together the Puppet configuration. In this example, we'll use a bit of reusable code downloaded from the Puppet Forge to install the Apache web server.

1. Open Puppet Forge (`http://forge.puppetlabs.com`) in a web browser. The Puppet Forge contains a large number of reusable modules to install and configure many types of software.

2. Search for an `apache` module by entering the term `apache` in the search box. The search results will give you a large number of modules available to manage the Apache web server:

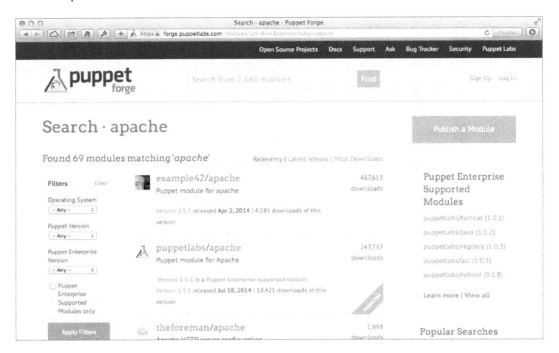

3. Select the `puppetlabs/apache` module. This module page will give you some information about the module as well as instructions on how to install the module and documentation on how to use the module in your environment:

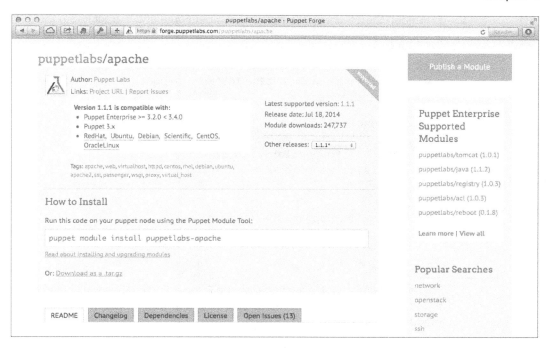

4. Install the `puppetlabs/apache` module into the `modules` directory. There are two ways you can do this:

    1. If you have puppet installed on your host machine (not in the Vagrant box), install the module with the `puppet module` command from the directory that contains the `puppet` directory, which was created in an earlier step:

        **puppet module install --modulepath=puppet/modules
        puppetlabs-apache**

        Note that the `puppet module` tool resolves dependencies and downloads them as well as the specified module itself. The output of the command will specify the dependencies downloaded to support the `apache` module:

        ```
        └─┬ puppetlabs-apache (v1.1.1)
          ├── puppetlabs-concat (v1.1.0)
          └── puppetlabs-stdlib (v4.3.2)
        ```

2. Download the `.tar.gz` file from the Puppet Forge and extract it into the `modules` directory. As this method does not resolve dependencies, this is something that will need to be done manually. In the `apache` module itself, there is a file named `metadata.json` (older modules might use a `Modulefile` instead). In this file, there is a snippet that contains the module dependencies:

```
"dependencies": [
  {
    "name": "puppetlabs/stdlib",
    "version_requirement": ">= 2.4.0"
  },
  {
    "name": "puppetlabs/concat",
    "version_requirement": ">= 1.0.0"
  }
]
```

These modules are also available on the Puppet Forge. These will have to be found, downloaded, and extracted similar to how the `puppetlabs-apache` module was installed.

 There is also a tool that can manage Puppet module dependencies called `librarian-puppet` that many Puppet developers find useful. We will cover the use of `librarian-puppet` in *Appendix B, A Puppet Development Environment*.

5. With the module dependencies installed, we need to create a *manifest* file that will govern how resources and modules are used. In the Vagrant provisioning snippet created earlier, a manifest file was specified:

```
puppet.manifest_file  = "site.pp"
```

We'll create this file now in the `manifests` directory, which was also created earlier. The code of this file (`manifests/site.pp`) will look like this:

```
node web {
  class{"apache":
    default_vhost => false,
  }

  apache::vhost{"default-host":
    docroot => "/var/www/html",
    docroot_owner => 'www-data',
    docroot_group => 'www-data',
    default_vhost => true,
```

```
        logroot => '/var/log/apache2',
        port => 80,
    }
}
```

This rather simple manifest file does three things: specifies an action for the `web` node (our Vagrant machine name), calls the `apache` class to install the Apache web server, and defines an `apache::vhost` type that will create a default virtual host for our web server.

> Note that the defined virtual host is specific to the `apache2` package present in the Ubuntu repositories. Puppet manifests and modules can be written to allow for different actions, based on facts, to be taken. Consult the Puppet documentation (`http://docs.puppetlabs.com`) to learn more about how to create Puppet modules.

6. With the manifest file in place, run the `vagrant up` command in our working directory (the one with the Vagrantfile). The Vagrant startup will output the results of the Vagrant startup as well as run the Puppet agent, once Puppet indicates the end of `catalog run`:

```
==> web: Notice: Finished catalog run in 9.93 seconds
```

Opening `http://localhost:8080` in a web browser will display the default Ubuntu start page:

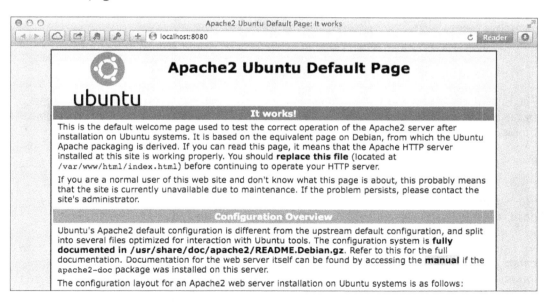

How it works...

The recipe presented here provisioned a Vagrant machine by interacting with a Puppet agent installed on the Vagrant machine with the Puppet provider. Specifically, we defined two separate folders to hold our Puppet logic:

- The `manifests` directory that holds Puppet manifests. These manifests are how the agent (or in a distributed case, the Puppetmaster) determines how the catalog will be compiled. In this case, note that our Vagrant machine hostname (`web`) matches the definition of a node:

```
node web {
...
}
```

By default, a `node` is identified by the hostname that is defined in our Vagrantfile:

```
web.vm.hostname = "web"
```

The manifest file can also use regular expressions to match defined hostnames to nodes.

- The Puppet `modules` directory contains Puppet modules and packaged reusable code. In this example, we used modules downloaded from the Puppet Forge (although, this directory could also hold modules developed for our own software projects). Puppet determines where to find these modules by the definition of a `modulepath`, which our Vagrantfile specifies with the definition:

```
puppet.module_path = "puppet/modules"
```

A Puppet `modulepath` can include multiple directories, something that can be used to separate modules downloaded from the Puppet Forge from modules being developed to support our own software projects.

The Puppet agent uses the node definition to determine the resources required to be defined by the manifest files and modules. The agent compiles a catalog of resources to be applied, then applies the catalog, creates resources, installs packages, and so on.

There's more...

Provisioning a Vagrant machine with Puppet can take a number of different forms. In this case, we've relied on using the masterless `puppet apply` command to compile and execute generated catalogs. If the purpose of Vagrant machines is not to develop system configurations, but rather to *publish* them to a larger team, it might be advantageous to have catalogs generated from a centralized location. Puppet does this through the Puppetmaster infrastructure. A Puppetmaster infrastructure will hold all the manifest and module code and accept requests from remote nodes to compile catalogs. A calling Puppet agent can execute catalogs created by Puppetmasters and report back on the results and success or failure of the catalog application.

To use a Puppetmaster, Vagrant also bundles a provisioner called the `puppet server` provisioner. If our web manifests and modules were hosted on a remote Puppetmaster (such as `puppetmaster.mycompany.com`), the provisioning section in the Vagrantfile would be:

```
web.vm.provision "puppet_server" do |puppet|
  puppet.puppet_server = "puppetmaster.mycompany.com"
end
```

Rather than applying local manifests, the Puppet agent in the Vagrant machine will attempt to retrieve a catalog rather than compiling one locally.

See also

There are many great resources and training opportunities to learn Puppet and the various components of the Puppet ecosphere. Here are a few resources to get you started:

- Puppet Labs: `http://www.puppetlabs.com`
- *Puppet Labs Documentation*: `http://docs.puppetlabs.com`
- *Puppet Apply Provisioner*: `https://docs.vagrantup.com/v2/provisioning/puppet_apply.html`
- *Puppet Agent Provisioner*: `https://docs.vagrantup.com/v2/provisioning/puppet_agent.html`

Configuring Vagrant environments with Chef

Vagrant environments can be provisioned using the **Chef** (`http://www.getchef.com/chef/`) configuration management tool. Chef is a configuration management tool that defines system resources with reusable components called recipes. The Chef client interprets these recipes into resources (such as packages, files, and so on) to be configured.

Chef recipes can also be applied in one of two ways:

- Applying local Chef recipes with the *chef-solo* tool
- Contacting a centralized Chef Server to obtain recipes to be applied to a local node by the client application

The client-server and local modes of Chef operation are very similar to the architecture deployed by Puppet in the previous recipe, with the architectural choices of solo or client-server operation being determined by project requirements.

This recipe will demonstrate the use of the Vagrant `chef-solo` provisioner to apply Chef recipes to install and configure a basic Apache web server.

Getting ready

Using the `chef-solo` provisioner requires that the Vagrant machine has a client application installed prior to executing the provisioner. The client can be installed in a Vagrant box prior to use, or we can enable Vagrant itself to manage the installation and configuration of the Chef client. The Chef project publishes an installation tool for the client called the **Chef Omnibus**, a script that performs all installation tasks for the Chef client. The Omnibus installer itself is a simple shell script that can be executed using the command:

```
curl -L https://www.getchef.com/chef/install.sh | sudo bash
```

This will install the Chef client on the machine where the command is executed. To ease the installation process in a Vagrant environment, there is a Vagrant extension (a Vagrant plugin) that we can install to enable some additional commands in our Vagrantfiles. This plugin is called the **vagrant-omnibus** plugin. (The *See also* section has links to the GitHub project with more information.)

Install the Vagrant plugin on your host machine by executing a Vagrant command:

```
vagrant plugin install vagrant-omnibus
```

This will download the plugin code and install it locally for use in our projects.

Additionally, when developing Chef code, we might want to install Chef on our host machine as well as the Vagrant guests. This allows us to use the `knife` tool on the host machine to download reusable code and dependencies. Install the Chef development tools on your workstation by following the instructions for your platform at `http://downloads.getchef.com/chef-dk`.

If the tools are installed correctly, you should be able to use `knife` from the command line. Executing `knife --version` should yield the following output (for the version of Chef at the time of this writing):

```
► knife --version
Chef: 11.14.6
```

How to do it...

In this example, we'll do things a bit *manually*, adding cookbooks locally using the `knife` tool. This will demonstrate the functions of cookbooks and how they can be reused for basic tasks in Chef provisioning.

Setting up the Vagrant environment

First, let's set up the Vagrant environment. Our Vagrant environment will perform three tasks: booting a machine, bootstrapping with the Chef client, and executing the `chef-solo` provisioner.

1. In a new directory, create a Vagrantfile. To start, this will be a pretty basic Vagrantfile using `chef/ubuntu-14.04` box:

```ruby
# -*- mode: ruby -*-
# vi: set ft=ruby :
VAGRANTFILE_API_VERSION = "2"

Vagrant.configure(VAGRANTFILE_API_VERSION) do |config|
  config.vm.define "web", primary: true do |web|
        web.vm.box ="chef/ubuntu-14.04"
        web.vm.network "forwarded_port", guest:80, host:8080
  end

end
```

   This Vagrantfile defines a `web` server and forwards the default HTTP port (`80`) to our localhost port `8080`.

2. Install the latest version of the Chef client. Using the `vagrant-omnibus` plugin installed in the *Getting ready* section, Omnibus can be executed with a new `web.omnibus.chef_version` property in the web machine definition:

```ruby
config.vm.define "web", primary: true do |web|
  web.omnibus.chef_version = :latest
  web.vm.box ="chef/ubuntu-14.04"
  web.vm.network "forwarded_port", guest:80, host:8080
end
```

   This will prompt the installation of the latest version of the Chef client on the `web` machine.

3. Define the `chef-solo` provisioner along with a single cookbook named `webserver` in the web machine definition:

```ruby
config.vm.define "web", primary: true do |web|
  web.omnibus.chef_version = :latest
  web.vm.box ="chef/ubuntu-14.04"
  web.vm.network "forwarded_port", guest:80, host:8080
  web.vm.provision "chef_solo" do |chef|
    chef.add_recipe "webserver"
  end
end
```

   This will instruct the provisioner to apply the cookbook named "`webserver`" to the Vagrant environment. With this defined, we now need to set up Chef provisioning.

Setting up Chef provisioning

Setting up the Chef provisioner will require us to create our new *webserver* cookbook and the dependencies required for the web server.

1. Create a directory in the working directory called `cookbooks`. By default, the Vagrant `chef-solo` provisioner searches for cookbooks to apply from this directory. The directory structure should look like this:

    ```
    ├── Vagrantfile
    ├── cookbooks/
    ```

2. In the `cookbooks` directory, create a new cookbook with the `knife` utility:

    ```
    knife cookbook create webmaster --cookbook-path .
    ```

    This will create a new folder named `webmaster` (this is where we will write our Chef code).

3. Find the `apache2` cookbook in the **Chef Supermarket**. To install an Apache web server, we'll want to find an appropriate cookbook. In a web browser, open the `https://community.opscode.com/cookbooks` URL. The Supermarket is a web application that allows you to browse and search for available cookbooks. Search for `apache2`.

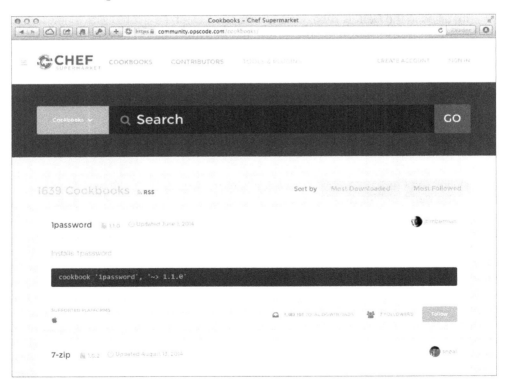

4. Take a look at the search result for `apache2`. The search result will link to a detailed page with information and instructions on how to use the `apache2` module:

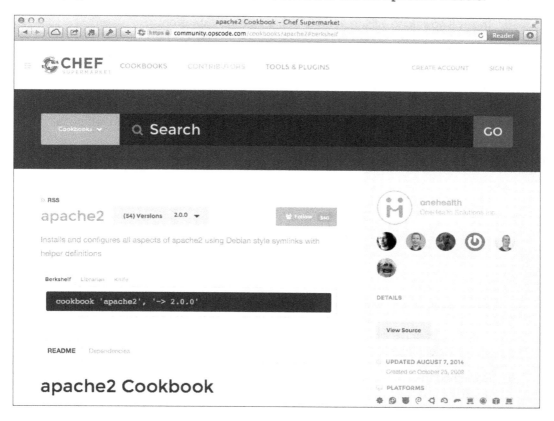

Note the two sections of the page shown in the preceding screenshot: the first tabbed interface with sections detailing how to use the module with **Berkshelf**, **Librarian**, or **Knife**, and a second tabbed interface with a **README** and defined **Dependencies**.

5. Find the command used to download the cookbook using `knife`. This appears in the tab called **Knife**. (Keep the browser window open at this step.)

```
knife cookbook site install apache2
```

```
knife cookbook site download apache2
```

6. In your local `cookbooks` directory, execute the `knife` download command:

```
knife cookbook site download apache2
```

This will download a file that ends with a `tar.gz` extension.

7. Extract the `tar.gz` file using the `tar` command. In this case:

```
tar xzvf apache2-2.0.0.tar.gz
```

This will extract the contents of the file into a directory named `apache2`.

8. In the web browser, find the tab named **Dependencies** at the bottom tab panel:

This is a list of the other cookbooks we will need to download in order to support the `apache2` cookbook.

9. Download the other dependencies with the `knife` utility. Do this by executing three commands:

```
knife cookbook site download iptables
knife cookbook site download logrotate
knife cookbook site download pacman
```

This will download three `tar.gz` files, one for each cookbook.

10. Extract the downloaded files with the `tar` utility, specifically:

```
tar xzvf iptables-0.14.0.tar.gz
tar xzvf logrotate-1.6.0.tar.gz
tar xzvf pacman-1.1.1.tar.gz
```

After extracting all cookbooks, we will have four directories: `apache2`, `iptables`, `logrotate`, and `pacman`.

11. With a text editor, open the default recipe file created when we used the `knife` utility to generate the `webserver` cookbook. After the cookbook generation, the file is in our created `webserver` folder: `webserver/recipes/default.rb`. The contents of this file are boilerplate code generated by the `knife` utility:

```
#
# Cookbook Name:: webserver
# Recipe:: default
#
# Copyright 2014, YOUR_COMPANY_NAME
#
# All rights reserved - Do Not Redistribute
#
```

12. Add some code to include our `apache2` module, define a virtual host, and instruct the `apache2` service to start. This will be added after the comment blocks in `default.rb`:

```
include_recipe "apache2"

web_app "localhost" do
  docroot "/var/www/html"
  cookbook 'apache2'
end

service "apache" do
  action :start
end
```

 Note that the Chef code here looks like the Ruby code that defines our Vagrantfiles. Chef itself uses the Ruby language and a Ruby object model to define the provisioning actions.

13. Once we have defined the use of the `apache2` cookbook, we'll want to add this dependency to our `webserver/metadata.rb` file. Add our dependency at the end of the file:

```
depends "apache2"
```

14. With all files saved, return to the directory where our Vagrantfile is and execute the `vagrant up` command. The Vagrant command should return text relaying the status of the provisioner and the output of the Chef provisioning run.

15. Once the provisioning run is complete, open `http://localhost:8080` in a web browser. This should display the default Ubuntu Apache2 holding page:

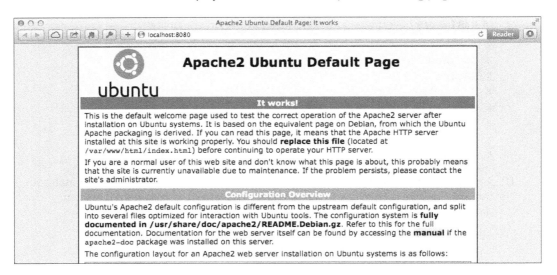

We have now completed our first provisioning run with the `chef-solo` provisioner.

How it works...

When using the `chef-solo` provisioner, we've seen a few features of Vagrant.

▶ Rather than a fully Chef-enabled Vagrant box, we've *bootstrapped* a new instance using a Vagrant plugin. A Vagrant plugin is a way to extend Vagrant to provide more functions, namely:

```
web.omnibus.chef_version = :latest
```

A Vagrant plugin can save a few steps in environment bootstrapping. Even if you are planning to use your scripts to bootstrap server instances, you might want to write and execute bootstrap scripts using the shell provisioner.

▶ We used the Chef `knife` tool to download open source cookbooks from the Chef Supermarket. Chef comes with a rich set of tools to manage virtual environments; we've only seen a small bit of what `knife` can do, and will mention briefly a cookbook management tool called `Berkshelf` in the following *There's more...* section.

▶ We used the `chef-solo` provisioner to provision an Apache web server in our virtual environment.

Chef is a large and varied project with many tools and options that cannot be covered here, but even the basic provisioning options available make Chef a useful tool when provisioning Vagrant environments.

There's more...

Chef is a very powerful tool for managing systems with many features. Vagrant developers may wish to be aware of two important techniques for combining Chef and Vagrant.

Managing environments with Berkshelf

When using Chef, there are a number of alternative tools to set up and use Vagrant environments.

A prominent example is the Berkshelf tool (`http://berkshelf.com`) that is included in the Chef Development Kit, which we installed on our host machine in the *Getting ready* section. When creating a new cookbook, the `berks init` function to generate cookbook stubs automatically includes a Vagrantfile to run and test the cookbook. In our case, as we created a new cookbook called `webserver`, we could start a new project by simply executing:

```
berks init webserver
```

A new Vagrantfile is created that performs all the preceding listed steps—adds the Omnibus installer: an appropriate Vagrant box, and executes the `chef-solo` provisioner. Berkshelf also manages cookbook dependencies, making individual download and extraction of Chef cookbooks unnecessary. When starting new cookbooks (or development environments), using Berkshelf to generate the entire environment might be your preferred option.

Provisioning with Chef Server

Along with the `chef-solo` provisioner, Chef environments can also be managed with a Chef Server: a centralized resource to store and manage cookbooks. A machine can retrieve provisioning instructions from the server and apply them using the `chef-client` tool. Vagrant contains a separate `chef-client` provisioner to interact with Chef Servers. Interacting with the server requires two items of information:

- A valid Chef Server URL
- A valid PEM key to authenticate with the Chef Server

With both these items, a `chef-client` provisioner can be configured as follows:

```
Vagrant.configure("2") do |config|
  config.vm.provision "chef_client" do |chef|
    chef.chef_server_url = "SERVER URL"
    chef.validation_key_path = "<PATH TO KEY>/validkey.pem"
  end
end
```

In this case, the Chef client in the Vagrant machine (which still requires the `vagrant-omnibus` plugin) can contact the Chef server to obtain a run list for the client. There are also other options to configure the client interaction with the server (see the Vagrant documentation for the provider for a list of options available to use the `chef-client` provisioner):

```
https://docs.vagrantup.com/v2/provisioning/chef_client.html
```

See also

▶ The Chef provisioner: `http://www.getchef.com/chef/`

▶ The Chef Omnibus installer: `https://docs.getchef.com/install_omnibus.html`

▶ Vagrant Omnibus plugin: `https://github.com/schisamo/vagrant-omnibus`

▶ Berkshelf: `http://berkshelf.com`

▶ Vagrant documentation – *Chef Client Provisioner*: `https://docs.vagrantup.com/v2/provisioning/chef_client.html`

Provisioning Vagrant environments with Salt

Vagrant machines can also be provisioned using **Salt** (`http://www.saltstack.com`). Salt is a combination of configuration management and system orchestration software. Salt relies on a *master/minion* architecture to enable configuration and control of large clusters of machines, but in this example, we will use *masterless* salt to provision a basic web server and develop our own salt *states* that define system configurations.

Getting ready

Compared to other configuration management provisioners, getting started with the Vagrant Salt provisioner is rather easy; the provisioner itself will check for the existence of the `salt-call` command. If the command does not exist in the Vagrant machine, the provisioner will bootstrap the environment without plugins or bootstrapping scripts.

In this example, we'll write a simple state to provision the `apache2` web server and apply the state using masterless Salt to apply our state.

How to do it...

Provisioning a Vagrant machine with Salt follows a similar approach to provisioning with Chef or Puppet tools. There are a few crucial differences in setting up Salt provisioning.

Configuring the Vagrant environment

1. As the Salt provisioner does not require bootstrapping or setup, we can start with a simple Vagrantfile. In this case, we'll use an Ubuntu 14.04 machine and forward the HTTP port on the guest machine to port `8080` on the host. The complete Vagrantfile is as follows:

```ruby
# -*- mode: ruby -*-
# vi: set ft=ruby :
VAGRANTFILE_API_VERSION = "2"
Vagrant.configure(VAGRANTFILE_API_VERSION) do |config|
  config.vm.define "web", primary: true do |web|
    web.vm.box ="puppetlabs/ubuntu-14.04-32-nocm"
    web.vm.network "forwarded_port", guest: 80, host:8080
  end
end
```

2. Create a folder to hold our Salt configurations and state files. This folder will be named `salt`, and will contain a folder named `roots` that will hold our state files. In our working directory (with the Vagrantfile), our working tree should look like the following code:

```
├── Vagrantfile
└── salt
    └── roots
```

3. Share the `salt` directory with our Vagrant machine. We will need to follow a convention for masterless Salt and mount our local `salt/roots` directory to the guest machine's `/srv/salt` directory. Add the synced folder configuration to our web definition:

```
web.vm.synced_folder "salt/roots/", "/srv/salt/"
```

4. Specify the Salt provisioner. We'll largely use default runtime here, specifying a configuration file (we'll add this in the next step) and specify that we should run *highstate*: the provisioning step for masterless Salt:

```
web.vm.provision :salt do |salt|
  salt.minion_config = "salt/minion"
  salt.run_highstate = true
end
```

This will trigger the Salt provisioning steps once we configure and create our state files.

Configuring Salt provisioning

1. Configure the Salt Minion. Minion is the process that will drive provisioning of the system and has a rather large set of configurations. For our purposes, the minion configuration can consist of two lines in a file named `minion` in the `salt/` directory. The file containing two lines is as follows:

```
master: localhost
state_top: top.sls
```

   This will specify that the file will run locally and look for the file `top.sls` to drive provisioning in a default directory. (The code examples included for this chapter include a complete minion configuration file.)

2. Create our `top.sls` file in the `salt/roots` directory in our working directory. This file will determine the application of other states applied to the Vagrant machine. These files are in YAML format, where spacing is important. Here is the complete `top.sls` file:

```
base:
  '*':
webserver
```

   The `top.sls` file here specifies that all machines (in this case, only a single Vagrant machine) apply the `webserver` state.

3. Create the web server state by creating the `webserver.sls` file in the same directory as `top.sls`, which was created in the previous step. The contents of `webserver.sls` will be:

```
apache2:            # ID declaration
  pkg:              # state declaration
    - installed     # function declaration
```

   This will declare that the `apache2` package should be installed in our environment.

4. With our state files now complete, start the environment with the `vagrant up` command. The command should return output about bootstrapping Salt. If the `salt-call` command is not present, then output information about the installation of the default Apache configuration.

5. Verify the environment by opening the `http://localhost:8080` page in a web browser. The Ubuntu Apache2 install page should be visible:

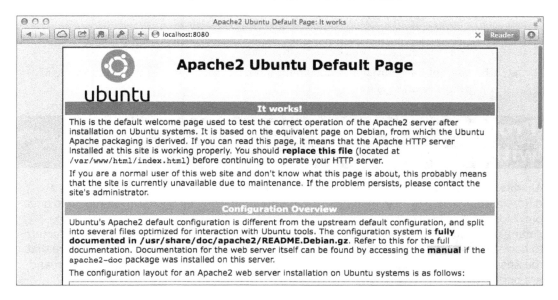

If the page is visible, then the Vagrant environment has been successfully provisioned with the Salt provisioner.

How it works...

What we've seen in this recipe is an example of using the Salt Minion to provision a Vagrant machine. The Salt Minion is somewhat similar to other provisioning agents, but the configurations can be somewhat different when using standalone mode. In particular:

▶ In this example, we relied on a default mount for the `root` directory that held the state files, these (and many other) configurations can be overridden in the minion configurations. The source code that accompanies this example contains a generated file with many other options and documentation of minion configurations.

▶ We created a few simple example state files that are executed using the `highstate` command. Salt configuration consists of a number of states, each with a different purpose. In practice, most configuration with Salt is done at the *sls* level with the `highstate` command executing the highest *state* in the Salt stack, which is typically `top.sls`.

The Salt provisioner also has many options to either bootstrap a Salt master, or interact with a master/minion architecture. The *Salt Provisioner* documentation (`https://docs.vagrantup.com/v2/provisioning/salt.html`) is a good place to get started with more advanced Salt configurations.

See also

▶ *SaltStack*: `http://saltstack.com`

▶ The *SaltStack Walk-through*: `http://docs.saltstack.com/en/latest/topics/tutorials/walkthrough.html`

▶ The Vagrant *Salt Provisioner* documentation: `https://docs.vagrantup.com/v2/provisioning/salt.html`

Provisioning Vagrant environments with Ansible

Ansible (`http://www.ansible.com`) is a configuration management tool that takes a different approach to system management. Rather than using an agent-driven model to drive provisioning, Ansible executes commands on remote nodes using SSH. For our purposes, setting up Ansible provisioning is somewhat simpler as there is not an agent or infrastructure to bootstrap, as there were in the previous three recipes. Ansible does, however, require that the Ansible software be installed on the host machine, as provisioning operations begin and are performed by the host on Vagrant machines.

 As Ansible is designed to execute commands using SSH; support for Windows operating systems is not currently available. At the time of writing this book, the Ansible team has announced some Windows support and plans to expand Ansible support for PowerShell infrastructure. See `http://www.ansible.com/blog/windows-is-coming` for further details. This recipe will apply only to Unix-based operating systems, mainly Linux and OS X.

Getting ready

To use Ansible, we first need to install Ansible on the host machine; there are no requirements to install software on the guest Vagrant machines. Ansible is widely distributed in package repositories and might be available for your platform. Consult the installation documentation (`http://docs.ansible.com/intro_installation.html#installing-the-control-machine`) for the instructions for your operating system.

If you wish to run the latest versions, Ansible can also be installed using the `python pip` command:

```
sudo pip install ansible
```

If you are running OS X, Ansible is also available from the **Homebrew** repositories (`http://brew.sh`) and can be installed with a simple command:

```
brew install ansible
```

There are also options to install from source, consult the Ansible installation documentation for information on how to build and deploy Ansible on your system.

This recipe will demonstrate the use of the Ansible provisioner to execute a simple playbook or set of Ansible commands.

How to do it...

To use the Vagrant Ansible provisioner, we'll need to set up a basic Vagrantfile as well as the Ansible playbooks.

Setting up the Vagrant environment

1. For this environment, we'll start with a simple Vagrantfile:

```
# -*- mode: ruby -*-
# vi: set ft=ruby :
VAGRANTFILE_API_VERSION = "2"

Vagrant.configure(VAGRANTFILE_API_VERSION) do |config|
  config.vm.define "web", primary: true do |web|
    web.vm.box ="puppetlabs/ubuntu-14.04-32-nocm"
    web.vm.network "forwarded_port", guest: 80, host:8080
  end

end
```

This Vagrantfile will start a base Ubuntu 14.04 machine and forward port 80 on the Vagrant machine to port 8080 on the localhost.

2. Create a directory to hold our Ansible playbooks. For this example, we'll name the directory `ansible` so that our working directory consists of our Vagrantfile and the `ansible` directory.

3. Configure the Ansible provisioner in our Vagrantfile by adding the provisioner code below the `web.vm.network` definition. The provisioner code that we'll add specifies our playbooks to run. It also specifies that Ansible should execute with the `sudo` command in the virtual machine:

```
web.vm.provision "ansible" do |ansible|
  ansible.playbook="ansible/playbook.yml"
  ansible.sudo = true
end
```

Once this is in place, we can proceed to write our Ansible playbook.

Setting up Ansible playbooks

1. Create a playbook file by creating the `playbook.yml` file (a YAML-formatted document) in the `ansible` directory:

    ```
    ---
    - hosts: all
      remote_user: vagrant
      tasks:
      - name: Install apache2 web server
        apt: name=apache2 state=present
    ```

    This playbook will instruct Ansible to apply this to all hosts with the vagrant user and a single task in order to install the Apache web server.

2. With this playbook in place, execute the `vagrant up` command to boot and provision the Vagrant environment. Vagrant will then output information about booting the machine and the output of the Ansible provisioner.

3. Verify that the command is completed successfully by opening `http://localhost:8080` in a web browser:

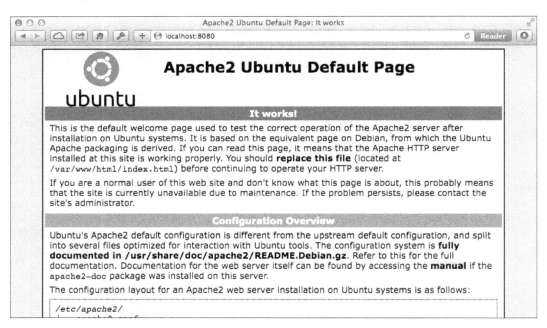

How it works...

As we noted in the *Getting ready* section, Ansible operates by issuing SSH commands to run from our host machine to the guest (Vagrant) machines. Setting up SSH in most situations can be a little tricky, as there are often a few steps involved in setting up users and the required private/public key infrastructure. Our Vagrant environment can use Ansible quite simply for two main reasons:

- When setting up the Ansible playbook, we choose to execute commands as the Vagrant user (the user that is typically present in publically distributed Vagrant boxes). If you are using a custom box, you'll want to be sure that your user is added to the playbook files.

- The Vagrant user can use `sudo` commands without the need to type a password. Again, this is true for most publically distributed Vagrant boxes.

Ansible interprets the playbook documents (written in YAML format) into a series of SSH commands that are used to provision the Vagrant machine.

See also

- Ansible: `http://www.ansible.com/home`
- Installing Ansible: `http://docs.ansible.com/intro_installation.html#installing-the-control-machine`

5
Networked Vagrant Environments

In this chapter, we will cover the following topics:

- ► Creating a local network
- ► Defining a multimachine environment
- ► Specifying the order of machine provisioners
- ► Creating clusters of Vagrant machines

Introduction

Standalone Vagrant environments can meet the needs of a variety of use cases. A common case would be using Vagrant to facilitate web and application development. In this case, forwarding the Vagrant guest web server port (usually port 80) to a port on the localhost would allow applications hosted on the web server to be accessed through a localhost address. (For example, opening `http://localhost:8080` in a browser.)

The port forwarding model might not work well for a few use cases. For example:

- ► Situations where a machine must be addressed using a real hostname, either in cases where a web application requires it or when a machine is using SSL certificates.

- ► Modeling deployment environments where different services are installed on dedicated machines. A common example would be developing a web application where a web application is installed and configured on a machine that connects to a database running on a separate virtual machine.

- ▶ Modeling clustered environments where virtual machines might register themselves for discovery. As an example, Vagrant can be a useful tool to model and develop systems with **Consul** (`https://consul.io`) or **CoreOS** (`http://coreos.com`).

- ▶ Vagrant can be used to assign IP addresses or set up service discovery that allows virtual machines to have fixed (or discoverable) IP addresses to be used by other services. This chapter contains recipes with basic Vagrant networking and use cases where a network of virtual machines is required.

 While Vagrant networking makes setting up networks rather simple, keep in mind that virtual machines will still use the local system's RAM and CPU. The number of virtual machines that can be used in a Vagrant network are limited by the resources of the host machine. If you have the need to create larger networks of machines, Vagrant can facilitate the use of cloud providers to create virtual machines using the compute resources of cloud services. This effectively allows you to *rent* computing space for a development environment. These use cases will be covered in the next chapter.

Creating a local network

Creating a local network is the process of assigning an IP to a Vagrant machine.

Getting ready

Before setting up a network, you might want to consider the type of network you wish to create. Vagrant essentially offers two options:

- ▶ A **local** network that limits access to **Virtual Machines** (**VMs**) running on the host computer. The hypervisor software typically specifies an address range.

- ▶ A **bridged** network that will obtain an IP address from outside the local range. This means that the Vagrant machine can be accessed as any other machine on the host computer network. You can, for example, specify bridged networking if you want your Vagrant machine to be a shared resource among many different people in your office. The downside is that the Vagrant machine will obtain an IP that cannot be controlled by the Vagrant environment and will rely on the larger network environment. This will make it difficult to create machine networks and we will not cover bridged networking in any depth here.

In this recipe, we'll create a simple Vagrant machine running Ubuntu 14.04 LTS and assign an IP to the machine. We'll also discuss how we can use these machines on our host environment.

A quick note regarding static IP addresses

When using a static IP address on a local machine, we'll want to ensure that we are using IP ranges reserved for private networks to avoid any possible collisions with our outside environment. The IP ranges for private networks are established by the Internet Engineering Task Force and are reserved for use by private networks. The three ranges are defined in RFC1918 (`http://tools.ietf.org/html/rfc1918`) as:

- `10.0.0.0-10.255.255.255` (10/8 prefix)
- `172.16.0.0-172.31.255.255` (172.16/12 prefix)
- `192.168.0.0-192.168.255.255` (192.168/16 prefix)

When assigning static IPs in a Vagrantfile, choose one of these ranges to assign IPs in. More specifically, you'll likely want to assign ranges in either the `172` or `192` ranges, many corporate (or even home) networks use the `10` range for resources located within the wider network by default. Your hypervisor software will typically alert you if you are running into an IP address conflict.

How to do it...

1. Start with a simple Vagrantfile. In this case, we'll start with a basic machine definition:

```ruby
# -*- mode: ruby -*-
# vi: set ft=ruby :

VAGRANTFILE_API_VERSION = "2"

Vagrant.configure(VAGRANTFILE_API_VERSION) do |config|
  config.vm.box = "puppetlabs/ubuntu-14.04-64-nocm"
end
```

2. To this configuration, assign an IP to the Vagrant machine using the `config.vm.network` parameter. Add this parameter after the box definition:

```ruby
config.vm.network "private_network", ip: "192.168.99.100"
```

This will assign the `"192.168.99.100"` IP to the Vagrant machine.

3. Start the machine with the `vagrant up` command.

4. Once the machine starts, verify that the IP address has been set by using `vagrant ssh` to access the machine. Once at a command prompt for the Vagrant machine, verify the IP ranges of the machine by using the `ifconfig` command. This will display information about the machine's network environment. For this example, the `inet addr` sections are the most important.

```
● ○ ●                        2. vagrant@localhost: ~ (bash)
vagrant@localhost:~$ ifconfig
eth0      Link encap:Ethernet  HWaddr 00:0c:29:e1:d4:2d
          inet addr:192.168.30.129  Bcast:192.168.30.255  Mask:255.255.255.0
          inet6 addr: fe80::20c:29ff:fee1:d42d/64 Scope:Link
          UP BROADCAST RUNNING MULTICAST  MTU:1500  Metric:1
          RX packets:1154 errors:0 dropped:0 overruns:0 frame:0
          TX packets:890 errors:0 dropped:0 overruns:0 carrier:0
          collisions:0 txqueuelen:1000
          RX bytes:134072 (134.0 KB)  TX bytes:99865 (99.8 KB)

eth1      Link encap:Ethernet  HWaddr 00:0c:29:e1:d4:37
          inet addr:192.168.99.100  Bcast:192.168.99.255  Mask:255.255.255.0
          inet6 addr: fe80::20c:29ff:fee1:d437/64 Scope:Link
          UP BROADCAST RUNNING MULTICAST  MTU:1500  Metric:1
          RX packets:102 errors:0 dropped:0 overruns:0 frame:0
          TX packets:8 errors:0 dropped:0 overruns:0 carrier:0
          collisions:0 txqueuelen:1000
          RX bytes:21318 (21.3 KB)  TX bytes:648 (648.0 B)

lo        Link encap:Local Loopback
          inet addr:127.0.0.1  Mask:255.0.0.0
          inet6 addr: ::1/128 Scope:Host
          UP LOOPBACK RUNNING  MTU:65536  Metric:1
          RX packets:0 errors:0 dropped:0 overruns:0 frame:0
          TX packets:0 errors:0 dropped:0 overruns:0 carrier:0
          collisions:0 txqueuelen:0
          RX bytes:0 (0.0 B)  TX bytes:0 (0.0 B)

vagrant@localhost:~$ ▮
```

Note that the Vagrant machine has two separate IPs on different interfaces defined here as `eth0` and `eth1`. The machine can respond to either of the IPs (one is assigned by the hypervisor, while the other is defined in the Vagrant configuration).

It is entirely possible that there is only one (the assigned) IP address for our Vagrant machine. For this example, the hypervisor added our IP address as a second interface, while keeping the other address for internal consistency.

Using a static IP address with a hosts file

Now that we have a machine with an assigned static IP address, there are a few ways that can be used to access the machine. In many cases, with static IPs, we will want to refer to the machine with a *real* hostname (that is, referring to this as web.local rather than 192.168.99.100). Computers are usually assigned these addresses through the **Domain Name System** (**DNS**) where you register an address and hostname with a DNS entry, but for local development, DNS can be overridden with a local *hosts file*. On Unix (Linux and OS X included), the hosts file is /etc/hosts. Windows machines also have hosts files typically in the \Windows\system32\drivers\etc\hosts file, although this has been different for some versions; consult your system documentation for the proper path to the hosts file.

Warning!

You will require administrator privileges on your machine to modify your /etc/hosts file. Modifying this file can have some adverse effects on your system and even leave your computer open to attack, should an override be added to the hosts file. If you modify this file, make sure that the *localhost* entry is left untouched (with IP address 127.0.0.1).

You know about every entry added to this file (some system attacks attempt to add entries to the file in order to override DNS entries to sensitive sites in an attempt to trick a user into handing over sensitive data). By default, the only definition in the file is *localhost*, make sure that the only items in here are entries that are added by you or with your explicit permission.

To use our Vagrant machine as a *real* IP address (say, for instance, web.local), we can add a new entry with the IP address assigned in the Vagrantfile. A complete /etc/hosts file with only the addition of web.local assigned to our static IP of 192.168.99.100 would look like this:

```
                              2. vim /etc/hosts (vim)
##
# Host Database
#
# localhost is used to configure the loopback interface
# when the system is booting.  Do not change this entry.
##
127.0.0.1       localhost cthompson
192.168.99.100  web.local

255.255.255.255 broadcasthost
::1             localhost
fe80::1%lo0     localhost

"/etc/hosts" [readonly] 13L, 275C
```

The Vagrant machine can then be accessed using the `web.local` name address. (For example, opening a default web server on the Vagrant machine would be `http://web.local` rather than a forwarded port address of something like `http://localhost:8080`.)

How it works...

In this recipe, we assigned a static IP address to a Vagrant address and assigned a URL to this IP. Assigning a static IP address requires a Vagrantfile parameter with an unused IP address on a local network. (Be sure to use addresses in the *local* range as specified in the *Getting ready* section of this recipe.)

Vagrant itself will use an internal network defined by the hypervisor software. IP routing is managed by a virtualized infrastructure embedded in the hypervisor. You might have noticed this when Vagrant outputs messages about `vmnet` (if using VMware – other messages for different hypervisors) during the bootup cycle.

One issue that you might encounter when starting or stopping many Vagrant hosts (or virtual machines in general) is that an occasional error can be thrown when the virtual networking infrastructure runs into collisions assigning IPs. In these cases, it might be okay to restart the affected virtual machine, but in many cases, a clean reboot of the host system might be required to *reset* the hypervisor network.

There's more...

There are a few different ways that we could manage static IPs and *real* URLs without manually editing the `/etc/hosts` file, with some simple methods using Vagrant plugins. There are many plugins to choose from and we will not be able to cover all the options. See `https://github.com/mitchellh/vagrant/wiki/Available-Vagrant-Plugins` for an up-to-date list of available plugins. Plugins dealing with assigning *real* addresses fall into two categories:

> ▶ **Using /etc/hosts files**: There are a number of plugins available to manage host machine's `/etc/host` files. One of the most commonly used plugins is the **vagrant-hosts** plugin that can be installed with the command:
>
> ```
> vagrant plugin install vagrant-hosts
> ```
>
> The `vagrant-hosts` plugin will supply another option, available in the Vagrantfile, that allows assigned IPs to be added to the host machine's `/etc/hosts` files with an additional attribute added along with an IP assignment:
>
> ```
> web.vm.provision :hosts
> ```

When starting a Vagrant machine with a plugin that edits the `/etc/hosts` file, Vagrant will prompt for a password; editing the hosts file will always require administrator privileges. Using plugins to manage this file might be simpler for frequent use, but be sure that all users of the created Vagrantfile have the plugin installed.

▶ **Using /etc/resolver for local DNS**: There are also Vagrant plugins that create local DNS servers and modify the *resolver* files on the guest and host operating systems. Some of them (such as *landrush*) are quite fully featured and can cover many complex scenarios for local development. Again, these plugins might require administrator privileges as DNS configuration can also have some adverse effects. You might wish to consider the type of network that you are establishing (whether or not it is a *host only* DNS setting or a setting shared between guests and hosts) and the operating systems supported by the plugins before choosing an appropriate one.

See also

▶ IETF RFC 1918: *Address Allocation for Private Internets* (`http://tools.ietf.org/html/rfc1918`)

▶ Wikipedia *hosts (file)* entry is a nice summary of how you can override DNS settings on your local machine: `http://en.wikipedia.org/wiki/Hosts_(file)`

▶ Currently available (and listed) Vagrant plugins are at `https://github.com/mitchellh/vagrant/wiki/Available-Vagrant-Plugins`

Defining a multimachine environment

The primary reason we wish to create networks of Vagrant machines is often because we wish to model an environment of more than one machine. A common example might be the desire to model a web application with dedicated web server machines and database machines, or even an environment that creates a cluster of identical virtual machines.

In this recipe, we will create a simple multimachine environment as well as look at techniques to create clusters of Vagrant machines.

Getting ready

Before we start with creating an environment of many machines, let's review the technique of defining machine names. When creating a multimachine environment, we'll want to ensure that each machine has a unique name. A unique name can be assigned by *defining* a new Vagrant machine:

```
Vagrant.configure(VAGRANTFILE_API_VERSION) do |config|
  config.vm.define "definedmachine" do | definedmachine |
```

```
    << Actions >>
  end
end
```

The `config.vm.define` method is how we define machines and specify actions that will be performed on a specific host.

How to do it...

In this example, we will create a small network of two virtual machines that defines a simple two-tier web application with a web server and a database server. These two servers will be defined in a single Vagrantfile, and we will manage our networks using `/etc/hosts` methods rather than using DNS.

1. Start with a simple Vagrantfile without a machine or box definition:

```
# -*- mode: ruby -*-
# vi: set ft=ruby :

VAGRANTFILE_API_VERSION = "2"
Vagrant.configure(VAGRANTFILE_API_VERSION) do |config|
end
```

2. In the `|config|` section, define a database server using a Vagrant machine definition. We'll add some detail about this machine, namely, the box that it will use to boot the machine, and a unique hostname. In a multimachine environment, we'll usually want to define a machine IP (particularly in the case where one Vagrant machine (a web server) will need to connect to another (a database server)):

```
config.vm.define "database" do |db|
  db.vm.box = "puppetlabs/ubuntu-14.04-64-nocm"
  db.vm.hostname = "db01"
  db.vm.network "private_network", ip: "192.168.55.100"
end
```

3. Create a second defined machine in a block after the `|db|` code block. This will be the `web` machine:

```
config.vm.define "web" do |web|
  web.vm.box = "puppetlabs/ubuntu-14.04-64-nocm"
  web.vm.hostname = "web01"
  web.vm.network "private_network", ip:"192.168.55.101"
end
```

4. Verify that both these machines are defined using the `vagrant status` command. This command will provide a list of all defined Vagrant machines in the file:

```
● ● ● 2. cothomps@cthompson: ~/vagrantbook/vagrantbook-examples/Chapter5/1.2 Defining a Multi-Machine Environent (zsh)
▶ vagrant status
Current machine states:

database                    not created (vmware_fusion)
web                         not created (vmware_fusion)

This environment represents multiple VMs. The VMs are all listed
above with their current state. For more information about a specific
VM, run 'vagrant status NAME'.

vagrantbook-examples/Chapter5/1.2 Defining a Multi-Machine Environen46d  ✖ ⊨ ⬤
▶ []
```

The `vagrant status` command will provide a list of defined machines, and their status, as well as the provider that will be used.

5. To complete the example, we'll use the shell provisioner to define the `/etc/hosts` file in the web server. This allows the web server to refer to the database server with the `db01` hostname. The complete web server definition will include this provisioning command. (In this case, we will overwrite the `/etc/hosts` file, which will allow our provisioning to be idempotent, although we will need to take care to define the *localhost* entry):

```
config.vm.define "web" do |web|
  web.vm.box = "puppetlabs/ubuntu-14.04-64-nocm"
  web.vm.hostname = "web01"
  web.vm.network "private_network", ip:"192.168.55.101"
  web.vm.provision "shell",
      inline: "echo '127.0.0.1 localhost web01\n192.168.55.100
db01' > /etc/hosts"
  end
```

6. Start both machines by executing the `vagrant up` command. This command will return the startup commands of both machines. (In the case of using local hypervisors such as VMware Fusion, the machines will also boot in the order that is specified in the Vagrantfile.)

```
2. vagrant up (bash)
▶ vagrant up
Bringing machine 'database' up with 'vmware_fusion' provider...
Bringing machine 'web' up with 'vmware_fusion' provider...
==> database: Cloning VMware VM: 'puppetlabs/ubuntu-14.04-64-nocm'. This can tak
e some time...
==> database: Checking if box 'puppetlabs/ubuntu-14.04-64-nocm' is up to date...
==> database: Verifying vmnet devices are healthy...
==> database: Preparing network adapters...
==> database: Starting the VMware VM...
==> database: Waiting for machine to boot. This may take a few minutes...
```

There might be cases where we wish to start a single machine in the Vagrantfile. This can be accomplished by defining the machine that will be booted or provisioned. For example, to only boot the database server, we would execute the `vagrant up database` command.

7. Once the machines have booted, the status can be verified once again using the `vagrant status` command:

```
2. cthomps@cthompson: ~/vagrantbook/vagrantbook-examples/Chapter5/1.2 Defining a Multi-Machine Environent (zsh)
▶ vagrant status
Current machine states:

database                  running (vmware_fusion)
web                       running (vmware_fusion)

This environment represents multiple VMs. The VMs are all listed
above with their current state. For more information about a specific
VM, run `vagrant status NAME`.

vagrantbook-examples/Chapter5/1.2 Defining a Multi-Machine Environen46d ✖ ≈ ◓
▶
```

8. Access the web machine by using the `vagrant ssh` command, specifying that we wish to connect to the web machine:

```
● ● ●                    2. vagrant@web01: ~ (bash)
▶ vagrant ssh web
Welcome to Ubuntu 14.04 LTS (GNU/Linux 3.13.0-24-generic x86_64)

  * Documentation:  https://help.ubuntu.com/
vagrant@web01:~$ ▯
```

9. Verify that the web server can contact the database with the `db01` hostname:

```
● ● ●                    2. vagrant@web01: ~ (bash)
vagrant@web01:~$ ping db01
PING db01 (192.168.55.100) 56(84) bytes of data.
64 bytes from db01 (192.168.55.100): icmp_seq=1 ttl=64 time=0.465 ms
64 bytes from db01 (192.168.55.100): icmp_seq=2 ttl=64 time=0.487 ms
64 bytes from db01 (192.168.55.100): icmp_seq=3 ttl=64 time=0.497 ms
64 bytes from db01 (192.168.55.100): icmp_seq=4 ttl=64 time=0.791 ms
64 bytes from db01 (192.168.55.100): icmp_seq=5 ttl=64 time=0.739 ms
^C
--- db01 ping statistics ---
5 packets transmitted, 5 received, 0% packet loss, time 3998ms
rtt min/avg/max/mdev = 0.465/0.595/0.791/0.142 ms
```

With this network in place, we can proceed to the task of setting up our web application by using Vagrant provisioners (such as shell scripts, Puppet, Chef, and so on) to install and configure database and web servers with the appropriate software and configurations for your application.

How it works...

Setting up multimachine environments in this simple context works by:

▶ **Defining specific hosts and hostnames**: In the example, we defined a specific *web* server and a specific *database* server.

▶ **Defining the network settings required to make our environment work**: Specifically, we gave our web server the ability to locate the database server by modifying the web server's `/etc/hosts` file. This allows the web server to find the database server, but it will not allow the database server to contact the web server.

As such, this environment is relatively static, but will not require additional infrastructure to manage network and/or DNS; we have an environment where a web (or application server) can connect to a database server using a hostname defined in an `/etc/hosts` file. For many scenarios, this is sufficient to allow for local development.

Defining different machines locally will also allow for separation of concerns. There might be cases where a developer is actively doing web server development using local provisioners, but the details of how the database is created are not particularly important. In this case, it might be desirable to allow the web server to use local provisioning scripts, allowing the database server to be provisioned using a centralized provisioning tool such as a **Puppet master**. Using separate machines allows developers to model entire systems while working, hopefully mimicking a production deployment early in the development process.

Specifying the order of machine provisioners

When setting up multimachine environments, it is often important to specify how machines will provision and the order in which they will provision.

Getting ready

Before we start with an example, there are a few important things to keep in mind about the ordering of Vagrant resources:

> Ordering and dependencies in Vagrant environments are often dependent on the type of resource being provisioned. In the case of desktop hypervisors, a Vagrant boot cycle will proceed in the order in which resources are defined as the Vagrantfile will wait for the process to exit. In the case of provisioning cloud environments, the return to the calling Vagrant process will be nearly immediate (as the call itself is to an asynchronous RESTful API), so the boot order can be difficult to enforce without modifying the Vagrantfile to use cloud service APIs in order to check for boot health.

> Vagrant will also evaluate code blocks from the *outside in* order with the code in the inner blocks either overriding (should the property be the same) or in an *outside in* order, which is especially important for provisioners.

In this recipe, we will demonstrate overriding and ordering in a simple Vagrantfile.

How to do it...

1. Start with a simple Vagrantfile. In this case, simply a Vagrantfile with a default box name (something that could be generated with a `vagrant init` command):

```
# -*- mode: ruby -*-
# vi: set ft=ruby :
VAGRANTFILE_API_VERSION = "2"
```

```
Vagrant.configure(VAGRANTFILE_API_VERSION) do |config|
  config.vm.box = "puppetlabs/ubuntu-14.04-64-nocm"
end
```

2. Add a default hostname and provisioner to the Vagrantfile below the box definition:

    ```
    config.vm.hostname = "override_me"
    config.vm.provision "shell", inline: "echo 'First Command to
    Execute'"
    ```

    With this file, a `vagrant up` command would boot with a hostname of `override_me` and text from the first provisioner would be output to the console.

3. Add a machine definition block with an override for the hostname and box type. In this case, we will name the machine `second`, override the box type (to a box with Puppet installed), and execute a second provisioner. Our complete Vagrantfile looks like this:

    ```
    # -*- mode: ruby -*-
    # vi: set ft=ruby :

    VAGRANTFILE_API_VERSION = "2"
    Vagrant.configure(VAGRANTFILE_API_VERSION) do |config|
      config.vm.define "second" do |second|
        second.vm.box      = "puppetlabs/ubuntu-14.04-64-puppet"
        second.vm.hostname = "second"
        second.vm.provision "shell", inline: "echo 'Second Command to
    Execute'"
      end
      config.vm.box = "puppetlabs/ubuntu-14.04-64-nocm"
      config.vm.hostname = "first"
      config.vm.provision "shell", inline: "echo 'First Command to
    Execute'"
    end
    ```

4. Execute this Vagrantfile with the `vagrant up` command. The output will show us the results of our hostname and the order of provisioning:

```
● ● ● 2. cothomps@cthompson: ~/vagrantbook/vagrantbook-examples/Chapter5/1.3 Ordering Provisioning (zsh)
▶ vagrant up
Bringing machine 'second' up with 'vmware_fusion' provider...
==> second: Cloning VMware VM: 'puppetlabs/ubuntu-14.04-64-puppet'. This can tak
e some time...
==> second: Checking if box 'puppetlabs/ubuntu-14.04-64-puppet' is up to date...
==> second: Verifying vmnet devices are healthy...
==> second: Preparing network adapters...
==> second: Starting the VMware VM...
==> second: Waiting for machine to boot. This may take a few minutes...
    second: SSH address: 192.168.30.129:22
    second: SSH username: vagrant
    second: SSH auth method: private key
==> second: Machine booted and ready!
==> second: Forwarding ports...
    second: -- 22 => 2222
==> second: Setting hostname...
==> second: Configuring network adapters within the VM...
==> second: Waiting for HGFS kernel module to load...
==> second: Enabling and configuring shared folders...
    second: -- /Volumes/WD HDD/vagrantbook/vagrantbook-examples/Chapter5/1.3 Ord
ering Provisioning: /vagrant
==> second: Running provisioner: shell...
    second: Running: inline script
==> second: stdin: is not a tty
==> second: First Command to Execute
==> second: Running provisioner: shell...
    second: Running: inline script
==> second: stdin: is not a tty
==> second: Second Command to Execute                                    46d ✖ ⌐ ◕


vagrantbook-examples/Chapter5/1.3 Ordering Provisioning   master ✗   46d ✖ ⌐ ◕
▶ ▯
```

Note a few results from this Vagrantfile:

▶   Despite an initial name defined outside a block, the booted machine (and in this case, there is only one) is referred to by the `second` hostname

▶   The second host booted with a Vagrant box that has Puppet installed

▶   Two separate provisioners executed on our box (one defined *globally* and one defined within our |second| code block)

The ordering of execution and overriding is important in multimachine environments, as we can define provisioners that can run globally on all machines (such as an `apt-get update` command to be executed prior to other provisioning on a network of Ubuntu machines) or to define global rules with a few exceptions, such as the type of Vagrant box that will be available in the network.

How it works...

Vagrant defines variables and executions using ID fields for each parameter. Some parameters can only be defined once, such as the rule that *each Vagrant machine can only be started from a single box*, which causes box definitions in code blocks to override global parameters. In this case, we have a box override defined in our Vagrantfile:

```
config.vm.box = "puppetlabs/ubuntu-14.04-64-nocm"
config.vm.define "second" do |second|
  second.vm.box      = "puppetlabs/ubuntu-14.04-64-puppet"
end
```

The override specifies that the `second` box will use the `puppetlabs/ubuntu-14.04-64-puppet` box file.

Provisioners, on the other hand, are not overwritten as they are executed in an *outside in* order. Provisioners defined in a code block are executed after other provisioners outside the block are executed in a top-down manner. In this case, the order specified in the Vagrantfile caused the output of `First Command to Execute`, although it was listed below the code block:

```
config.vm.define "second" do |second|
  second.vm.provision "shell", inline: "echo 'Second Command to
Execute'"
end
config.vm.provision "shell", inline: "echo 'First Command to Execute'"
```

By default, provisioners are assigned different IDs, so overriding a provisioner requires specification of an ID in the Vagrantfile. Specifying an ID parameter will cause provisioners of identical IDs to perform an override. In this example, we can modify our provisioners to include the `shell_provisioner` ID definition:

```
config.vm.define "second" do |second|
  second.vm.provision "shell", inline: "echo 'Second Command to
Execute'", id:"shell_provisioner"
end
config.vm.provision "shell", inline: "echo 'First Command to
Execute'", id:"shell_provisioner"
```

With identical ID tags, executing a Vagrant provision operation only echoes output from the provisioner in the |second| code block:

```
==> second: Second Command to Execute
```

The ordering and overriding of provisioners and variables is especially important in multimachine Vagrant environments. A multimachine Vagrantfile can specify global parameters (such as boxes or common provisioning tasks) that allow for individual machines to override the global parameters.

Creating clusters of Vagrant machines

While the scenario of mimicking defined application architectures (for example, the two-tier or three-tier web application) can be accomplished using simple hosts files and hosts file modifications, creating *clusters* of Vagrant machines will require a bit of additional complexity, namely, the ability for machines to discover one another using either DNS servers or through service discovery.

In this example, we will create a cluster of Vagrant machines that can communicate with DNS connections using two additional tools:

▶ **Consul** (`https://consul.io`): This is a tool that allows services and machines to discover one another over a distributed network. In our case, we will use Consul very simply and set up a single Consul server that will serve multiple agents. We will, for this example, also limit our use of Consul to *node* discovery. This will essentially define a local DNS infrastructure.

▶ **Dnsmasq** (`http://www.thekelleys.org.uk/dnsmasq/doc.html`): This is a utility that allows local services (such as Consul) to serve DNS requests from local processes. In this case, Dnsmasq allows our system to use the DNS interface of a local Consul agent in order to serve DNS requests.

Getting ready

This recipe will install a number of different services using the combination of shell provisioners and Puppet. We will highlight some of the important aspects of the approach (the full source code is available in examples provided in the book).

How to do it...

1. Start our example with a simple Vagrantfile. This Vagrantfile will define a global box file that will be used to start all our machines. We'll choose a box that has the Puppet provisioner installed, as this is how we will provision the Consul server and agents:

    ```
    # -*- mode: ruby -*-
    # vi: set ft=ruby :
    ```

```
VAGRANTFILE_API_VERSION = "2"
Vagrant.configure(VAGRANTFILE_API_VERSION) do |config|
  # Define a global box file to be used by all machines.
  config.vm.box = "puppetlabs/ubuntu-14.04-64-puppet"
end
```

2. Define our Consul server. In this case, we're also going to use a variable to define a static network IP that we can point our cluster members to in order to join the cluster. On the server, we will also add provisioners that will execute an `apt-update` command (and install an unzip program) prior to executing the `puppet run` command. The Puppet scripts will install and initialize the Consul server (see the code example for full details):

```
VAGRANTFILE_API_VERSION = "2"
$consul_server_ip = "192.168.30.130"

Vagrant.configure(VAGRANTFILE_API_VERSION) do |config|
  # Define a global box file to be used by all machines.
  config.vm.box = "puppetlabs/ubuntu-14.04-64-puppet"
  # Create and provision a Consul server machine.
  config.vm.define "consul" do |consul|
    consul.vm.hostname = "consul"
    consul.vm.network "private_network", ip: $consul_server_ip
    consul.vm.provision "shell", inline: "apt-get update && apt-
get install -y unzip"

    consul.vm.provision "puppet" do |puppet|
      puppet.manifests_path = "puppet/manifests"
      puppet.module_path    = "puppet/modules"
      puppet.manifest_file  = "site.pp"
    end
  end
```

3. Define a variable that allows us to create an arbitrary number of cluster members in our system. Add this variable before the definition of the `consul_server_ip` variable in the previous step. These variables are global throughout the Vagrantfile and can be used by each Vagrant machine defined. In fact, we will use the `consul_server_ip` variable when we instruct our cluster members to join the cluster in this example:

```
# Define a variable - the number of web nodes.
$cluster_nodes = 3
$consul_server_ip = "192.168.30.130"
```

4. Define the Consul server and provisioning steps. This will include two provisioning steps: a shell script that updates the `apt-repositories` command (this is a step that is only necessary on Ubuntu or Debian Linux distributions) and installs the `unzip` package. The second runs the `puppet apply` provisioner against the Vagrant machine. The Puppet scripts will install and start the Consul server:

```
config.vm.define "consul" do |consul|
  consul.vm.hostname = "consul"
  consul.vm.network "private_network", ip: $consul_server_ip
  consul.vm.provision "shell", inline: "apt-get update && apt-get install unzip"

  consul.vm.provision "puppet" do |puppet|
    puppet.manifests_path = "puppet/manifests"
    puppet.module_path    = "puppet/modules"
    puppet.manifest_file  = "site.pp"
  end
end
```

5. With the Consul server in place, we'll now define the cluster members. Recall that we defined a parameter named `$cluster_nodes` (we'll use this to create a number of Vagrant machines). We'll do this by using a Ruby iterator. Create a new code block that contains this iterator:

```
(1..$cluster_nodes).each do |i|
  << Code To Define Nodes>>
end
```

This will create an execution loop that will define the number of desired machines.

6. In the loop, define a virtual machine by using the `i` iterator to define a unique name to the cluster. We can define the `vm_name` constant and assign this constant as the hostname of our machine:

```
config.vm.define vm_name = "cluster%02d" % i do |cluster|
  cluster.vm.hostname = vm_name
end
```

With the definition of the cluster machines in place, the Vagrantfile can be verified by executing the `vagrant status` command. This command should return a list of all the defined machines, including those defined in our looping construct:

```
● ● ● 2. cothomps@cthompson: ~/vagrantbook/vagrantbook-examples/Chapter5/1.4 Creating a Network of Vagrant Machi...
▶ vagrant status
Current machine states:

consul                    not created (vmware_fusion)
cluster01                 not created (vmware_fusion)
cluster02                 not created (vmware_fusion)
cluster03                 not created (vmware_fusion)

This environment represents multiple VMs. The VMs are all listed
above with their current state. For more information about a specific
VM, run `vagrant status NAME`.

vagrantbook-examples/Chapter5/1.4 Creating a Network of Vagrant Machines   master
  ✗                                                                46d ✖ ↳ ◓
▶ ☐
```

7. Now, define the provisioning steps required to join the `cluster` virtual machines to the Consul cluster. We'll do this in three steps for a client: the update for our Ubuntu/Debian machines, a `puppet run` command to install and configure the clients, and finally a step to execute a `join` command using the defined server IP:

```ruby
(1..$cluster_nodes).each do |i|
  config.vm.define vm_name = "cluster%02d" % i do |cluster|
    cluster.vm.hostname = vm_name
    cluster.vm.provision "shell", inline: "apt-get update &&
apt-get install -y unzip"
    cluster.vm.provision "puppet" do |puppet|
      puppet.manifests_path = "puppet/manifests"
      puppet.module_path    = "puppet/modules"
      puppet.manifest_file  = "site.pp"
    end
    cluster.vm.provision "shell", inline: "consul join
#{$consul_server_ip}"
  end
end
```

8. With all the provisioners (including our Puppet modules) in place, start the environment with the `vagrant up` command. This command should note that four machines will start:

```
●  ◉  ●                          2. vagrant up (bash)
▶ vagrant up
Bringing machine 'consul' up with 'vmware_fusion' provider...
Bringing machine 'cluster01' up with 'vmware_fusion' provider...
Bringing machine 'cluster02' up with 'vmware_fusion' provider...
Bringing machine 'cluster03' up with 'vmware_fusion' provider...
==> consul: Cloning VMware VM: 'puppetlabs/ubuntu-14.04-64-puppet'. This can tak
e some time...
▯
```

Starting these separate machines could take a while to boot, but after a few minutes, the Vagrant startup should complete.

9. Access the first cluster machine with the `vagrant ssh cluster01` command.

10. Verify that a Consul cluster is active by executing the `consul members` command. This should return the list of three servers:

```
●  ◉  ●                       2. vagrant@cluster01: ~ (bash)
vagrant@cluster01:~$ consul members
Node        Address             Status  Type    Build  Protocol
cluster01   192.168.30.129:8301 alive   client  0.4.0  2
consul      192.168.30.130:8301 alive   server  0.4.0  2
cluster02   192.168.30.131:8301 alive   client  0.4.0  2
cluster03   192.168.30.132:8301 alive   client  0.4.0  2
vagrant@cluster01:~$ ▯
```

11. The individual cluster members can also be pinged using the Consul DNS interface. From the `cluster01` machine, the `cluster02` machine can be *pinged* with the `cluster02.node.vagrant.consul` hostname:

```
●  ◉  ●                       2. vagrant@cluster01: ~ (bash)
vagrant@cluster01:~$ ping cluster02.node.vagrant.consul
PING cluster02.node.vagrant.consul (192.168.30.131) 56(84) bytes of data.
64 bytes from 192.168.30.131: icmp_seq=1 ttl=64 time=0.335 ms
64 bytes from 192.168.30.131: icmp_seq=2 ttl=64 time=0.680 ms
64 bytes from 192.168.30.131: icmp_seq=3 ttl=64 time=0.378 ms
^C
--- cluster02.node.vagrant.consul ping statistics ---
3 packets transmitted, 3 received, 0% packet loss, time 2001ms
rtt min/avg/max/mdev = 0.335/0.464/0.680/0.154 ms
vagrant@cluster01:~$ ▯
```

12. Verify that other nodes can be pinged by using the `<hostname>.node.vagrant.consul` pattern. In this case, we should be able to ping `consul.node.vagrant.consul` and `cluster02.node.vagrant.consul` with them responding as a *normal* host. In this case, however, rather than using a centralized DNS server, the hosts in the `consul` domain are identified by the DNS interface of a local Consul agent.

With the machines running and responding to DNS, the machines consist of an effective cluster. We can expand our provisioning to install software that we wish to run on clustered machines (such as load-balanced web servers or shared database instances).

How it works...

In this example, the cluster is effectively bound together with Consul. In our simple environment (only a handful of machines), we created a dedicated Consul server and connected agents through this server IP. It should be noted that a larger Consul deployment would use a number of servers possibly spread across geographic distributions and data centers. Consul is designed to allow for service discovery and failover for large clusters.

In our recipe, we are using Consul to provide flexible DNS services to a number of cluster members. There is no requirement (other than host system resources) on the number of servers that can join the cluster. In each case, the DNS entry follows the pattern:

```
<hostname>.node.vagrant.consul
```

The hostname can also be discovered without prior knowledge for the rest of the cluster by using the `cluster members` command to retrieve a list of hostnames that are present in the cluster. The reason for the longer DNS name is that the DNS interface to Consul will define machines by hostname (defined by the machine), the type of service being accessed (in this case, a `node`), the definition of a data center (`vagrant`), and the standard top-level domain defined by the Consul interface of `consul`. The `datacenter` parameter is defined in Consul configurations present on the agent and server. We simplify the deployment by specifying a single data center (or cluster of machines) named `vagrant`.

The Consul environment is defined by using the Puppet scripts executed by the `puppet apply` provisioner. The Puppet scripts are shared by all environments with each environment being given a catalog by definitions in the `site.pp` file. The `site.pp` file defines two types of hosts: servers and cluster members:

```
node /^consul/{
  class{"consul::server": }
}
node /^cluster/{
  include consul
}
```

The Consul module referenced in this recipe does four basic things:

▶ Installs the Consul software from a released ZIP package

▶ Configures Consul to run as a service

▶ Configures Consul to run in server or agent mode through configuration files

▶ Installs and configures Dnsmasq to forward DNS requests for the `consul` domain to the Consul agent

With a simple Consul server/agent configuration, we can create clusters of Vagrant machines without configuring DNS servers or relying on machine-specific configurations. We can also use this infrastructure to expand our Vagrant environment to different hypervisor or cloud computing environments.

There's more...

There are many different ways we could implement similar solutions, Consul is only one of the choices. This list is not an exhaustive list of possibilities, but there are some more popular methods to manage clusters of machines, including our clustered Vagrant environment.

Configuring DNS with plugins

There are a number of Vagrant plugins that create lightweight DNS servers to serve hostnames and IP addresses to servers configured to use the lightweight DNS server. This would be sufficient for simple local clusters, although plugins might not be accessible in all deployment environments.

Configuring a cluster with etcd

Another solution to cluster machines is provided by the CoreOS project (`http://coreos.com`). CoreOS aims to create massive clusters of CoreOS machines that operate nearly entirely by managing Docker container deployments with **etcd** acting as a service discovery layer for the containers as well as the fleet orchestration tool. The CoreOS project hosts a project demonstrating this type of clustering with CoreOS at `https://github.com/coreos/coreos-vagrant`.

Clustering with Apache Mesos

Another popular method for clustering and cluster management is **Apache Mesos**. The Mesos project also provides a Vagrant-based project to learn how to manage servers using Mesos at `https://mesosphere.com/docs/getting-started/`.

See also

▶ *Consul* (https://consul.io): a tool for service discovery. Consul is also sponsored by HashiCorp, the same company that supports Vagrant itself.

▶ *Dnsmasq* (http://www.thekelleys.org.uk/dnsmasq/doc.html): a network utility to forward and serve DNS requests.

▶ *Running CoreOS on Vagrant* (https://coreos.com/docs/running-coreos/platforms/vagrant/): a project provided by the CoreOS project to start clusters of CoreOS machines.

▶ *Apache Mesos* (http://mesos.apache.org) and *Mesosphere* (https://mesosphere.com).

6
Vagrant in the Cloud

In this chapter, we will cover the following topics:

- ▸ Using Vagrant with Amazon Web Services
- ▸ Using Vagrant with DigitalOcean
- ▸ Sharing local machines with HashiCorp Atlas
- ▸ Sharing web applications with HashiCorp Atlas

Introduction

While developing applications with local Vagrant machines is a very handy tool for development, there are a few cases where our local environments can be somewhat limited. Cloud-based services can be utilized with Vagrant to create more powerful development environments or perhaps even simply share resources with other developers.

This chapter contains recipes that address two primary use cases:

- ▸ The case where our development environments of one (or multiple) machines require more computational resources that are available on a development workstation
- ▸ The case where we wish to share our environments with other developers or end users

These cases can be met by using cloud services (such as Amazon Web Services or DigitalOcean) for greater computational power and a publically accessible deployment. Simple cases of sharing and demonstrating resources can also be accomplished fairly simply by using another HashiCorp service: Atlas (`http://atlas.hashicorp.com`).

This chapter will cover how to create and launch Vagrant machines with two fairly large cloud service providers. One is Amazon Web Services that provides a full feature set of private clouds and security rules and the second is DigitalOcean that provides simpler and cheaper computational instances without other infrastructure offerings. There are also many other cloud providers, such as **Rackspace** (`https://github.com/mitchellh/vagrant-rackspace`), the **Google Compute Engine** (`https://github.com/mitchellh/vagrant-google`) and, even a provider created by Microsoft for use with **Microsoft Azure** (`https://github.com/MSOpenTech/vagrant-azure`). It seems that getting started with Amazon Web Services and Digital Ocean will provide a jumping-off point to understand how Vagrant could also be used with these other cloud providers.

> Nearly all cloud providers will require some type of billing information in order to charge for computational resources. Take care in making sure that instances you launch with Vagrant are also destroyed after use. It might even be useful to verify that in your cloud provider's console the instances you have created have been destroyed. Leaving instances running can often lead to a rather surprising month-end bill.

Using Vagrant with Amazon Web Services

One of the more popular cloud platforms in recent years has been Amazon Web Services (`http://aws.amazon.com`), an **Infrastructure as a Service** (**Iaas**) platform that has several categories of services, ranging from simple computational instances (**Elastic Compute Cloud** or **EC2**) to fully managed application deployment services such as Amazon Beanstalk.

Vagrant can be used with **Amazon Web Services** (**AWS**) as either an extension of a desktop computing environment, using AWS to provide more computational power and better networking than you might have available in a desktop environment, or as a way to develop and test code written to interact with other Amazon applications or data services.

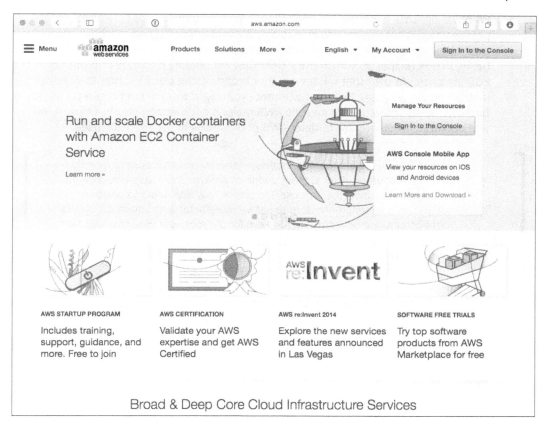

Getting ready

Before we can spin up and use EC2 instances with Vagrant, we'll need to set up an account with Amazon Web Services. While setting up the initial account is beyond the scope of this recipe, we can note a few practices that you will want to be aware of before starting with AWS:

- Signing up for an AWS account is relatively straightforward (Amazon Web Services makes this process as simple as possible). At the time of writing this book, get started by clicking on the **Get Started for Free** button on the AWS homepage at `http://aws.amazon.com`. This setup allows you to create an account and associate a billing method with your new account.

- When creating resources (which you can do outside of Vagrant), note that AWS provides a *free tier* for beginners. New accounts can launch and run certain services free of charge. The free tier is typically limited to smaller resource sizes (such as **t2.micro** EC2 instances, and single Availability Zone database instances, and so on). Amazon also offers very inexpensive storage for files using the **Simple Storage Service** (**S3**) that can be used to store and serve large files (such as Vagrant boxes).

- ▶ When using AWS, it is always a good idea to limit users to a 'least privilege' set of permissions. What this means is that only allow users (including machine 'users' for automated scripts or Vagrantfiles) the privileges they require to perform their required tasks. In this recipe, we will create a user that will be able to create and manage EC2 instances (a user that will have rather broad permissions in order to execute instructions in general). In a 'real' scenario, you might want to limit these permissions further to restrict the user to specific AWS regions or other conditions. Consult the IAM documentation on how to tailor AWS permissions to your specific uses.

An important corollary here is that never use the root account to directly manage resources. After signing up for an Amazon Web Services account, use this single user (the root user) to create new IAM users to perform actions. In addition, make sure to set up multifactor authentication on the root account and never create API keys for the root user. See the AWS *IAM Best Practices* document for information on how to safely set up and use your new account at `http://docs.aws.amazon.com/IAM/latest/UserGuide/IAMBestPractices.html`.

If you suspect suspicious activity in your AWS account, contact AWS customer support immediately as they can help you sort out what happened and can help settle any financial issues related to unauthorized use.

- ▶ Make sure that any unused resources (including Vagrant boxes) are not left running. The largest costs often encountered in typical AWS usage are associated with running EC2 instances. If your instance does not need to run constantly, feel free to either stop (or terminate) the instance in order to avoid being charged for the use of computational resources. Consult the EC2 pricing guide for an overview of instance types and their associated costs at `http://aws.amazon.com/ec2/pricing/`.
- ▶ If you do frequently use EC2 instances (including Vagrant use), you can consider instance reservations. Reserving an instance includes an up-front fee, but can yield cost savings in hourly charges later on.

In this recipe, we'll look at setting up an AWS account to launch Vagrant machines, which allows us to control a *cloud-based* environment as simply as a desktop-based one.

How to do it...

Before we can spin up Vagrant instances in AWS, we'll need to prepare a little groundwork. What we'll do in preparation is as follows:

1. We'll create an Amazon **Identity and Access Management** (**IAM**) account that will be used to create our Vagrant boxes. Creating separate accounts is also a good idea, as the credentials that will be needed to create EC2 instances could be used to potentially create instances that you will be billed for. It is critically important that the credentials you use to create instances have limited access and should never be credentials that can access your root account.

2. Set up a **Virtual Private Cloud** (**VPC**) to host our Vagrant instances. A VPC can be used to isolate cloud resources, giving us the ability to define security rules around the resources that we will create. It's a good idea to isolate the ability to access the EC2 instances that we will create to a fixed set of IP addresses (or in many cases, a single IP address).

Creating a Vagrant IAM account

Creating an IAM account and assigning credentials is part of the AWS IAM service, available under the **Administration & Security** menu. This example will show you how to create a new user with credentials that requires either the Amazon root account (the account created when you signed up with AWS) or another IAM user with administrative privileges to the account.

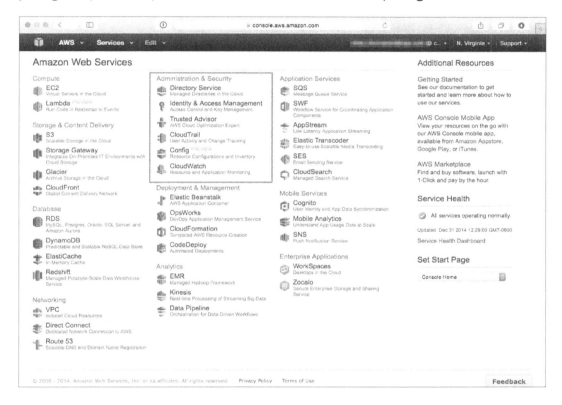

3. In the IAM console, choose **Users** from the navigation menu:

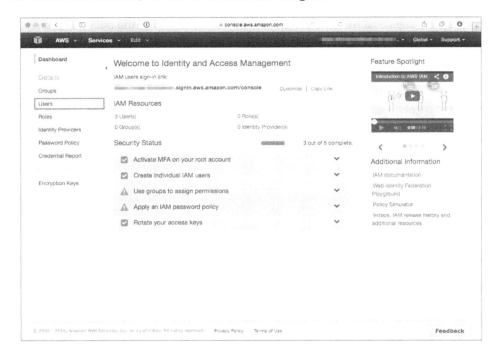

4. The users page will have an option to create new users. Select this option.

5. Create a new user with the username `vagrant-user`. There will be an option (checked by default) to generate an access key for each user. The access keys generated in this step will be the credentials that will be required for Vagrant to create new instances (ensure that this box is checked). We can also modify the access credentials of this user later on, should we wish to create or revoke these credentials.

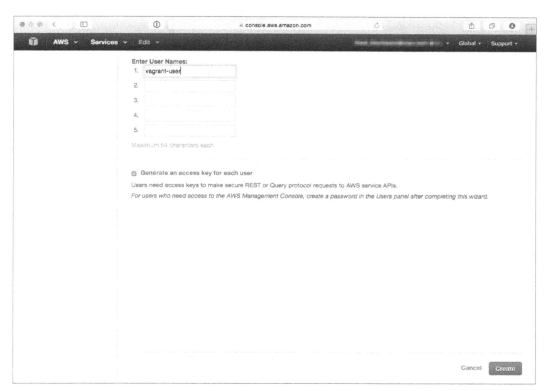

6. After creating the users, the next page will display two options immediately on the page along with an option to download credentials in a text file to manage the newly created credentials. Either way, this will be the last time that the new credentials will be available. After this step, credentials will need to be revoked and recreated. At this point, our new user does not have permissions to perform any action. We will need to grant permissions for this new user to create EC2 instances. It's a good idea at this stage to download the credentials file and store it in a safe location.

7. Now that the user has been created and we've downloaded the user credentials (save these for later), we'll want to grant permissions to our new user. Return to the **Users** page that we saw in step 2 (we can get there with the left-hand navigation). On the **Users** page, our new `vagrant-user` will be present. Click on the user to bring up the **Details** page:

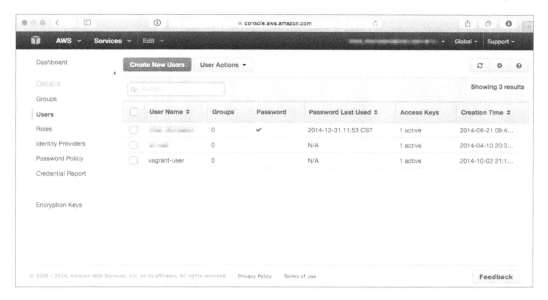

8. Clicking on the user brings up a user detail page. The detail page will have some general detail about the user (an ARN identifier, password settings, and so on). Scroll down the page until we come to the permissions section, and in particular the section labeled **User Policies**. Click on this button to add new permissions:

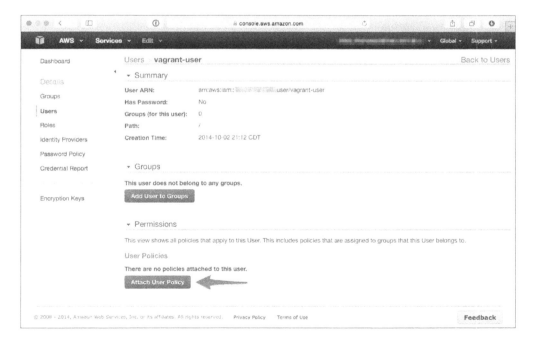

9. For this example, we are going to grant our `vagrant-user` fairly expansive permissions to EC2 in our account. The **Manage User Permissions** page will present a list of options. In our example, we are going to select the **Amazon EC2 Full Access** policy template:

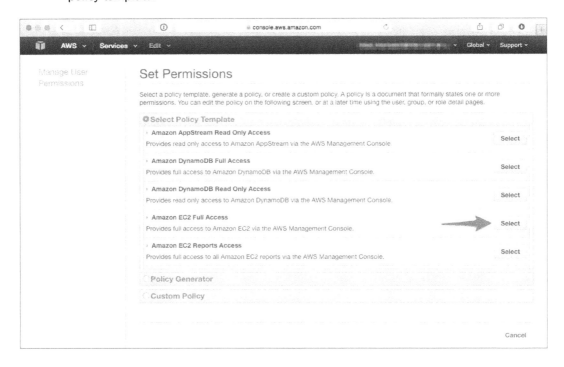

 You will often not wish to grant your users full access to EC2. Instead, you'll want to limit user access based on both permission sets (creating, assigning IPs, and so on) and geography (choosing a region that you will launch your instances into). In this case, *full access* is granted that allows you (the reader) to start with Vagrant/EC2 without implementing security for specific AWS regions. You might be in the situation where you are launching instances into the AWS Singapore region, others might be launching into AWS Ireland, and so on. Be aware that granting full access to users increases the chance that computational resources could be created (intentionally or unintentionally) that you will be charged for. Make sure that your access credentials are secure and that you review the number of EC2 instances you are running frequently.

With an account set up with credentials, we'll want to do one last thing before launching EC2 instances with Vagrant: securing our Vagrant machines from the outside world with a VPC.

Setting up a VPC

Amazon has recommended the creation of **Virtual Private Clouds** (**VPCs**) for all EC2 instances created in the AWS cloud, including the Vagrant machines that we will be launching. A VPC gives us the ability to control access to AWS resources from both the open Internet and other AWS resources by defining subnets. For example, a VPC could be set up to service a large number of developers and development services (or even production resources) with subnets restricting access from certain classes of Virtual machines (such as our Vagrant machines) to specific resources (such as an Amazon RDS database that is set up specifically for development or QA access while isolating production databases in the same VPC).

We'll set up a simple VPC that allows full access from the VPC to our development workstation. There are many resources (including the Amazon Web Services documentation) to help set up VPCs for more complex use cases. If you use AWS resources extensively, you'll also want to automate the creation of networks and resources using **CloudFormation** templates. In this example, we'll create our VPC using the web console in our account.

1. Access the VPC settings in the AWS Management Console. You'll find the VPC link under **Networking**:

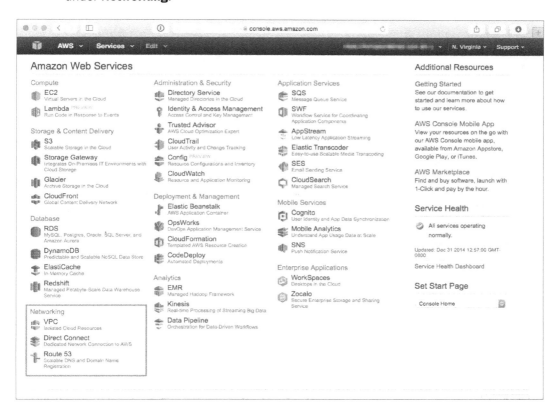

2. We'll use the simplest approach to create our VPC with the VPC wizard. There should be an option to start the wizard from the VPC console:

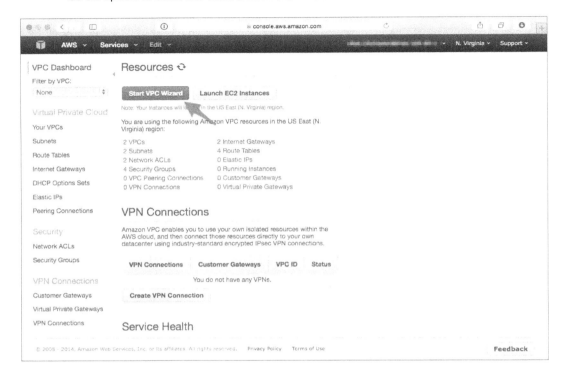

3. The VPC that we are going to create is the simplest type (a single public subnet within a VPC). We'll control access with security groups, but our Vagrant machines will require direct access to the Internet to retrieve software packages and configurations. This configuration of having machines able to access the outside Internet without NAT network setups is what AWS refers to as a *public* subnet. The wizard has a preconfigured VPC for this purpose:

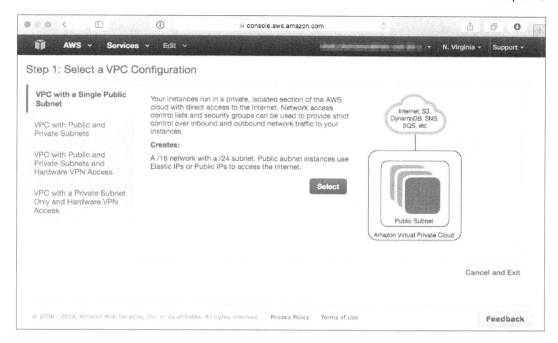

4. The final step in the wizard will prompt you to assign some names and network information about our new VPC. In this case, we'll name our VPC `vagrant-vpc` with a single subnet named `Vagrant Subnet`. For our case, the default network settings will work. These would likely only change if our new VPC is designed to connect to a local network using VPN connections between the VPC and a hardware (or software) router.

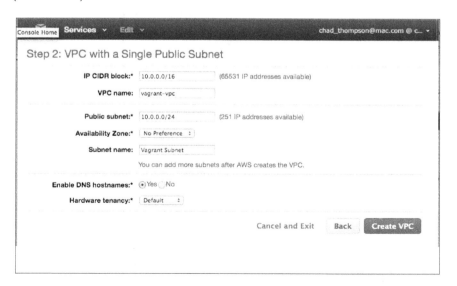

Once the **Create VPC** button is pressed, a dialog box appears with information about the VPC and the resources that it requires.

 Amazon has not been charging for the creation of VPCs themselves. The only billing related to VPCs are EC2 instances launched into the VPC and VPN connection bandwidth into and out of the VPC.

5. Once the VPC has been created, we'll make one last change (we'll restrict access to VPC resources to our current IP address). There are two ways we could do this: through access control lists to the entire network or through security group rules. It's often simpler to set up and modify security group rules in our simple case. To do this, open the **EC2** console, you can get to this from the main console or the dropdown under the **Services** menu:

6. In the EC2 console, select the **Security Groups** option from the left-hand navigation:

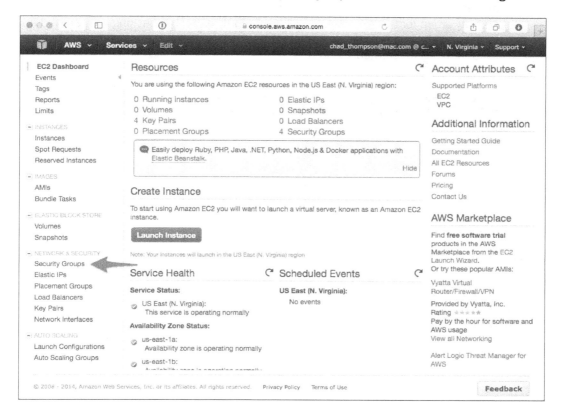

7. The **Security Groups** list will display a list of available security groups in the account, one of them will be a security group assigned to our VPC. There should be only one security group for this example. Select the security group by checking the box on the left-hand side. In this case, we'll select the security group that has an assigned VPC ID for the VPC we created:

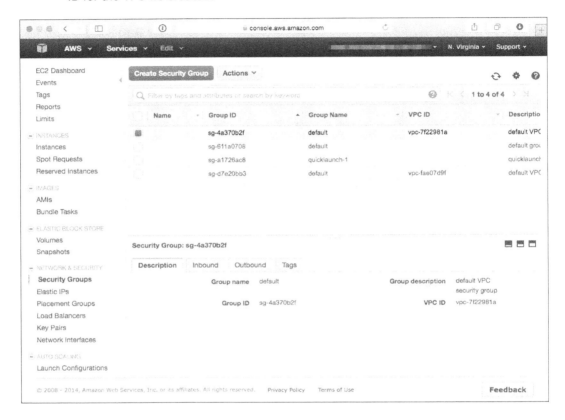

8. With the security group selected, choose the **Inbound** tab. The tab will show a list of security groups:

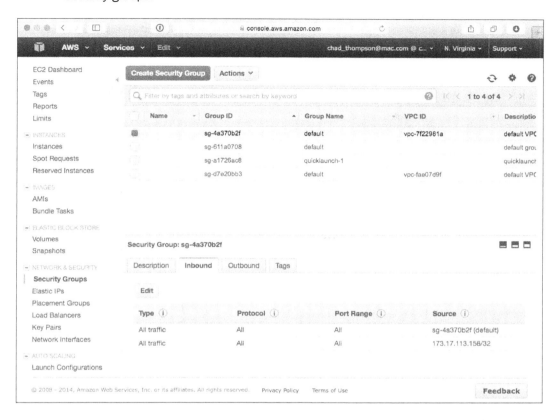

9. Add a new security group by clicking on the **Edit** button to open a pop up with a list of security rules. Select **Add Rule** and create a rule that allows for all traffic from the IP you are connecting from. Security rules can, of course, be more complicated and allow for different levels of access, but this will be enough for us to launch Vagrant machines into a VPC.

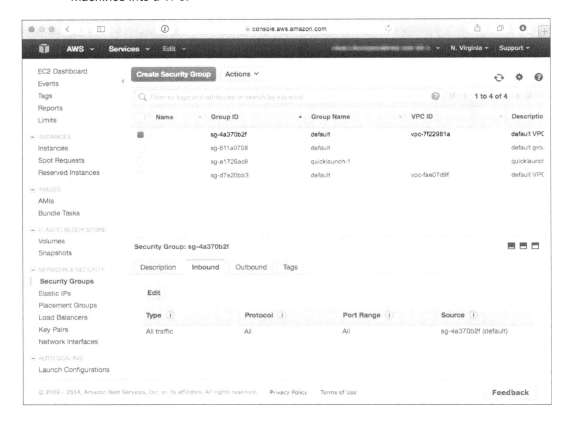

This will create a security group to launch Vagrant resources. Now, we need only one additional item: a security key to access our AWS boxes.

Creating a security key for Vagrant instances

EC2 instances are accessed by the use of a private key that is created specifically to access the instance. We will create (and keep!) a private key for our Vagrant instances. Like other AWS credentials, this key can only be generated once—the keys cannot be recovered.

1. Access the **Key Pairs** option in the EC2 dashboard under the **NETWORK & SECURITY** menu:

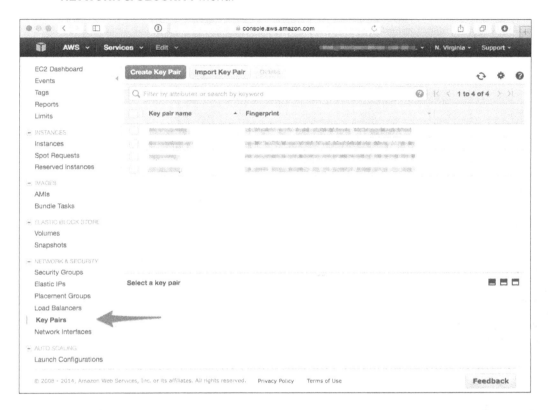

2. The key pair interface will have a button to create a new key pair instance. Select the **Create Key Pair** button and give our new key pair a name (in this case, `vagrantkey`):

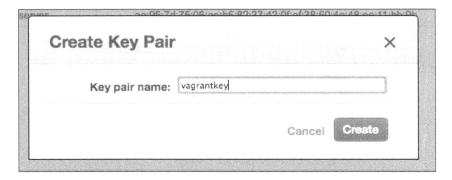

3. On creating the key pair, a file should download from AWS that contains the content of our new key pair. Save this to a secure location on your system.

With the VPC, security group and key pair created, our Amazon account is ready to host our Vagrant machines.

Installing the Vagrant-AWS plugin

The Vagrant AWS functionality is a part of the Vagrant plugin. To install the plugin and prepare Vagrant to use AWS, we will need to install the plugin by executing the following command from the command prompt:

```
vagrant plugin install vagrant-aws
```

We'll also need to install a *dummy* box for use with the provider. Install the dummy box with the command:

```
vagrant box add dummy https://github.com/mitchellh/vagrant-aws/raw/
master/dummy.box
```

(Up-to-date documentation on the plugin is available at `https://github.com/mitchellh/vagrant-aws`)

Gathering required information for the provider

Finally, we'll need to gather a bit of information for the AWS provider, much of this is created earlier in this section:

▶ The AWS access key or secret key for your account.

▶ The name of the EC2 key pair (in this case `vagrantkey`).

▶ The name of the region you wish to launch instances into. This will be the same region where you created your VPC.

▶ The AMI ID of the instance type you wish to launch. This can be found by choosing **Launch Instance** in the EC2 dashboard. You won't complete the launch process here, but you can find the AMI ID of the instance type that you would like to create. In this case, we'll grab the AMI ID of the latest version of Ubuntu supported by AWS:

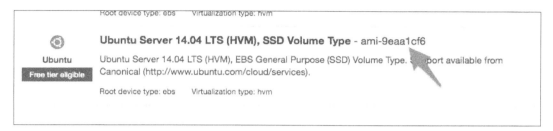

▶ The instance type that you would like to launch. You can find a list of instance types and pricing at `http://aws.amazon.com/ec2/instance-types/`. In this case, we'll use the *free tier* available type of t2.micro. Be sure to match your instance size for the workload you are planning to use (make sure that you understand the pricing or cost ramifications of launching new instances). Amazon's pricing model will incur an hourly cost for each instance launched.

▶ The Subnet ID of our public subnet.

▶ The security group ID of our public security group (added in the preceding section).

With these seven points, we can begin to set up our Vagrant AWS provider.

Setting up the Vagrant AWS environment

With the rather considerable setup to using AWS securely, we can start launching Vagrant machines into our new subnet.

1. Let's start this project by creating a directory structure to hold a few files. In a working directory (which will eventually hold our Vagrantfile), create a directory named `aws`. In this example, I'm copying the security key generated as `vagrantkey` in the *Getting ready* section to a file called `vagrantkey.pem`.

2. In the `aws` directory, create a file called `config.rb`. This file will have the configuration variables we'll need to launch instances. It will also likely have information that you will not want to check for version control. The content of the file will look like this:

```
$aws_options = {}
$aws_options[:access_key] = "ACCESS_KEY"
$aws_options[:secret_key] = "SECRET_KEY "
$aws_options[:ec2_keypair] = "vagrantkey"
$aws_options[:region] = "us-east-1"
$aws_options[:ami_id] = "ami-9eaa1cf6"
```

```
$aws_options[:instance_type] = "t2.micro"
$aws_options[:subnet_id] = "subnet-17a37860"
$aws_options[:security_group] = "sg-4a370b2f"
```

(These values will, of course, be different for different VPC environments.)

3. With the two files in the `aws` directory, place a Vagrantfile in the main working directory. For this example, the Vagrantfile will look like this:

```ruby
# -*- mode: ruby -*-
# vi: set ft=ruby :

# Vagrantfile API/syntax version. Don't touch unless you know what
you're doing!
VAGRANTFILE_API_VERSION = "2"

CONFIG = "#{File.dirname(__FILE__)}/aws/config.rb"
if File.exist?(CONFIG)
  require CONFIG
end

Vagrant.configure(VAGRANTFILE_API_VERSION) do |config|
  config.vm.define "web" do |web|
      web.vm.box                = "dummy"
      web.vm.provider "aws" do |aws, override|
        override.ssh.username           = "ubuntu"
        override.ssh.private_key_path = "#{File.dirname(__
FILE__)}/aws/vagrantkey.pem"
        aws.access_key_id     = $aws_options[:access_key]
        aws.secret_access_key = $aws_options[:secret_key]
        aws.keypair_name      = $aws_options[:ec2_keypair]
        aws.region            = $aws_options[:region]
        aws.ami               = $aws_options[:ami_id]
        aws.instance_type     = $aws_options[:instance_type]
        aws.subnet_id         = $aws_options[:subnet_id]
        aws.associate_public_ip  = "true"
        aws.security_groups   = $aws_options[:security_group]
        aws.tags = {
            'Name' => 'Vagrant Web Server',
        }
    end
  end
end
```

4. With this Vagrantfile in place (and the configuration variables in our `config.rb` file), start the environment with the command:

   vagrant up web -provider=aws

   This should start the Vagrant environment. If everything starts correctly, the startup should exit with a final message about syncing the vagrant folder from the local system to the new AWS machine.

5. Verify that you can access this AWS instance with both `vagrant ssh web` to access the instance with SSH and by verifying that an instance is running in the AWS EC2 console:

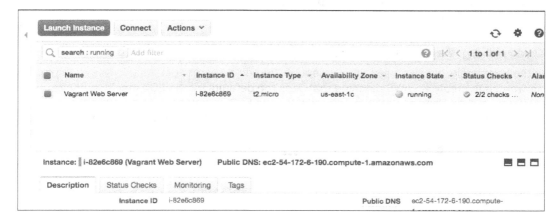

6. When you're finished with the instance, be sure to take it down with the vagrant destroy command to avoid incurring charges to run an on-demand instance in EC2. After destroying the instance with Vagrant, it should appear in the AWS console as *terminated*. Halting will also stop the instance for a later restart without incurring the full cost of running EC2 instances.

How it works...

As we've seen in the previous two sections, there can be quite a bit of setup work with AWS to use Vagrant machines, but this setup allows us to launch virtual instances securely. Our Vagrantfile does contain a few new items that require a bit of explanation.

Saving configuration data outside the Vagrantfile

One of the primary additions to our Vagrantfile is the inclusion of an *external* file: a configuration file that holds specific account details. Storing these type of details in an external file allows you to keep these details confidential, while at the same time it allows you to share your Vagrantfile. Including this file is done with a Ruby style include statement:

```
CONFIG = "#{File.dirname(__FILE__)}/aws/config.rb"
if File.exist?(CONFIG)
  require CONFIG
end
```

Including this file allows the main Vagrant file to access the details in the `$aws_config` object that is defined in the `config.rb` file.

Overriding Vagrantfile defaults

In the Vagrantfile, we also used the concept of overriding Vagrant defaults. In this example, we wanted to create an AWS machine that uses the defaults for the EC2 machine image (AMI) rather than Vagrant defaults. In particular, the EC2 instance would not have the default user (`vagrant`) installed, nor would it have the private key that is used for published Vagrant boxes. To change this behavior, an override was specified, overriding both the default username (in this case, `ubuntu`, on Red Hat-based EC2 types, the value would be `ec2-user`) along with the private key created in the AWS console:

```
web.vm.provider "aws" do |aws, override|
    override.ssh.username       = "ubuntu"
    override.ssh.private_key_path = "#{File.dirname(__FILE__)}/
aws/vagrantkey.pem"
```

Specifying AWS details

The final item in the Vagrantfile is the specification of AWS details. The information related to account details, private key names, and so on, is common for any AWS connection, but there are a few variables that we specified to meet a particular need:

▶ We require that our Vagrant box receive a *public* IP address. In our VPC, the public address is what allows Vagrant to connect to the machine running in AWS. If we wish to use private IP addresses (in the `10.*` range), we need to establish an active VPN connection to our VPC.

▶ We specified an AWS *tag* for our instance, in this case, simply giving our instance a name. AWS provides the ability to tag resources for later use and reporting (if we needed to separate our main account from billing chargebacks, tags could identify machine owners and accounts).

The one item here that we did not do to our instance is specify a private IP. Although, we cannot access the machine directly with a private IP, machines in the subnet (such as multiple Vagrant machines) can access each other with private `10.*` addresses.

There's more...

Workflows and deployment with Amazon Web Services is a vast topic (a full treatment of EC2 patterns, security requirements and deployment workflows are somewhat beyond the scope of this recipe.) A good place to start on a general introduction to Amazon Web Services (and the features offered) is the official documentation at `http://aws.amazon.com/documentation/`.

See also

▶ The Amazon Web Services homepage (`http://aws.amazon.com`) is where you will need to go to sign up for an account and get started with using Amazon Web Services. Similar to most cloud services, you will need to have a source of payment on file, although Amazon does offer a *free tier* for new users that will help you get started with using AWS (and use this example) free of charge.

▶ *IAM Best Practices* (`http://docs.aws.amazon.com/IAM/latest/UserGuide/IAMBestPractices.html`)—AWS strongly recommends the use of IAM users when creating and using AWS resources.

▶ The Vagrant AWS plugin (`https://github.com/mitchellh/vagrant-aws`) will need to be installed in order to use the AWS provisioner.

▶ A handy guide to EC2 instance types, which includes information about the machine specifications (RAM/CPU) along with pricing information is available at `http://aws.amazon.com/ec2/instance-types/`.

▶ When getting started with AWS Services, the *AWS Documentation* (`http://aws.amazon.com/documentation/`) provides a useful overview and introduction to available services.

Using Vagrant with DigitalOcean

DigitalOcean (`http://digitalocean.com`) is a cloud computational service provider that has quickly gained a positive reputation among many development communities for fast, reliable, and inexpensive compute instances (virtual machines). DigitalOcean has also implemented a rich API layer to access compute instances, making it easy for developers to integrate with DigitalOcean.

This recipe will require a DigitalOcean account (sign up at `http://digitalocean.com`). Note that a new account will require a method of payment as DigitalOcean does not offer a free tier.

Getting ready

To use DigitalOcean as a provider, we'll need to install the provider as a plugin. The plugin is available with a simple install:

```
vagrant plugin install vagrant-digitalocean
```

(More detail about the plugin, installation, and options is also available at the GitHub site: `https://github.com/smdahlen/vagrant-digitalocean`.)

Once the plugin is downloaded, there are only two other items that you will need to create.

Creating a DigitalOcean API token

The Vagrant DigitalOcean plugin uses the DigitalOcean API to launch new *droplets* for use with Vagrant. To use the API, we will need to generate an API token.

1. After creating a DigitalOcean account, logging in to DigitalOcean will display a control panel. The default view will list any running droplets:

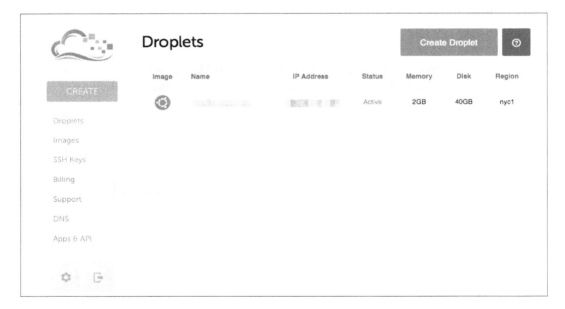

2. From the console, select **Apps & API**. This dialog box has a function that allows for the creation of a **Personal Access Token** (if one is not already present) that can be used to access the DigitalOcean API:

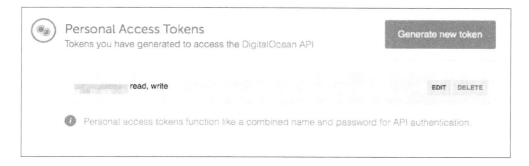

3. Select the **Generate new token** option. On the new token screen, give the token a name and allow the token to write (the write permissions will be needed to launch instances):

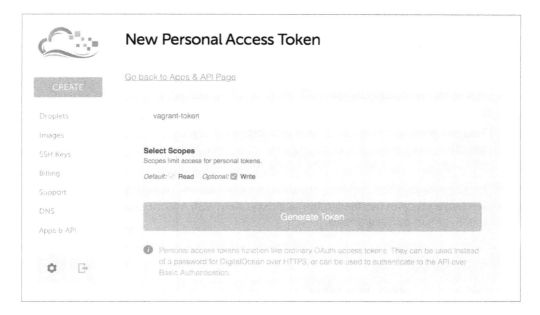

> This new token can access the API and launch instances that could be billed under your account. Take care to protect generated tokens as you would protect a username/password. If a token is inadvertently shared, make sure to revoke the token to keep your account safe.

4. Select the **Generate Token** button after the name and permissions are set. This will create a new token with read/write permissions. We'll need this token for our later Vagrant configuration. Copy and save this token now as it will not be available after leaving the generation page:

Creating a new SSH key pair

The last setup step we'll need to do is the generation of a new key pair to connect with a DigitalOcean instance. This key pair will be used to enable SSH communication between your workstation and the remote DigitalOcean droplet.

1. In a working directory (where we'll create our Vagrantfile), create a new key pair with the `ssh-keygen -f vagrant` command.

    This will generate a key pair with a public/private key. (For more information on generating key pairs, see `http://www.openssh.com/`. It's likely that OpenSSH is either in use or available for your platform.)

2. Do not enter a passphrase for these keys except for the default (blank) values. This will leave you with two files in the directory: `vagrant` and `vagrant.pub`. We'll use these keys in our Vagrantfile.

How to do it...

Now that we have the setup steps completed, we can create a Vagrantfile to start a DigitalOcean droplet. Our Vagrantfile will need to override some default behavior as well as specify some variables that are unique to a DigitalOcean configuration.

1. Start with a basic Vagrantfile. In this example, we will create a single machine Vagrantfile, so we can begin by defining the file along with an override section for our provider:

    ```
    # -*- mode: ruby -*-
    # vi: set ft=ruby :
    ```

```
VAGRANTFILE_API_VERSION = "2"
Vagrant.configure(VAGRANTFILE_API_VERSION) do |config|
  config.vm.provider :digital_ocean do |provider, override|
  end
end
```

2. In our provider block, specify a few override parameters. The first will be a path to the private key (the private and public keys must be kept in the same directory). If the keys are in the same directory as the Vagrantfile, we can specify this location by using the Ruby `File.dirname` method to obtain the current working directory. We will also need to override the box to use a *dummy* box for Vagrant operation. Setting the hostname will also correspond to the name of the machine in the DigitalOcean console:

```
override.ssh.private_key_path = "#{File.dirname(__FILE__)}/
vagrant"
override.vm.box = 'digital_ocean'
override.vm.hostname = 'vagrantbox'
override.vm.box_url = "https://github.com/smdahlen/vagrant-
digitalocean/raw/master/box/digital_ocean.box"
```

3. Following the overrides, specify a few parameters for the provider:

```
provider.ssh_key_name = "vagrant-key"
provider.token = '<< TOKEN >>'
provider.image = 'Ubuntu 14.04 x64'
provider.region = 'nyc2'
provider.size = '512mb'
```

The SSH key name will be used to name and submit the public key portion of our generated key pair to DigitalOcean (which will be available in the console). The `provider.token` variable will be the token we generated earlier. The image, region, and size are specific to the type of droplet you would like to launch. We'll discuss how to find these values in the next section.

4. Once the override and provider sections are complete, the instance should launch with the command:

vagrant up --provider=digital_ocean

Once this instance is launched, it should be accessible with a `vagrant ssh` command and be listed in the Vagrant console:

Droplets

Image	Name	IP Address	Status	Memory	Disk	Region
◎			Active	2GB	40GB	nyc1
◎	vagrantbox	162.243.41.146	Active	512MB	20GB	nyc2

Once we are finished with our droplet, a `vagrant destroy` command will destroy the droplet. Be sure to verify that the droplet has been destroyed (DigitalOcean will charge for any operational droplet on an hourly basis). Once we have a working Vagrantfile, we can create and destroy DigitalOcean droplets as needed, using provisioners to install and configure software and applications. The provider will also use the rsync protocol to copy the entire working directory (where the Vagrantfile is) to the `/vagrant` directory in the DigitalOcean droplet.

How it works...

The DigitalOcean provider makes use of the DigitalOcean API to launch and manage Droplets. When we generated a token for use with Vagrant, we generated a general use API token. The DigitalOcean provider uses this token to create instances, but we can also use the API to find information about our droplets and functions that are available to us. For example, we can use the API token to retrieve a list of images, regions, and sizes available for us to use in our Vagrantfile. Simply execute a curl command to access the API:

```
curl -X GET "https://api.digitalocean.com/v2/images/" \
    -H "Authorization: Bearer << TOKEN >>"
```

Where our API token is used in place of `<< TOKEN >>`. This will return a rather large JSON file, but we can find an entry with information about the name and available regions for an image. One example is:

```
{"id":6918735,
"name":"Ubuntu 14.04 x32",
"distribution":"Ubuntu",
"slug":"ubuntu-14-04-x32",
"public":true,
```

```
"regions":["nyc1","ams1","sfo1","nyc2","ams2","sgp1","lon1","nyc3","a
ms3","nyc3"],"
created_at":"2014-10-17T20:13:41Z"}
```

In our Vagrantfile, `provider.image` will be the name of the image and the regions where the image can be launched are in the regions array. The image size, however, can be found on the pricing page (`https://www.digitalocean.com/pricing/`) with the size being the amount of RAM for the droplet (for example, `512mb`, `1gb`, `2gb`, `4gb`, `8gb`).

There are also more options available to interact with the DigitalOcean API through the provider, see the plugin homepage (`https://github.com/smdahlen/vagrant-digitalocean`) for more information.

See also

- ▶ Vagrant DigitalOcean plugin: `https://github.com/smdahlen/vagrant-digitalocean`
- ▶ The DigitalOcean API: `https://developers.digitalocean.com`

Sharing local machines with HashiCorp Atlas

One of the reasons that we might use cloud providers is due to their ability to share Vagrant resources with outside users (either at the machine (SSH) level, or even to simply demonstrate progress on web applications). HashiCorp has launched its Atlas project to support the use of Vagrant (along with other HashiCorp tooling) to develop and deploy infrastructure. Atlas supports several features that are useful for Vagrant users. These include:

- ▶ A repository of Vagrant boxes that can be downloaded for use for a number of providers
- ▶ Sharing features that allow Vagrant users to share HTTP services between Vagrant machines
- ▶ Sharing features that allow Vagrant users to access remote Vagrant machines with the SSH protocol

 The features supported by Atlas and the prior Vagrant Cloud product require a version of Vagrant later than version 1.6. Versions prior to 1.7 will also likely yield messages that refer to Vagrant Cloud rather than Atlas. In any case, the APIs have remained identical, although the naming conventions have changed.

Using Atlas to share virtual machines is a free service, but does require an Atlas account.

Getting ready

Joining Atlas is simple, especially for the free account tier.

> At the time of writing this book (early 2015), Atlas is still in a technical preview state. The functions described here are carried over from the prior *Vagrant Cloud* product and will be available for some time to come. As HashiCorp develops Atlas, there will be more features added (some freely available and some only available with a payable account). While the processes described here should remain in use for the foreseeable future, keep in mind that some of the specifics could change as more features and products are added to Atlas. Consult the Atlas documentation for up-to-date information.

1. Open `http://atlas.hashicorp.com` in a web browser.

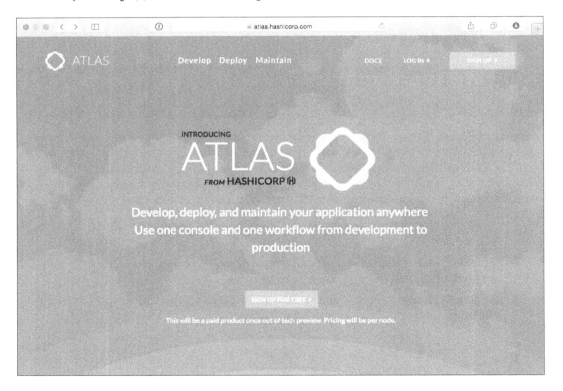

2. Select the option (there are a few ways) to **SIGN UP FOR FREE**.

3. This signup will prompt you to choose a username and enter a valid e-mail address and password. This username and password will be used to log in from the Vagrant application later on.

How to do it...

To demonstrate the use of Vagrant Share, we'll create a simple Vagrant machine (with a local provider) that installs the Apache web server and installs a simple web page. We'll enable machine sharing that allows another user to access the machine via SSH.

1. Start with a simple Vagrantfile that defines a machine and a shell provisioner. The complete Vagrantfile is as follows:

```ruby
# -*- mode: ruby -*-
# vi: set ft=ruby :

$script = <<SCRIPT
apt-get update
apt-get install -y apache2
echo "Shared With Atlas" > /var/www/html/index.html
SCRIPT

VAGRANTFILE_API_VERSION = "2"

Vagrant.configure(VAGRANTFILE_API_VERSION) do |config|
  config.vm.box = "puppetlabs/ubuntu-14.04-32-nocm"
  config.vm.provision "shell" , inline: $script
end
```

2. Before launching the Vagrant machine, log in to your Atlas account using your existing account, or perhaps the credentials created in the *Getting ready* section. Do this by running the vagrant login command.

   Vagrant will prompt you for a username and password. It will display a success message (**You're now logged in!**) if the login is successful:

```
  ●  ●  ●   2. cothomps@cthompson: /Volumes/WD HDD/vagrantbook/vagrantbook-examples/Chapter6/1-3-vagrant-share (zsh)
▶ vagrant login
In a moment we'll ask for your username and password to Vagrant Cloud.
After authenticating, we will store an access token locally. Your
login details will be transmitted over a secure connection, and are
never stored on disk locally.

If you don't have a Vagrant Cloud account, sign up at vagrantcloud.com

Username or Email:
Password (will be hidden):
You're now logged in!                                              46d  ✻  ⊾  ●

vagrantbook-examples/Chapter6/1-3-vagrant-share   master  X        46d  ✻  ⊾  ●
▶ ▯
```

3. Start the machine with the `vagrant up` command. The box should proceed to boot normally, outputting the results of the installation commands.

4. Once the box has booted (and Atlas login was successful), start a sharing session by executing the `vagrant share --ssh` command.

   This will output some information about sharing the session and will leave the sharing session open (and active) in the foreground. Before the share is available, Vagrant will also prompt for a key password. When sharing the machine, a remote user will require this password to log in to the machine.

   When sharing, the output will remain in the terminal window, while the Vagrant *sharing* process remains in the foreground:

```
                          2. vagrant share --ssh (bash)
▶ vagrant share --ssh
==> default: Detecting network information for machine...
    default: Local machine address: 192.168.30.129
    default: An HTTP port couldn't be detected. Since SSH is enabled, this is
    default: not an error. If you want to share both SSH and HTTP, please set
    default: an HTTP port with `--http`.
    default:
    default: Local HTTP port: disabled
    default: Local HTTPS port: disabled
    default: SSH Port: 22
==> default: Generating new SSH key...
    default: Please enter a password to encrypt the key:
    default: Repeat the password to confirm:
    default: Inserting generated SSH key into machine...
==> default: Checking authentication and authorization...
==> default: Creating Vagrant Share session...
    default: Share will be at: happy-blizzard-5953
==> default: Your Vagrant Share is running! Name: happy-blizzard-5953
==> default:
==> default: You're sharing with SSH access. This means that another user
==> default: simply has to run `vagrant connect --ssh happy-blizzard-5953`
==> default: to SSH to your Vagrant machine.
==> default:
==> default: Because you encrypted your SSH private key with a password,
==> default: the other user will be prompted for this password when they
==> default: run `vagrant connect --ssh`. Please share this password with them
==> default: in some secure way.
▯
```

5. The SSH information can be shared with a remote user. The output of the share command gives instructions on how to connect with a machine shortname. A remote user who also has an account (and is logged in!) to Atlas can access the machine with the command:

```
vagrant connect -ssh happy-blizzard-5953
```

The name of the machine (in this case, `happy-blizzard-5953`) will be unique for each share session. Connecting to the machine remotely requires that remote users have:

- ❏ A current (later than 1.6) version of Vagrant installed

- ❏ SSH installed (particularly for Windows machines)

- ❏ A valid login to Atlas

When connecting to the machine, remote users will be prompted for the password entered when the initial share was created. After connecting, Vagrant will give the user shell access to the remote machine:

```
                          3. vagrant@localhost: ~ (bash)
▶ vagrant connect --ssh happy-blizzard-5953
Loading share 'happy-blizzard-5953'...
The SSH key to connect to this share is encrypted. You will require
the password entered when creating to share to decrypt it. Verify you
access to this password before continuing.

Press enter to continue, or Ctrl-C to exit now.
Password for the private key:
Executing SSH...
Welcome to Ubuntu 14.04 LTS (GNU/Linux 3.13.0-24-generic i686)

 * Documentation:  https://help.ubuntu.com/
Last login: Wed Dec 31 12:21:26 2014 from 192.168.30.1
vagrant@localhost:~$ []
```

6. The created share will also be visible in the Atlas console. The **SHARES** interface displays a list of active shares that your account has created:

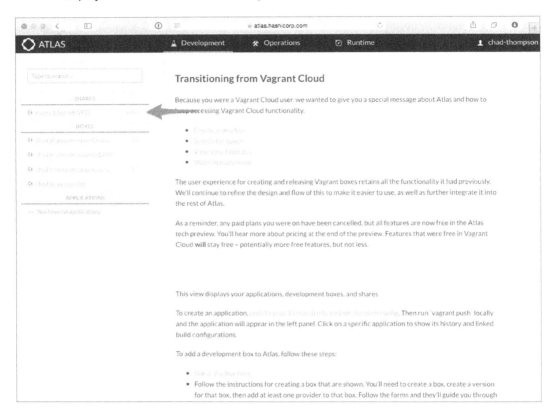

Note that shares will expire after eight hours. Although, using Atlas to share is useful for short sessions (or a day's work), Atlas is not designed to allow permanent access to a Vagrant machine.

The sharing session can be terminated from our Unix terminal with the *Ctrl + C* key command to exit the sharing session.

How it works...

Atlas provides a very useful service for Vagrant users: a proxy layer that allows machines created by Vagrant with desktop software to be shared with other users. Atlas only allows two modes of sharing: by SSH (a command-line session) or a *normal* sharing over port 80 that is ideal to demonstrate local web applications to a remote audience.

► HashiCorp Atlas: `http://atlas.hashicorp.com`

Sharing web applications with HashiCorp Atlas

Atlas is a useful tool to share environments with other developers or colleagues when solving environment issues. Atlas can also be used to share web applications with a remote audience, something that can often be difficult to do when demoing experimental features without setting up new infrastructure.

Getting ready

Before we can share with Atlas, we'll need a valid Atlas account. Signing up for an Atlas (`http://atlas.hashicorp.com`) account is fairly straightforward. The details of signing up are discussed in the Getting ready section of the previous recipe.

How to do it...

Web development with Vagrant is a fairly common task. Atlas allows you to share and demonstrate any HTTP application (a typical web application, or perhaps even an API) to a remote audience.

1. First, start with a Vagrantfile that provisions an application to run on port `80`. In this case, we'll install the Apache web server and demonstrate a simple static web page. (The simple page will also keep our Vagrantfile small for demonstration purposes):

```ruby
# -*- mode: ruby -*-
# vi: set ft=ruby :

$script = <<SCRIPT
apt-get update
apt-get install -y apache2
echo "Shared With Atlas" > /var/www/html/index.html
SCRIPT

VAGRANTFILE_API_VERSION = "2"

Vagrant.configure(VAGRANTFILE_API_VERSION) do |config|
  config.vm.box = "puppetlabs/ubuntu-14.04-32-nocm"
  config.vm.provision "shell" , inline: $script
end
```

2. Make sure that we are logged in to our Atlas account through Vagrant. Log in using the `vagrant login` command.

   This will prompt for the account username and password. A success message is displayed if the authentication is successful.

3. Start the Vagrant machine with the `vagrant up` command.

4. Once the machine is booted and provisioned, run the `vagrant share` command.

   Vagrant will output information about authentication and will end with a random URL that can be shared with remote users. During the sharing session, Vagrant will run in the foreground as the command will not exit back to the terminal:

```
                          2. vagrant share (bash)
▶ vagrant share
==> default: Detecting network information for machine...
    default: Local machine address: 192.168.30.129
    default: Local HTTP port: 80
    default: Local HTTPS port: disabled
==> default: Checking authentication and authorization...
==> default: Creating Vagrant Share session...
    default: Share will be at: lazy-mittens-7743
==> default: Your Vagrant Share is running! Name: lazy-mittens-7743
==> default: URL: http://lazy-mittens-7743.vagrantshare.com
```

5. Open the provided URL in a web browser. This will be random for every share:

6. Share the URL with remote users. This same URL should be accessible to remote users.

7. It's also possible to access shared machines through the Atlas console. This allows you (or those you have sharing enabled with) to access the machine through the Atlas navigation menu.

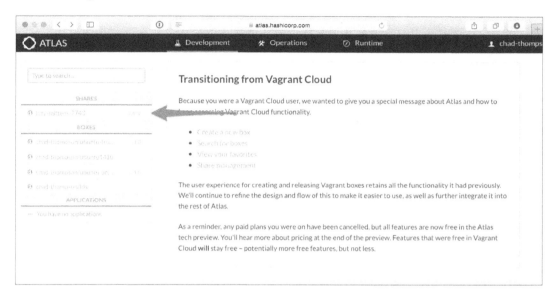

8. Terminate the sharing session in the Unix terminal with a *Ctrl + C* key command to exit back to the shell.

How it works...

Atlas creates a proxy that is available for web applications to be shared with other users, even with users that are not using Vagrant or have an Atlas account.

In this example, we used the same Vagrantfile as the previous recipe to share a web application, whereas other users with Vagrant (and an Atlas account) can share SSH sessions, but any user can access web applications, which makes Vagrant a useful tool to demonstrate or use web applications on a temporary basis.

Atlas does terminate share sessions after eight hours, and there is no particular expectation of application performance. Sharing in this manner is effective to demonstrate or simple development (perhaps testing an API for a mobile application), but setting up an environment that can be shared or used more heavily will likely require using a different cloud deployment method.

See also

▶ Atlas: `http://atlas.hashicorp.com`

▶ The *Sharing local machines with HashiCorp Atlas* recipe

7
Packaging Vagrant Boxes

In this chapter, we will cover the following topics:

- ▶ Packaging Vagrant boxes from ISO files
- ▶ Building Vagrant boxes with Packer
- ▶ Sharing Vagrant boxes
- ▶ Sharing Vagrant boxes with Atlas

Introduction

In many scenarios, using a basic Vagrant environment is an acceptable method to create and destroy development environments. Most of the recipes in this book focus on this type of development environment: downloading a base box from the Atlas box repository, booting the box, then executing provisioners to install and configure software. In each case, the entire development environment is recreated every time a new environment is launched from the Vagrantfile. In some cases, this workflow can be cumbersome for users. There are a few reasons that you might want to re-evaluate when building environments on every launch:

- ▶ Provisioning an entire environment can be time consuming, particularly if there is a large amount of software to install and configure. Internet bandwidth might also be a concern – downloading files from package repositories can be
- ▶ There can be reasons to *freeze* an environment at specific software versions rather than relying on versions present in package repositories.
- ▶ There might be software required (such as a commercial database package) that cannot easily be installed in an automated fashion.

In each of these cases, it might be desirable to distribute our environment not only as a Vagrantfile, but also as a Vagrantfile with a packaged box file. A box file can be distributed with software installed and configured, allowing users to start quickly and easily without requiring Vagrant to perform a complete provisioning cycle. In this chapter, we will look at the creation and packaging of Vagrant boxes, from creation of boxes in a manual fashion (from ISO files) to more automated ways of creating Vagrant boxes. Finally, we will demonstrate and discuss methods to share Vagrant boxes with others.

Packaging Vagrant boxes from ISO files

Packaging Vagrant environments for others is a very common problem. Packaging an environment can start from creating a simple base box with an operating system installed to repurposing existing virtual machines for use as Vagrant boxes. In either case, Vagrant can be a solution to the problem of sharing virtual machines with other team members.

In this example, we will create a Vagrant box from a machine (CentOS) created with VMware Fusion. The same method will apply to VMware Workstation (Windows and Linux) with similar steps required for VirtualBox.

 This recipe requires the use of the commercial VMware Fusion provider. For more information on this provider, see the provider homepage at `https://www.vagrantup.com/vmware`. For instructions on using VirtualBox to create virtual machines, see the *Using existing virtual machines with Vagrant* recipe of *Chapter 1, Setting Up Your Environment*. In the first chapter, an existing virtual machine was exported for use with VirtualBox using the vagrant package command.

Getting ready

Before starting this exercise, we will need to create a new virtual machine using our hypervisor software, in this case, VMware Fusion. For this chapter, I will assume that:

- You are able to download an ISO distribution of your desired operating system or are otherwise able to create a virtual machine on your desktop machine.

- You are able to install an operating system on your virtual machine. Booting and installing from ISO files can be different for various operating systems. Be sure to consult the documentation for your distribution and hypervisor software.

Creating virtual machines with hypervisor software is quite different for various combinations of hypervisors and OS distributions. VMware has created several *easy install* paths for some of the popular Linux distributions: easy installation for Ubuntu and CentOS can configure user accounts and VMware Tools distributions required for Vagrant. Other distributions (such as Fedora and Oracle Enterprise Linux with the *unbreakable* kernel) might require some manual configuration and compilation of tool suites.

It is possible to create Windows Vagrant boxes using these methods as well, although there are two things that can make sharing Windows Vagrant boxes somewhat difficult:

▶ Most desktop Windows installations can be rather large in size. Where many Vagrant box publishers aim to keep box distributions small enough to download over public Internet, packaging a desktop Windows distribution can create very large (in excess of 20 GB) files that can be difficult to share in some circumstances.

▶ Desktop Windows distributions can also have licensing requirements that make sharing box files difficult.

In 2014, Microsoft experimented with Vagrant distributions by releasing a 180-day evaluation of Windows Datacenter 2012 in Vagrant box format and is currently distributing Vagrant boxes through the modern IE program. Using those boxes might be a good starting point for Windows projects rather than packing your own files.

How to do it...

Before we start with packing a virtual machine as a Vagrant box, we will need to configure our virtual machine for use by Vagrant.

Preparing a virtual machine

1. Create a virtual machine by creating a new machine from an ISO file. Consult your hypervisor documentation on creating virtual machines.

> You might also want to consider requirements for memory and disk space based on development requirements. The Vagrant documentation specifies some basic minimum requirements recommended for boxes that will be publically distributed at `https://docs.vagrantup.com/v2/boxes/base.html`.

2. Ensure that your virtual machine has a user account named `vagrant`. By convention, most box packagers also use the `vagrant` string as passwords for any required accounts. If you are using an installation that allows for *easy install*, you can create the vagrant user on initial installation.

3. Make sure that your operating system (for Linux machines) has the SSH daemon running and that it is configured to run on system startup. (For example, with CentOS or Red Hat derivatives, make sure that you issue the `chkconfig sshd on` command as root).

> The following steps (4-9) are specific to Unix boxes, where the primary means of accessing the box is the **Secure Shell** (**SSH**).

4. In the `vagrant` user directory, create a directory called `.ssh` and ensure that this directory has `700` permissions. As the Vagrant user, this can be done with:

   `mkdir ~/.ssh&&chmod 700 ~/.ssh`

5. Install the *insecure key pair* if you want your new box to be used by Vagrant users without modification of the Vagrantfile. The Vagrant insecure key pair is available on GitHub at `https://github.com/mitchellh/vagrant/tree/master/keys`. Install the keys by saving them to the `.ssh` directory created in the previous step:

   `cd ~/.ssh&& curl -O https://raw.githubusercontent.com/mitchellh/vagrant/master/keys/vagrant`

   `cd ~/.ssh&& curl -O https://raw.githubusercontent.com/mitchellh/vagrant/master/keys/vagrant.pub`

6. Copy the public key to the `authorized_keys` file as well:

   `cp ~/.ssh/vagrant.pub ~/.ssh/authorized_keys`

7. Ensure that all keys are read-only by only the Vagrant user:

   `chmod 400 ~/.ssh/*`

8. As the root user, modify the sudo permissions of the Vagrant user. Using the `visudo` command, add a line defining sudo permissions for the Vagrant user without password. On CentOS (and most Linux operating systems), become the root user and execute `visudo`. This will open the `suoders` file with a vi text editor interface. This is one case where the use of `vi` is largely dictated, nearly all Linux distributions recommend modifying permissions files with only the `visudo` editor. In the editor, add a line (you might wish to do this after the typical root user permission entry) for the Vagrant user. The block of the file will look like this:

   `## Allow root to run any commands anywhere`

   `root      ALL=(ALL)        ALL`

   `vagrant ALL=(ALL)        NOPASSWD: ALL`

9. While in the `visudo` editor, look for a line that might require *tty* for connection and disable this requirement by commenting out the `requiretty` line. (This might be different depending on your operating system):

   `#Defaults     requiretty`

10. A recommended tweak when using Vagrant is to also add an additional line to the SSH configuration (typically `/etc/ssh/ssh_config`) in order to disable SSH clients from attempting a reverse DNS lookup. Add a single line to the `ssh_config` file to disable the lookup:

    `UseDNS no`

11. After these configuration items have been completed, save all the files you have edited and shut down the virtual machine.

Packaging the virtual machine as a Vagrant box

Packaging a virtual machine will have steps that are dependent on individual providers. For example, a VMware Fusion box will have different packaging steps than a VirtualBox box file. Consult the provider documentation at `http://docs.vagrantup.com/v2/providers/index.html` for more information about packaging the box for your provider. For this example, we will be creating a Vagrant box to be used with VMware Fusion, the procedure for exporting a box using VirtualBox was demonstrated in the *Using existing virtual machines with Vagrant* recipe of *Chapter 1, Setting Up Your Environment*.

1. On the host system, find the directory that contains the virtual machine files. On OS X, a VMware Fusion virtual machine is presented as a file. We'll need to view the package contents of a virtual machine file.

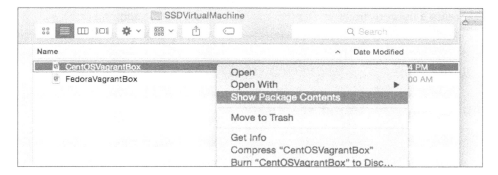

Revealing package contents of the folder will display files related to the virtual disk (`vmdk`) and other definitions. If you intend to distribute this box to the general public, it's recommended that you compress the disk files and remove unnecessary files for box distribution. In practice, you will likely use automated tools to help with these tasks, for this example, we'll leave the virtual machine files as it is.

 It will also be simpler to execute most of the tasks in this section from the command line, as we will be packaging the box file with the Unix *tar* command in a later step. For example, when OS X displays virtual machines as a single file, most OS X applications are also accessible as folders. For instance, to get to the folder that is the virtual machine above executing the `cd` command (`cd ~/SSDVirtualMachine/CentOSVagrantBox.vmwarevm`) will take you to the directory with the virtual machine files.

2. Create the required `metadata.json` file that describes the box contents and the provider required to execute the box file. At minimum, the `metadata.json` file must define the box provider, in this case, `vmware_fusion`:

```
{
   "provider": "vmware_fusion"
}
```

3. With the metadata file in place, we can package the box from the terminal with the *tar* command:

```
tarczvf  vagrant-example.box <<path_to_virtual_machine>>/*
```

The box file is a Unix *tarball*: a file in a gzipped TAR (Tape ARchive) format with the virtual machine files at the *root* level of the box. In this specific example, we can create a new box from our CentOS virtual machine with the command:

```
tarczvfcentos7_vmware_fusion.box ~/SSDVirtualMachines/
CentOSVagrantBox.vmwarevm/*
```

With the box file created, we can now install and use the box locally.

Installing the new Vagrant box

With our new box file in hand, we can now add a new box to our local Vagrant cache.

1. Add the new box with the `vagrant box add` command. In our example (creating a CentOS 7) box, (and from the same directory we were in when executing step 3), add the box to our local cache by specifying the file location and a name for the box:

```
vagrant box add centos7_vmware_fusion.box --name=centos7
```

2. Verify the addition of the box with the `vagrant box list` command. If our new box is added successfully, it will be listed with our other locally installed boxes:

```
▸ vagrant box list
centos64                              (virtualbox, 0)
centos7                               (vmware_fusion, 0)
```

3. In a new working directory, we'll test our new box by initializing a Vagrantfile with the box. The `vagrant init` command can be used with our box name to generate a new Vagrantfile. For example, we can initialize a new Vagrantfile with our `centos7` box:

```
vagrantinitcentos7
```

4. Once the Vagrantfile has been created, test our new box by executing the `vagrant up` command. Vagrant should output startup information and exit to the command line, allowing us to access our new environment with `vagrant ssh`.

How it works...

In this example, we have packaged a new Vagrant box manually, configured the vagrant user access, set up SSH keys, and configured *super user* access. The steps presented will create a Vagrant box that can be shared publicly. Further, users should be able to start the machine with a simple Vagrantfile using default settings.

Creating boxes is also a provider-specific task. The process of packaging a box for VMware Desktop software will be different than packaging boxes for VirtualBox due to different methods of creating virtual hard drives (VMware uses a `vmdk` file format and VirtualBox uses `ovf`) and settings to operate virtual machines in a hypervisor. The first chapter of the book details the use of existing machines with VirtualBox using the `vagrant package` command. This example detailed the more complex process of exporting a Vagrant box for a VMware provider.

There's more...

When creating virtual machines to be used by others, it is often useful to create these machines using automation tools such as Packer (`http://packer.io`), which can be used to execute scripts in order to build Vagrant boxes. Building virtual machines automatically is the topic of the next two recipes.

See also

▶ The Vagrant VMware provider: `https://www.vagrantup.com/vmware`

▶ The *Using existing virtual machines with Vagrant* recipe of *Chapter 1, Setting Up Your Environment*, for instructions on how to export virtual machines created with VirtualBox

▶ Vagrant documentation on *Creating a Base Box*: `https://docs.vagrantup.com/v2/virtualbox/boxes.html`

▶ Vagrant documentation on the `package` command for VirtualBox Vagrant boxes: `https://docs.vagrantup.com/v2/cli/package.html`

Building Vagrant boxes with Packer

While packaging boxes from ISO images and manual provisioning can be a useful solution to share virtual machines, manual maintenance and updating of virtual machines can be time consuming and difficult to manage.

HashiCorp (the company that provides Vagrant) created a project solely for the purpose of creating and packaging virtual environments for a variety of virtualization platforms. This product is aptly named **Packer** (`http://packer.io`). Packer uses configuration files to specify the end result of a packaged virtual machine. In particular, Packer groups commands into:

 ▶ **Builders**: These are commands and instructions to build a virtual machine using ISO files and bootstrapping commands. A builder can specify instructions for a number of platforms, such as using preseed files to create Ubuntu machines or API information to create Amazon Web Services AMI files. A Packer file might specify multiple Builders in the same file, allowing several virtual machine formats to be created in the same build process.

 ▶ **Provisioners**: This is a Packer provisioner that is very similar to a Vagrant provisioner, allowing a number of provisioning environments to operate on a newly created Packer image. Packer includes a number of provisioners for different configuration management approaches that includes many of the same configuration management languages used by Vagrant.

 ▶ **Post-Processors**: There are a number of post-processing steps that can be used in a Packer build to package environments. In this example, we'll look at using the Vagrant post-processor to compress and package a machine.

Packer contains a number of features that can make the packaging of virtual environments simpler to maintain. For more information (and documentation), see the Packer homepage at `http://packer.io`.

In this recipe, we will create an Ubuntu 14.10 box packaged for the VMware Fusion provider, using a combination of Packer templates and an Ubuntu preseed configuration.

Getting ready

Before we can create Vagrant boxes with Packer, we'll first need to install Packer to our workstation. Packer is distributed as a binary distribution for Linux, OS X, Windows, and BSD operating systems.

1. Download the binary package appropriate for your operating system from `https://packer.io/downloads.html`. The binary file will be a file in ZIP format that contains compiled binaries for your operating system.

2. Place the binaries in a common location. I prefer to install Packer binaries (on a Unix system) in `/usr/local/packer`, but you might wish to keep them in your user directory. Copy the contents of the ZIP file (or extract the contents of the ZIP file) to this directory.

3. Add the directory where the Packer binaries are extracted to your user `PATH` variable. On a Unix-based system using the bash shell (which is the default for many modern Unix distributions), add the following line to the `.bash_profile` configuration in your home directory:

```
export PATH=/usr/local/packer:$PATH
```

There might already be an `export PATH` command in your profile, feel free to add your Packer directory to this command. On a Windows machine, path settings are typically kept in your system (or user) environment variables.

4. Check to see whether Packer is configured correctly by opening a new terminal window and running the `packer version` command. If the paths are configured correctly, you will see the version information about Packer:

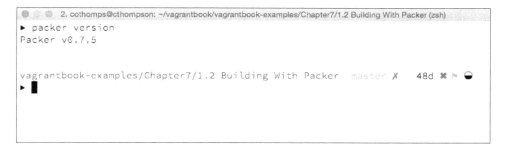

The hypervisor for which a box is being packaged (if using Packer with a desktop hypervisor) must also be installed. Packer can also be used to build cloud images and other types of cloud machines, but this recipe will focus on building a desktop hypervisor box, specifically, we'll use Packer to build the Ubuntu 14.10 box for the VMware Fusion provider.

How to do it...

To build an image, there are a few items that we will need to bootstrap a virtual machine from an ISO file:

- ▶ The ISO file itself. In this case, we'll start with an ISO image downloaded from the Ubuntu website (`http://ubuntu.com`).

- ▶ We'll need to know how to automatically install an operating system from an ISO file in an automated fashion. This typically involves a *boot command* that is a script that the installer uses to begin the installation process and a *preseed* file that specifies information that the installation process requires to install the operating system. While these files can be written from scratch, it's typically best to find examples from the operating system provider or, perhaps, from other open source projects to build on.

Packer will build the Vagrant box by booting the operating system, running the basic installation, and then executing provisioning steps specified in the file.

1. Download an ISO file for the distribution you wish to install. In this case, an ISO file for the Ubuntu 14.10 server distribution (`ubuntu-14.10-server-amd64.iso`) has been downloaded from the Ubuntu website (`http://ubuntu.com`).

2. Before we can use the ISO file, we'll also need to obtain the MD5 checksum of the file; for Ubuntu, these are published separately at `https://help.ubuntu.com/community/UbuntuHashes`. The md5 checksum allows Packer to validate that the ISO file being used is authentic.

3. Create a working directory for all our Packer files to be kept in. We will create a Packer template and two directories, one for HTTP bootstrap files and a second to hold a provisioning script. The directory will look something like this (once our `unicorn64_vmware.json` Packer template is created):

```
.
├── http/
├── shell/
├── unicorn64_vmware.json
```

4. Create a template file (seen in the previous step) called `unicorn64_vmware.json`. This file will specify how we will create our Vagrant box. It (in it's entirety) is a JSON file that describes how to build our Vagrant box:

```
{
  "builders":[
    {  "type": "vmware-iso",
      "iso_url": "file:///<<PATH_TO_ISO_DIRECTORY>>/ubuntu-14.10-server-amd64.iso",
        "iso_checksum": "91bd1cfba65417bfa04567e4f64b5c55",
        "iso_checksum_type": "md5",
        "ssh_username": "vagrant",
        "ssh_password": "vagrant",
        "ssh_wait_timeout": "300s",
        "shutdown_command": "echo vagrant | sudo -S shutdown -P now",
        "output_directory": "ubuntu-1410",
        "http_directory": "http",
        "tools_upload_flavor": "linux",
        "boot_command": [
          "<esc><wait>",
          "<esc><wait>",
          "<enter><wait>",
          "/install/vmlinuz<wait>",
          " auto<wait>",
```

```
            " console-setup/ask_detect=false<wait>",
            " console-setup/layoutcode=us<wait>",
            " console-setup/modelcode=pc105<wait>",
            " debconf/frontend=noninteractive<wait>",
            " debian-installer=en_US<wait>",
            " fb=false<wait>",
            " initrd=/install/initrd.gz<wait>",
            " kbd-chooser/method=us<wait>",
            " keyboard-configuration/layout=USA<wait>",
            " keyboard-configuration/variant=USA<wait>",
            " locale=en_US<wait>",
            " netcfg/get_hostname=unicorn64<wait>",
            " netcfg/get_domain=vagrantup.com<wait>",
            " noapic<wait>",
            " preseed/url=http://{{ .HTTPIP }}:{{ .HTTPPort }}/
preseed.cfg<wait>",
" --<wait>",
            "<enter><wait>"
        ]
        }
    ],

    "provisioners": [
      {
          "type"  : "shell",
          "script": "shell/base.sh",
          "execute_command": "echo 'vagrant' | sudo -S sh '{{ .Path
}}'"

      }
    ],
    "post-processors":[
      {
          "type": "vagrant",
          "output": "unicorn_{{.Provider}}.box"
      }
    ]
}
```

5. Now, we'll need to add a file in our `http` directory named `preseed.cfg`. This preseed file is rather lengthy and can be found with the code examples for this chapter. A preseed file for Ubuntu specifies system settings required to install the operating system and is not specific to Packer. In fact, each operating system (and operating system installer) will have different methods to define files required for automatic installation. For example, Red Hat Linux derivatives use a *Kickstart* file specific to the Anaconda installer packaged with Red Hat and related Linux distributions. What is important is that this file is located in the directory specified by two variables in the Packer template. The Packer directive is `"http_directory"`: `"http"` and the line in the `boot_command` directive is `"preseed/url=http://{{ .HTTPIP }}:{{ .HTTPPort }}/preseed.cfg<wait>"`.

6. Create a simple provisioning script that will install the Vagrant public keys into a newly booted virtual machine:

```
#!/bin/sh
apt-get update
apt-get install -y wget
if ![ -d /home/vagrant/.ssh ]; then
  mkdir -p /home/vagrant/.ssh
chownvagrant:vagrant /home/vagrant/.ssh
fi
if ![ -f /home/vagrant/.ssh/authorized_keys ]; then
  wget --no-check-certificate https://raw.github.com/mitchellh/
vagrant/master/keys/vagrant.pub -O /home/vagrant/.ssh/authorized_
keys
chownvagrant:vagrant /home/vagrant/.ssh/authorized_keys
fi
echo "vagrant ALL=(ALL) NOPASSWD: ALL\n" >> /etc/sudoers
```

Place this file in the `shell` directory and name the file as `base.sh`. It's important that this file echoes the provisioner block in the Packer template:

```
"provisioners": [
  {
     "type"  : "shell",
     "script": "shell/base.sh",
     "execute_command": "echo 'vagrant' | sudo -S sh '{{ .Path
}}'"
  }
],
```

7. With these files in place, execute the Packer build using the command:

```
packer build unicorn64_vmware.json
```

8. The output of this command should detail the steps taken and you should note a VMware Fusion (in this example) window start and several automated steps happen in the window. When the install window appears, this Packer build should proceed automatically with no intervention required. You should notice, however, that the installer proceeds through all the steps in a virtual machine installation:

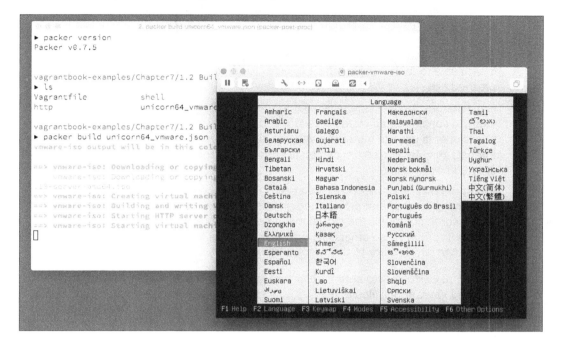

9. After the Packer command exits (and this should take several minutes), a file will be left in the working directory called `unicorn_vmware.box`. Add this file to your local Vagrant cache with the command:

vagrant box add unicorn_vmware.box –name unicorn_vmware.

10. Verify that the box works correctly by initializing a Vagrantfile (`vagrant initunicorn_vmware`) and executing the `vagrant up` command. The newly packaged box should boot and provide a working Ubuntu 14.10 Vagrant box.

How it works...

We've seen how to create and package a Vagrant box using Packer (the templates, bootstrapping, and application of a simple shell provisioner to our new machine). Let's take a look at a few details.

The building blocks of Packer templates

A Packer template consists of a few major sections. In this example, we use three of them:

- **Builders**: We specified a single builder (of type `vmware-iso`) for this template. A template can consist of multiple builders that allows for a single template to define (and create) many different virtual environments or Vagrant boxes. The builder specifies the basic steps required to start a virtual machine, including initial users and the `boot_command` that specifies the steps required to start the installation. The builder also includes an HTTP directory. Packer creates a local http server that is available to the virtual machine in order to serve configuration files (such as the preseed file).

- **Provisioners**: A provisioner is similar to the concept in Vagrant (*provisioners* define steps to configure and install software into an image). In this example, a simple shell provisioner is used to install the Vagrant public keys. Other provisioners (including Puppet, Ansible, and so on) can be used to install and configure software in the newly created box.

- **Post-processors**: Post-processors specify Packer to take actions once the virtual machine is created and provisioned. In this example, we're using the *Vagrant* post-processor to compress the virtual machine disk files and create a file in the box format. There are also other post-processors available for certain tasks, such as publishing our new box to the Vagrant Cloud.

Packer is a very powerful tool to automate virtual (and even cloud) image creation. This example created Vagrant *box* files to use Vagrant with local hypervisors, but Packer can also be used to create image files for cloud providers such as custom **Amazon Machine Images** (**AMIs**) to launch EC2 instances.

Building Vagrant boxes with VeeWee

Another popular method of building Vagrant boxes is a tool called **VeeWee** (`https://github.com/jedi4ever/veewee`) that predates the publication of Packer. VeeWee is a Ruby-based tool to build Vagrant (and other types) of virtual machine formats. This tool installs with the gem package manager if your system meets specific requirements for Ruby versions and development environments. See the documentation at `https://github.com/jedi4ever/veewee` for more on building boxes with VeeWee.

See also

- Packer: `http://packer.io`—the official website has documentation related to using Packer in different situations (and with different cloud providers)

- VeeWee: `https://github.com/jedi4ever/veewee`

- Ubuntu preseeding: `https://help.ubuntu.com/lts/installation-guide/i386/apb.html`—Packer uses operating system utilities to automate the installation of an operating system

▶ Red Hat Kickstart installations: `https://access.redhat.com/documentation/en-US/Red_Hat_Enterprise_Linux/7/html/Installation_Guide/sect-kickstart-syntax.html`—Kickstart is the automated method to install Red Hat-derived operating systems that will be necessary to automate the installation of Red Hat-derived operating systems

Sharing Vagrant boxes

Once a Vagrant box has been built, the next challenge is sharing this Vagrant box with others. When sharing Vagrant boxes, there are a few things to take into account:

▶ Who are you going to be sharing this box with? Is the box meant for public distribution, or is it something that is specific to the needs of a particular development team?

▶ How big is the box? Most public base boxes are rather small, but in the case of boxes created for a development team, the box size can be rather large depending on the amount of software and configuration that was done to the box. Keep in mind that any software installed on the box will also add to the size of the box file itself. For example, creating a development box with an enterprise database installed and configured will be large enough to make *public* hosting options difficult.

▶ Is there any sensitive data, material, or software licenses configured on the box itself?

While an easy option for box hosting is the public Vagrant cloud (there are also paid options to host *private* boxes), large file storage will still have the issues encountered when serving large (multigigabyte) files over HTTP. A general thumb rule is that the longer the process of downloading a box takes, the less likely it is that your development team will be able to update and iterate frequently (a box that downloads to development workstations more quickly will be updated and iterated on more frequently).

This recipe will demonstrate storing and serving a box with a local HTTP server and integrating this hosting solution into a Vagrantfile.

Getting ready

Before we can demonstrate how to serve a Vagrantfile, we'll need to install an HTTP server that can be accessed by all the members of a development team. Keep in mind that the eventual goal is to make possible the quick download of large files (the best option if developers are all co-located would be to set up an HTTP server *internally* that can be accessed over a local LAN). For teams that consist of remote workers or offices, there can be issues with a LAN-based web server; hosting files on external servers, running WAN optimization, or even running mirrors from one location to another can be good options.

For this example, we'll assume that you have set up a web server (it doesn't matter what flavor as long as it can host large files) at an Internet address that can be reached by the intended audience.

How to do it...

1. Have a web server available that can hosts files. Also, keep the Vagrant box handy that you wish to publish.

2. Copy the Vagrant box to the web server. It might be available at a URL such as:

   ```
   http://vagrantboxes.mydomain.com/project/ubuntu_1404.box
   ```

3. With the Vagrant box published to a web server, create a new Vagrantfile to use the HTTP-hosted Vagrant box:

   ```ruby
   # -*- mode: ruby -*-
   # vi: set ft=ruby :

   # Vagrantfile API/syntax version. Don't touch unless you know what
   you're doing!
   VAGRANTFILE_API_VERSION = "2"

   Vagrant.configure(VAGRANTFILE_API_VERSION) do |config|
     config.vm.box = "ubuntu_1404"
     config.vm.box_url = "http://vagrantboxes.mydomain.com/project/
   ubuntu_1404.box"
   end
   ```

   The main addition here is the use of the `config.vm.box_url` parameter to point the Vagrantfile at the hosted box. Additional provisioners can be used like any other Vagrantfile.

4. Start the box with the `vagrant up` command. If the box is not present on the user system, Vagrant will download the box from the specified URL and boot the machine.

How it works...

The Vagrant `config.vm.box_url` directive allows Vagrantfiles to automatically download and manage boxes specified by Vagrantfiles. This allows for ease of sharing boxes and development environments. Rather than specifying a set of instructions to a development team, a single Vagrantfile can be used to specify the entirety of the development environment.

There are other options to host box files that might make download times faster, but HTTP is a protocol that Vagrant understands natively.

Sharing Vagrant boxes with Atlas

Following the release of Vagrant 1.5, HashiCorp introduced a new service to support the publication and sharing of Vagrant boxes either for public or private collaboration. In late 2014, this functionality was folded into HashiCorp's Atlas project (http://atlas.hashicorp.com). In earlier recipes, we used the Atlas repository to discover boxes, whereas now we wish to publish our own boxes to share it with others.

Following the release of Vagrant 1.5, HashiCorp introduced a new service to support the discovery and publication of Vagrant boxes: the Vagrant Cloud (http://vagrantcloud.com). The Vagrant Cloud was introduced to share Vagrant environments in *Chapter 6, Vagrant in the Cloud*. In this recipe, we will create a box file for distribution to a wider audience.

Getting ready

Before we can share boxes using Atlas, there are a few things to keep in mind about how to use your the Atlas account:

- ▶ Hosting (uploading) boxes to Atlas itself will require a paid account. At the time of writing this book, Atlas has opened these function for *free* access during a technical preview period. However, it is likely that Atlas will continue to require payment to host boxes (along with deployed box environments). An Atlas account will cover any fees used to host and transfer data related to the Vagrant box.

- ▶ Atlas continues to support the listing of boxes that are hosted externally. In the previous Vagrant Cloud product, these listings were provided as a free service to the community and most likely will continue to remain freely available for box publishers and users. Using the listing only will require you to find hosting with an external provider with either an existing web host or quite often with storage services such as Amazon Web Services' **Simple Storage Service (S3)** offering. As long as the box can be accessed with a publically available HTTP URL, it can be listed (and versioned) using Atlas.

- ▶ Atlas will also continue to provide private box hosting and collaboration for a fee, likely continuing the previous Vagrant Cloud model of hosting cost being based on the number of collaborators that access a central account.

Atlas will also provide a number of services for not only hosting Vagrant environments, but also for deploying and monitoring application infrastructure. Visit http://atlas.hashicorp.com for more details on Atlas, the technical preview period, and the products and services that Atlas will support.

In this recipe, we will list a box with the Atlas repository, while hosting the box file itself with the relatively inexpensive Amazon S3 service. This example will use the web console (advanced users might wish to investigate using either the Atlas API to publish box files or Packer post-processors in order to simplify the workflow to publish Vagrant boxes as part of a build pipeline).

How to do it...

1. Create a box using an automated tool (such as Packer) or package the box by hand. Copy this box to a publically accessible web server or S3 bucket. For this example, a box has been created and uploaded to Amazon S3. The box is available (on S3) at the public URL:

   ```
   https://s3.amazonaws.com/vagrantcookbook/boxes/
   ubuntu/1410/0_1_0/unicorn_vmware.box
   ```

2. Log in to Atlas (`http://atlas.hashicorp.com`) with your user credentials. (See *Chapter 6, Vagrant in the Cloud* for directions on registering an Atlas account.) Select the **Create a new box** option:

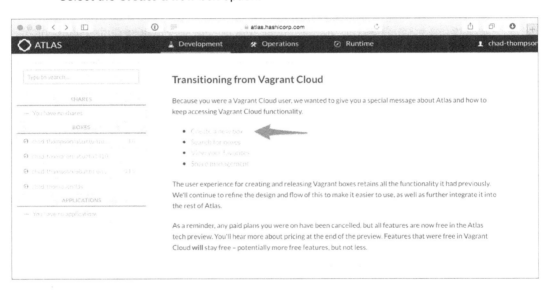

The transitional period of the Atlas launch will likely see some major changes to the interface (make sure to consult the Atlas documentation for updated information on publishing boxes and using the Atlas interface).

3. The box creation screen will require a name for the box (the first part of the name is the name of your Atlas account).

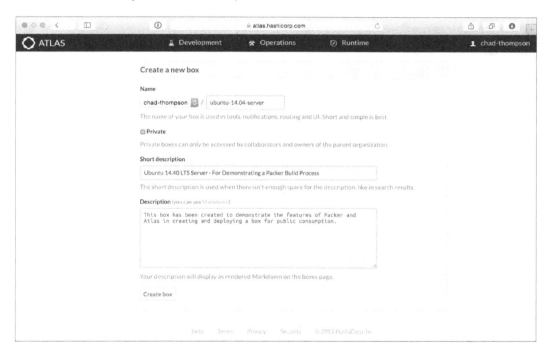

4. Once the box name and description is entered, the next screen will prompt you to choose a version name for the box and a description of the version. Box versions allow you to create updated versions of existing boxes (a good idea if you are publishing this box to support software development and deployment).

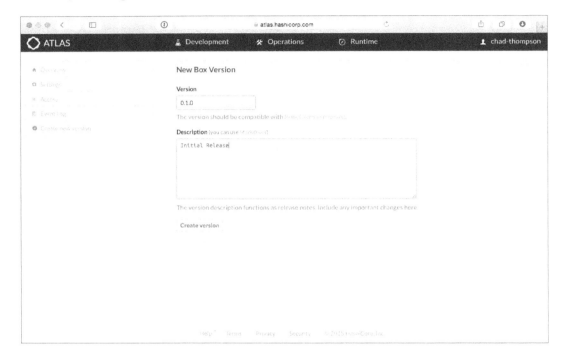

5. After creating a version, the next screen allows you to specify a required provider for the box, which is useful if your build scripts (such as Packer scripts) generate boxes with more than one provider (such as publishing a VirtualBox and a VMware environment with the same set of provisioning scripts):

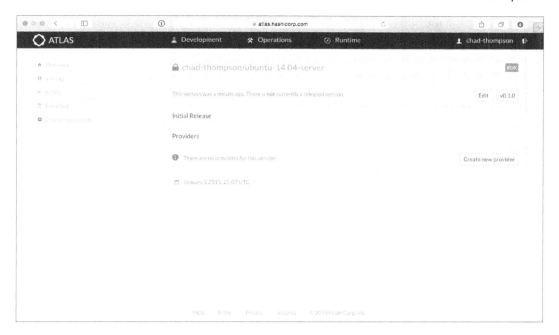

6. Adding a provider will require you to choose the appropriate provider (in this example, `vmware_desktop`) along with either an upload or a URL where the box file can be found. In our example, the box is available through Amazon S3.

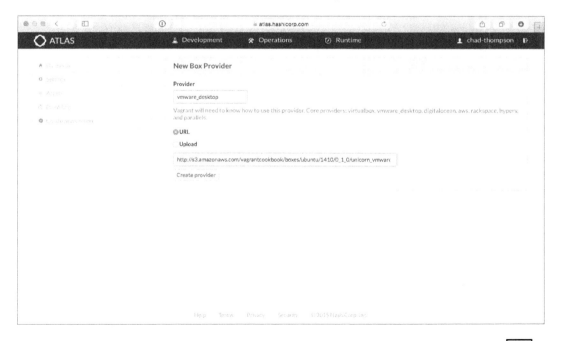

7. Once the providers and URLs have been entered, the next step is to release the box to the public and add it to the Atlas public index by choosing the **Release version** option:

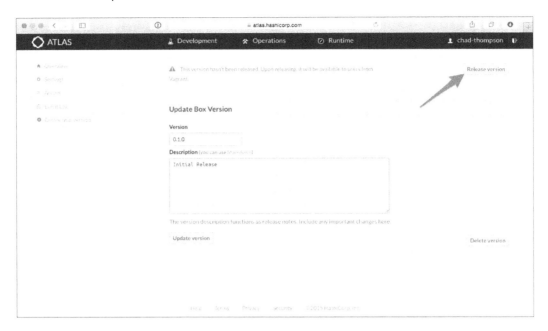

8. Once the box has been released, a new version is added to the timeline (a history) of the public box. This history of versions and updates is available to the public and users can specify these versions in Vagrantfiles.

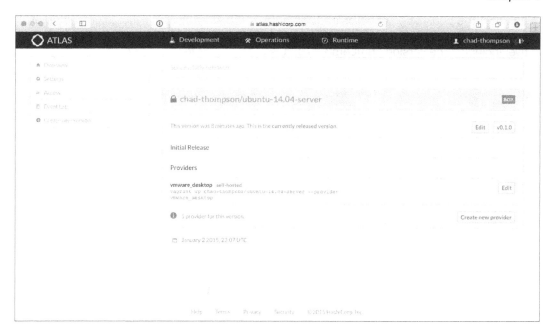

Once the box has been released, it can be discovered in the Atlas repository by users and other developers. Atlas will keep track of statistics as well, which lets popular box files become more prominent in search results and use.

In addition, the publication of boxes adds an entry in the Atlas *overview* that is presented on login, where you can see at a glance the boxes, shares, and applications that the account has active, including the version numbers and status of the boxes in the repository.

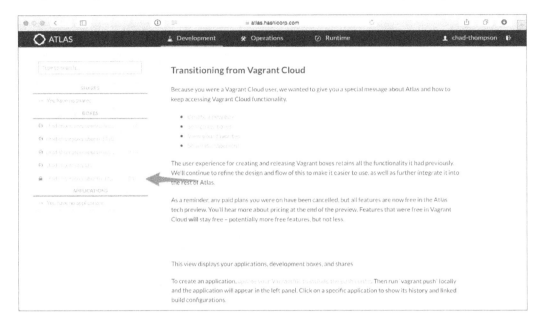

There's more...

If you are building boxes on a regular basis, you might want to make publication to the Atlas part of a build process. For boxes hosted in private accounts on Atlas, Packer (`http://packer.io`) offers a post-processor to publish Vagrant boxes.

 At the time of writing this book, the post-processor for Atlas still uses the name vagrant-cloud. This might be changing in coming months.

Adding the post-processor to a Packer build will automate the process of updating box files and allows development teams to update development environments within Vagrant itself.

See also

- ▶ Vagrant Cloud: `http://vagrantcloud.com`
- ▶ Packer: `http://packer.io`
- ▶ The *Vagrant Cloud Packer Post-Processor*: `https://www.packer.io/docs/post-processors/vagrant-cloud.html`

Vagrant Plugins

Vagrant itself has a highly extensible architecture that can be utilized to provide additional functionality. Vagrant extensions are written using Vagrant's *plugin* framework. Vagrant plugins are typically written to extend Vagrant by:

- ▸ Creating new providers that can execute commands and configure resources within the guest operating systems
- ▸ Adding or modifying resources on guest operating systems
- ▸ Adding or modifying resources on the host operating system

Plugins can also create new commands that can be executed within the Vagrant executable.

Vagrant plugins are written in the language of Vagrant itself: the Ruby programming language. Writing Vagrant plugins utilizes a framework to get started, but will be rather difficult unless you have a basic grasp of the Ruby programming language. This appendix will create and explain a simple example of a custom *provider*, one that allows us to add a new provisioner block to say *hello* to the provisioner. In the end, this block of code can be added to our Vagrantfile:

```
config.vm.provision :hello do |hello|
  hello.inline = 'Chad!'
end
```

This will produce the output on provisioning:

```
==> default: Running provisioner: hello...
[stdout] Hello Chad!!
```

Extending Vagrant in this way can be useful to publish extensions to Vagrant itself. Users might want to take care in creating new plugins rather than using existing provisioners for a few reasons:

- Provisioning operations are typically best done using existing provisioners. Ruby code written to support provisioning operations will not be typically portable in the way that provisioning code written using portable provisioning tools, such as Chef, Puppet, shell scripts, and so on.

- Vagrant plugins require additional complexity for end users to manage. A written Vagrantfile that requires a plugin also requires users to install plugins before the Vagrantfile itself is usable.

- When using Vagrant plugins, one must also take care to use Ruby features that are available in the Ruby runtime provided in Vagrant packages. There are ways of specifying these versions and failing the plugin, but care in compatibility is something that must be kept in mind. Developers should also note that the current versions of Vagrant are no longer distributed as RubyGems, so dependencies between Vagrant and Vagrant plugins (which are distributed as RubyGems) are implicit rather than explicitly defined in Gemfiles.

Setting up a Ruby runtime environment

Getting started to write Vagrant plugins is identical to setting up a Ruby development environment.

Getting ready

It's typically good practice to develop using the target runtime. Vagrant embeds a Ruby runtime in the installed operating system package that can be used to find the proper version of Ruby to use as a development target. You can set up a Ruby environment by performing the following steps:

1. Find the location of the Vagrant installation. On OS X for example, Vagrant is typically installed in `/Applications/Vagrant/`. The Vagrant installation contains a folder named `embedded/` that contains the Ruby runtime used by Vagrant.

2. In a terminal window, execute a version command on the embedded Ruby. To do this, change directories to `/Applications/Vagrant/embedded/bin` and execute:

```
./ruby -version
```

This will return a value of the Ruby runtime. In this case, OS X package, Vagrant 1.6.5) of:

```
2. cothomps@cthompson: /Applications/Vagrant/embedded/bin (zsh)
▶ ./ruby --version
ruby 2.0.0p353 (2013-11-22 revision 43784) [universal.x86_64-darwin12.5.0]

Vagrant/embedded/bin
▶ []
```

3. Set up a development version of Ruby. The simplest method can be to download, install, and configure a package from the Ruby website, but installing a tool such as **rbenv** (`http://rbenv.org`) can make Ruby development and installation of development tools much simpler. There are many ways to install rbenv; on OS X, it can be as simple as using the Homebrew package manager (`http://brew.sh`) to install using the `brew install rbenv` command.

    The companion **ruby-build** project (`https://github.com/sstephenson/ruby-build`) can also be installed using a Homebrew package:

    brew install ruby-build

> There are also other methods of installing rbenv and ruby-build for other platforms. In many recent Linux distributions, rbenv is available in package repositories. For example, installing on a recent version of Ubuntu is as simple as installing with the `apt-get install rbenv` command.
>
> Installing ruby-build in these cases is often recommended as a plugin to rbenv. Consult the documentation on GitHub for rbenv (`https://github.com/sstephenson/rbenv`) and ruby-build (`https://github.com/sstephenson/ruby-build`) for more information.

4. With rbenv/ruby-build installed and configured, we can install the desired version of Ruby with the installation command. In this case, we'll install the version we determined from the Vagrant runtime in an earlier step:

    rbenv install 2.0.0p353

5. With Ruby installed, we can then install the bundler gem that allows us to begin creating our own gems:

    gem install bundler

With these tools installed and a good text editor or Ruby Integrated Development Environment such as JetBrains' **RubyMine** (`https://www.jetbrains.com/ruby/`), we can start developing our own Vagrant plugin.

For this example, we'll develop a very simple plugin (a provisioner) with a single input variable that says "Hello" when the provisioner runs.

How to do it...

Developing a Vagrant plugin is identical to developing a Ruby gem and extending the Vagrant runtime by defining classes in the `VagrantPlugins` module. In practice, it is often useful to start by consulting other plugins to determine how to implement the plugin interfaces. This example relies heavily on the setup done in the `vagrant-aws` plugin (`https://github.com/mitchellh/vagrant-aws`) and the `vagrant-host-shell` plugin (`https://github.com/phinze/vagrant-host-shell`). You might find these two examples useful, but there are also many more plugins (nearly all of them open source) to use in starting a project.

This appendix will rely on code examples included with the book; we will highlight the steps required and a few important aspects of this simple plugin.

1. Create a new project in a working directory with the Ruby bundler tool, which might be the simplest way to start:

   ```
   bundle gem vagrant_hello
   ```

   There is a naming convention that Vagrant plugins typically use where Vagrant plugins start with `vagrant-`, but if you are starting with the bundle, the command bundler often interprets dashes to create folders within projects. When starting with the `gem` command, it might be simpler to create names with an underscore character, then rename them to fit the *dash* naming convention of Vagrant plugins.

   Once the folder structure has been renamed, we should have a file structure that looks like this:

   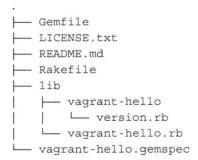

   ```
   .
   ├── Gemfile
   ├── LICENSE.txt
   ├── README.md
   ├── Rakefile
   ├── lib
   │   ├── vagrant-hello
   │   │   └── version.rb
   │   └── vagrant-hello.rb
   └── vagrant-hello.gemspec
   ```

2. With the gem dependencies in place, declare dependencies in our Gemfile and gemspec (`vagrant-hello.gemspec`).

    The Gemfile is fairly simple; we simply declare that we wish to use a gemspec file and we will declare the Vagrant source code as well. This gem is *not* added as a requirement to our plugin gem because we assume that a Vagrant plugin will run within the context of Vagrant itself at runtime. What we will need for development is the code that defines the `VagrantPlugin` module:

```
source 'https://rubygems.org'

# Specify your gem's dependencies in vagrant-hello.gemspec
gemspec

gem "vagrant", :git => "git://github.com/mitchellh/vagrant.git"
```

With the Gemfile written, we can edit the `vagrant-hello.gemspec` to define some information and development dependencies:

```
# coding: utf-8
$:.unshift File.expand_path("../lib", __FILE__)

require 'vagrant-hello/version'

Gem::Specification.new do |spec|
  spec.name           = "vagrant-hello"
  spec.version        = VagrantPlugins::Hello::VERSION
  spec.authors        = ["Chad Thompson"]
  spec.email          = ["chad_thompson@mac.com"]
  spec.summary        = "Say Hello"
  spec.description    = "Say Hello"
  spec.homepage       = ""
  spec.license        = "Apache2"
  spec.add_development_dependency "bundler", "~> 1.7"
  spec.add_development_dependency "rake", "~> 10.0"
end
```

Most of this is gem metadata that describes the gem itself and some information that could be published to a gem repository. We've also declared a few dependencies for development, ensuring that we have the `rake` and `bundle` tasks commands available to our project.

Two items to take note of are as follows:

❑ We require the version file in our `lib` directory named `vagrant-hello/ version`. This corresponds to the `version.rb` file present in this directory.

❑ The *version* itself will be part of the `VagrantPlugins` module.

With these dependency files in place, we can install the dependencies (bundler, rake) as well as the Vagrant source code with the simple command:

bundle install

This will download several Ruby gems as well as download the Vagrant source code from Git to our Ruby runtime.

> We might want to take care that our Vagrant runtime that we normally use is in our executable `PATH` user variable. Verify the version of Vagrant that your system will use with the `which vagrant` command.
>
> If the command returns the *normal* Vagrant, your system will continue to use the installed Vagrant executables. If the system returns a path that includes `.rbenv/shims`, you might wish to modify your executable `PATH` or simply make sure to delete the Vagrant executable in the rbenv environment.

3. Modify the version file to match the structure we declared in the gemspec file in the previous step:

```
module VagrantPlugins
  module Hello
    VERSION = "0.0.1"
  end
end
```

Note that our version file defines the `VERSION` variable to be in the `VagrantPlugins` *parent* module and the `Hello` submodule. This will ensure that our plugin defines an extension within the larger Vagrant plugins module that is part of the Vagrant runtime.

4. Define our "Hello" plugin by creating the `plugin.rb` file in the `lib/` directory. This Ruby file contains a bit of error handling (to ensure that Vagrant is present) and includes our plugin definition:

```
begin
  require 'vagrant'
  rescue LoadError
  raise 'The vagrant-hello plugin must be run within Vagrant.'
end
```

```
module VagrantPlugins::Hello
  class Plugin < Vagrant.plugin('2')
    name 'vagrant-hello'
    description <<-DESC.gsub(/^ +/, '')
      A simple plugin to say hello in the host OS.
    DESC

    config(:hello, :provisioner) do
      require_relative 'config'
      Config
    end

    provisioner(:hello) do
      require_relative 'provisioner'
      Provisioner
    end
  end
end
```

Note here a few items of syntax:

- The definition of the `HelloPlugin` class that inherits from a specific version of Vagrant. This allows future versions of Vagrant to identify and perhaps use your plugin without further modification. This extension guarantees that your plugin will *always* load and not potentially corrupt the operation of future versions of Vagrant.

- Note here the syntax used to call the `config` and `provisioner` methods, each will require a relative file (in this case, `config.rb` and `provisioner.rb`) and call the appropriate functions.

5. Define the configuration in `config.rb`. The config file typically defines how our Vagrantfiles will interact with the plugin. In this case, the `accessor :inline` attribute allows us to create a configuration parameter named `inline` in the provisioner block of our Vagrantfile:

```
module VagrantPlugins::Hello
  class Config < Vagrant.plugin('2', :config)
    attr_accessor :inline

    def initialize
      @inline = UNSET_VALUE
    end

    def finalize!
      @inline = nil if @inline == UNSET_VALUE
    end
```

```
    def validate(machine)
      errors = _detected_errors

      unless inline
        errors << ':hello provisioner requires someone to say
hello to!'
      end

    end
  end
end
```

6. Implement the actions of the provisioner in an additional file named
   `provisioner.rb`:

```
module VagrantPlugins::Hello
  class Provisioner < Vagrant.plugin('2', :provisioner)
    def provision
      result = Vagrant::Util::Subprocess.execute(
          'bash',
          '-c',
          "echo 'Hello #{config.inline}!'",
          :notify => [:stdout, :stderr]
      ) do |io_name, data|
        @machine.env.ui.info "[#{io_name}] #{data}"
      end
    end
  end
end
```

In this example, the provisioner is very basic; a *provision* method will simply execute
a Bash process within the guest that echoes the "Hello string " with the value of
`config.inline` appended to the output.

7. Create a simple Vagrantfile to test our new plugin. In this case, we'll also need to tell
   our Vagrantfile to load the local plugin (gem) file: `vagrant-hello`.

```
# -*- mode: ruby -*-
# vi: set ft=ruby :

$LOAD_PATH.unshift File.expand_path('../../lib', __FILE__)
require 'vagrant-hello'

Vagrant.configure("2") do |config|
  config.vm.box = "puppetlabs/ubuntu-14.04-32-nocm"
```

```
    config.vm.provision :hello do |hello|
      hello.inline = 'Chad!'
    end
  end
```

8. With everything in place, our file structure now looks like this:

```
.
├── Gemfile
├── Gemfile.lock
├── LICENSE.txt
├── README.md
├── Rakefile
├── Vagrantfile
├── lib
│   ├── vagrant-hello
│   │   ├── config.rb
│   │   ├── plugin.rb
│   │   ├── provisioner.rb
│   │   └── version.rb
│   └── vagrant-hello.rb
└── vagrant-hello.gemspec
```

Start this local environment with a slightly different command:

`bundle exec vagrant up -provisioner=virtualbox`

The `bundle exec` command will ensure that our Ruby runtime is defined locally. If you have defined a different default provisioner for Vagrant, you might also wish to define our box provisioner to be the `virtualbox` provisioner that is bundled with Vagrant.

The `vagrant up` command should proceed normally. The output will provision and boot a virtual machine as normal (using a base box), with the final output being that of our custom provisioner:

`==> default: Running provisioner: hello...`

`[stdout] Hello Chad!!`

We have now implemented a simple provisioner that can be built with a *rake* task and distributed as a RubyGem. Publishing the gem to RubyForge allows the following command to install the plugin to your local Vagrant installation:

`vagrant plugin install vagrant-hello`

How it works...

Developing a Vagrant plugin is very similar to developing a typical Ruby gem; if you are not familiar with Gem development, there are a variety of Ruby programming books that can help you get started. The structure of the Vagrant plugins allows you to define a few different types of functions:

- **Provisioners**: In this example, we defined a simple provisioner that executed a Bash script.

- **Guests and guest capabilities**: These functions allow plugin developers to both test for certain guest operating systems and add functions to guests without requiring additional provisioners.

- **Hosts and host capabilities**: These functions allow Vagrant to modify functions of the host operating system within the confines of operating system permissions. Primary examples are plugins that modify the host operating system's `/etc/host` files or DNS entries that allow other system services to refer to Vagrant machines by a defined name in a Vagrantfile.

- **Providers**: Defining providers allows Vagrant to provision and manage virtual environments other than VirtualBox. For example, Vagrant's support for VMware, Amazon Web Services, and DigitalOcean are all custom providers that use the APIs of each of these services.

The plugin framework allows developers to extend the Vagrant runtime that allows for additional capability. However, there is a downside to this feature: using a plugin requires end users to install it prior to executing Vagrantfiles that require the plugin, and code written in plugins can be nonportable if Vagrant is being used to support a full development lifecycle from Vagrant development boxes to production servers. In this specific case (executing a bash command), a simpler and more portable solution would be to use the existing shell provisioner. While there are some cases where plugin extensibility is desired, developing plugins is something that should be carefully considered in the majority of software development cases.

See also

- *The Ruby programming language*: `http://ruby-lang.org`

- *rbenv* (`http://rbenv.org`): a tool to set up Ruby development environments

- *ruby-build* (`https://github.com/sstephenson/ruby-build`): A companion to rbenv to install Ruby versions

- A list of currently available plugins published by the Vagrant project: `https://github.com/mitchellh/vagrant/wiki/Available-Vagrant-Plugins`

A Puppet Development Environment

While we covered the use of Puppet as a provisioning environment in *Chapter 4, Provisioning with Configuration Management Tools*, the use of Vagrant to create a development environment for configuration management is something that is worth covering in a little more depth. While this appendix will cover the use of Vagrant to create Vagrant development environment, many of the same principles apply to other configuration management environments (particularly the configuration management tools that rely on a master/agent architecture).

There are many ways to set up a Puppet development environment. A few common approaches are as follows:

- ▶ The use of a single machine environment and the `puppet apply` provisioner to develop single Puppet modules. This is a common setup to create and test a single module.

- ▶ The use of a multimachine environment to simulate a Puppetmaster or Puppet agent environment. This scenario allows for not only a full *test* of the interaction of agent and master, but also makes setting up a cluster of machines for software testing a bit simpler. (For example, a scenario that allows a developer to set up a multi-tier application or a load-balanced web cluster.)

Using configuration management tools can allow an entire development stack to be created *locally*, either as a development workstation or perhaps within a continuous integration environment. In this appendix, we'll take a deeper look at a few ways to use Vagrant as a Puppet development environment.

Before we can set up a development environment, we'll note the two ways that we can apply puppet manifests to a node:

- **With the puppet apply provisioner**: This allows us to apply a Puppet manifest
- **With the puppet agent provisioner**: This boots a virtual machine and configures a Puppet agent to retrieve a catalog from a remote Puppet server

In this example, we'll look at creating environments using these two techniques.

Setting up a Puppetmaster with the puppet apply provisioner

In the first scenario, we'll take a deeper look at how to set up a Puppetmaster with the *apply* provisioner—using Puppet to manage the Puppetmaster itself. We can start this project in a couple of ways:

- Bootstrap an entire Puppet environment by installing and configuring the Puppet Labs package repositories and installing Puppet
- Using the Vagrant images provided by Puppet Labs and available on the Vagrant Cloud

In this example, we'll start with the Puppet Labs images. These images will have the Puppet agent preinstalled and ready to use. Bootstrapping instances to install Puppet typically involves installation and startup with a shell script that can make a development environment more complicated.

A quick note on using Ubuntu images is that when using Debian-based boxes, it is typically a good idea (if not required) to execute an `apt-get update` command prior to executing package installations. As this often needs to be done prior to bootstrapping a Puppet install, it's often best to do this with an inline shell provisioner.

How to do it...

In this section, we'll discuss how we can set up a source-controlled Puppetmaster and also discuss how it can be bootstrapped. You will also learn how to create Puppet nodes. Let's begin.

Setting up a source controlled Puppetmaster

There are a few ways to start a Puppetmaster project with Vagrant, but I've found that it is often easiest to start with a working (if empty) Puppetmaster configuration and source control from a *new* Puppetmaster installation. To start a project:

1. Create a new Vagrant machine. Start by initializing a box from a box provided by Puppet Labs and is available on the Vagrant Cloud. For this example, we'll use:

    vagrant init puppetlabs/ubuntu-14.04-64-puppet

2. To start, we can add a simple shell provisioner to execute an `apt-get update` command (for Debian-based machines only) and execute the installation of a Puppetmaster:

    ```ruby
    # -*- mode: ruby -*-
    # vi: set ft=ruby :

    # Vagrantfile API/syntax version. Don't touch unless you know what
    you're doing!
    VAGRANTFILE_API_VERSION = "2"

    Vagrant.configure(VAGRANTFILE_API_VERSION) do |config|
    config.vm.box = "puppetlabs/ubuntu-14.04-64-puppet"

      config.vm.define "puppetmaster" do |puppetmaster|
        puppetmaster.vm.hostname = "puppet"
        puppetmaster.vm.provision "shell", inline: "apt-get update &&
    apt-get install -y puppetmaster"
      end
    end
    ```

    This will start a Vagrant box and install the `puppetmaster` package. We'll use this initial package installation to create an initial configuration directory.

3. Start the box with the `vagrant up` command.

4. Once the box has finished booting, copy the `/etc/puppet` directory to the `/vagrant` directory. Access the machine with the `vagrant ssh` command and copy the directory with the `cp /etc/puppet /vagrant` command.

    This will copy the contents of the configuration directory outside the virtual machine to the host machine. Verify that the contents of the working directory look something like this:

    ```
    ├── Vagrantfile
    ├── puppet
    │   ├── environments
    │   │   └── example_env
    │   │       ├── README.environment
    ```

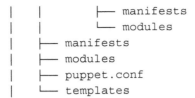

```
|  |          ├── manifests
|  |          └── modules
|  ├── manifests
|  ├── modules
|  ├── puppet.conf
|  └── templates
```

5. With our working directory set, destroy the Vagrant machine with the `vagrant destroy` command. This will leave a clean working directory to begin working.

6. Before starting with our Puppetmaster, let's also allow all certificate exchanges to be *signed* automatically. Create a file in the Puppet root directory (the directory with `puppet.conf`) named `autosign.conf` with a single line:

```
*
```

This allows all certificate requests to be allowed to our local Puppetmaster. This isn't a good idea in a *production* environment, but it will make our development processes a bit simpler.

Bootstrapping a Puppetmaster

Now that we have a working directory, we can start bootstrapping a Puppetmaster. In some cases, a Puppetmaster can be bootstrapped with a shell script, but it's far more fun (and useful!) to manage a Puppetmaster with the Puppet itself.

1. Start with our Vagrantfile in the previous step, but remove the step of installing the Puppetmaster itself:

```ruby
# -*- mode: ruby -*-
# vi: set ft=ruby :

# Vagrantfile API/syntax version. Don't touch unless you know what
you're doing!
VAGRANTFILE_API_VERSION = "2"
Vagrant.configure(VAGRANTFILE_API_VERSION) do |config|
  config.vm.box = "puppetlabs/ubuntu-14.04-64-puppet"
  config.vm.define "puppetmaster" do |puppetmaster|
    puppetmaster.vm.hostname = "puppet"
    puppetmaster.vm.provision "shell", inline: "apt-get update"
  end
end
```

This will start our Puppet machine and update the package repositories for use.

2. Let's start simply by creating a single manifest file to bootstrap our Puppetmaster. In the `manifests/` folder, add a new file named `site.pp`. This file is the manifest file for our Puppetmaster. Define the content of this file to simply output a notification. This will be the start of our iterative approach to develop puppet manifests:

```
node /^puppet/ {
  notify{"Install a Puppetmaster": }
}
```

3. Define a `puppet apply` provisioner in the Vagrantfile. Immediately after the shell provisioner, add the Puppet provisioner block:

```
puppetmaster.vm.provision "puppet"  do |puppet|
  puppet.manifests_path = "puppet/manifests"
  puppet.manifest_file  = "site.pp"
  puppet.module_path    = "puppet/modules"
end
```

This is a basic `puppet apply` provisioner block. It will look to begin catalog compilation with the `site.pp` file and use the `modules/` directory to hold reusable Puppet modules.

4. Start the virtual machine with the `vagrant up` command. The final step in booting the machine should be output from the Puppet provisioner:

```
==> puppetmaster: Notice: Compiled catalog for puppet.localdomain
in environment production in 0.09 seconds
```

```
==> puppetmaster: Notice: Install a Puppetmaster
```

```
==> puppetmaster: Notice: /Stage[main]/Main/Node[puppet]/
Notify[Install a Puppetmaster]/message: defined 'message' as
'Install a Puppetmaster'
```

```
==> puppetmaster: Notice: Finished catalog run in 0.01 seconds
```

Our output notification here notes that the `notify` resource was successfully called by the Puppet provisioner. The Puppet provisioner can be called subsequently with the `vagrant provision` command rather than doing a full restart.

5. With our initial Puppetmaster machine ready to provision, let's create an environment that allows us to modify the configuration of the Puppetmaster (and any Puppet modules) using a local text editor. To do this, we'll link our `puppet/` directory in our host working directory to the `/etc/puppet` configuration directory on the guest. (This was our reason to copy files in our first step.) To write this puppet module, we will have to:

   1. Install the Puppetmaster package.

   2. Connect to the Vagrant machine with the `vagrant ssh` command.

3. Remove the existing `/etc/puppet` directory installed as part of the Puppetmaster package. We will replace the installed directory with the one we created earlier in our Vagrant working directory.

4. Create a symbolic link in the guest from `/vagrant/puppet` to `/etc/puppet`.

5. Restart the Puppetmaster daemon with a `service puppetmaster restart` command. This will read any differences that are present in the symlinked working directory.

If you have done puppet development previously, you might recognize this as a potential use of the package-file-service pattern. We can replace the `notify` command in the `site.pp` file created previously with some Puppet code that reflects the installation of the Puppetmaster. The full `site.pp` manifest looks like this:

```
node /^puppet/ {
  package{"puppetmaster":
    ensure => '3.7.3-1puppetlabs1',
  }

  file{"/etc/puppet":
    ensure  => 'link',
    force   => 'true',
    target  => '/vagrant/puppet',
    require => Package["puppetmaster"],
    notify  => Service["puppetmaster"],
  }

  service{"puppetmaster":
    ensure => running,
    require => Package['puppetmaster'],
  }
}
```

This will install the Puppetmaster, link our Puppetmaster code, and start the Puppetmaster.

6. Execute the manifest by running `vagrant provision puppetmaster`. This will provision and start a Puppetmaster instance in the virtual machine.

7. Verify that the Puppetmaster is running successfully by logging in to the machine (`vagrant ssh puppetmaster`) and running the Puppet agent process. After logging in to the machine, become a *super user* by executing the following command:

sudo puppet agent -t

This will start the Puppet agent. The Puppet agent will attempt to communicate with a Puppetmaster at the default address (*Puppet*) and retrieve a catalog. The Puppet agent should return quickly, as no changes are registered between the run of the Vagrant provisioner and the agent run:

```
Info: Retrieving pluginfacts
Info: Retrieving plugin
Info: Caching catalog for puppet.localdomain
Info: Applying configuration version '1416969518'
Notice: Finished catalog run in 0.09 seconds
```

This Puppetmaster setup can be used to continue developing Puppet code in order to deploy using the masterless or agent approach (both should be usable interchangeably). When developing modules, it is often enough to develop using the masterless approach, but it can also be useful to see how nodes interact in a full master/agent environment.

Provisioning nodes with a Puppetmaster

Vagrant is a powerful tool to create multiple virtual machines. Puppet is an equally powerful tool to manage multiple nodes. Let's create a second node to be provisioned entirely from the Puppetmaster started in the previous section.

1. Define a second node in the Vagrantfile. We'll make sure that this second node can access the Puppetmaster as *Puppet* by adding a fixed IP for the Puppetmaster and creating an /etc/hosts/ entry that allows our new node to access the Puppetmaster at the default address of *Puppet*. A complete Vagrantfile with both nodes looks like this:

```
# -*- mode: ruby -*-
# vi: set ft=ruby :
# Vagrantfile API/syntax version. Don't touch unless you know what
you're doing!
VAGRANTFILE_API_VERSION = "2"
$puppetmaster_ip = "192.168.30.134"

Vagrant.configure(VAGRANTFILE_API_VERSION) do |config|
config.vm.box = "puppetlabs/ubuntu-14.04-64-puppet"
  config.vm.define "puppetmaster" do |puppetmaster|
    puppetmaster.vm.hostname = "puppet"
    puppetmaster.vm.network "private_network", ip: $puppetmaster_
ip
    puppetmaster.vm.provision "shell" , inline: "apt-get update"
    puppetmaster.vm.provision "puppet"  do |puppet|
      puppet.manifests_path = "puppet/manifests"
```

```
          puppet.manifest_file   = "site.pp"
          puppet.module_path     = "puppet/modules"
      end
    end
    config.vm.define "web01" do |web|
      web.vm.hostname = "web01"
      web.vm.provision "shell", inline: "apt-get update"
      web.vm.provision "shell", inline: "echo '#{$puppetmaster_ip}
puppet puppet.localdomain' >> /etc/hosts"
    end
end
```

This defines our second node as `web01`.

2. Start the node with the `vagrant up web01` command.

3. SSH into the `web01` node with the `vagrant ssh web01` command.

4. In the `web01` node, start the Puppet agent with the `sudo puppet agent -t` command. This will start the Puppet agent and quickly return an error as our Puppetmaster has not yet been configured to compile a catalog for web nodes.

5. Define a *web* node by editing the `puppet/manifests/site.pp` file (the Puppetmaster manifest file) in our working directory. We'll make this simple for now: simply install the Apache web server package. In this case, being *Ubuntu only* for now. The additional node looks like this:

```
node /^web/ {
  package{"apache2": ensure => installed, }
}
```

6. Configure the Vagrant Puppet agent provisioner in the Vagrantfile. Add a provisioning block to the `web01` machine definition:

```
      web.vm.provision "puppet_server" do |puppet|
        puppet.puppet_server = "puppet"
      end
```

This will start the Puppet agent using the machine name `puppet` to retrieve a catalog. It would also be possible to use the IP address of the Puppetmaster itself, but having the definition of the IP address in the `/etc/hosts` file allows the Puppet agent to run independently of Vagrant provisioners if desired.

7. Run the Puppet server provisioner with the `vagrant provision web01` command. This will produce provisioner output that ends in a notification that the Puppet agent is running:

```
==> web01: Running provisioner: puppet_server...
==> web01: Running Puppet agent...
```

 If you encounter issues related to *waitforcert* errors, be sure to verify that the Puppetmaster is configured to *autosign* certificates. While this might not be desirable in a real production environment, autosigning certificates can make development simpler. See `https://docs.puppetlabs.com/puppet/latest/reference/ssl_autosign.html` for more information on SSL and certificate verification options with Puppetmasters.

8. Log in to the web server (`vagrant ssh web01`) and verify that the `apache2` package has been installed:

```
vagrant@web01:~$ which apache2
/usr/sbin/apache2
```

The results of the Puppet run can also be verified through report creation on the node at `/var/lib/puppet/state/last_run_report.yaml` or any configured reporting on the Puppetmaster.

Now, we have a working node connecting to the Puppetmaster and retrieving catalogs. We can continue developing our manifests by adding more resources to our manifest, or by adding modules to the `puppet/modules` directory, and calling the appropriate classes in our manifest.

Using Vagrant as a development environment for either individual modules or entire infrastructures can take any one of a number of methods. This example is simply one configuration that can be used to develop and test a puppet infrastructure.

There's more...

There is another important use case to use Vagrant in conjunction with Puppet development: the use of Vagrant as part of an acceptance testing framework. Puppet Labs recently released an open source framework called **Beaker** (`https://github.com/puppetlabs/beaker/wiki`) to test puppet modules against a variety of operating systems. Beaker uses a number of *hosts* files to define virtual machines (or virtual environments) in order to test Puppet modules.

A quick way to get started with writing modules with Beaker tests is to install Gareth Rushgrove's **puppet-module-skeleton** project available at `https://github.com/garethr/puppet-module-skeleton`. The skeleton will extend the functionality of the `puppet module` command, generating stub files for configuration as well as a number of test files using `puppet-rspec` and `beaker` as test frameworks. Once the framework is installed, generating a module will also generate a few stub *hosts* files for Beaker. For example, the hosts file generated to test against a CentOS Vagrant box:

```
HOSTS:
  centos-64-x64:
    roles:
      - master
    platform: el-6-x86_64
    box : centos-64-x64-vbox4210-nocm
    box_url : http://puppet-vagrant-boxes.puppetlabs.com/centos-64-
x64-vbox4210-nocm.box
    hypervisor : vagrant
CONFIG:
  log_level: verbose
  type: foss
```

With these files in place (and proper role definition, and so on), the test framework will start Vagrant machines (or multiple Vagrant machines, depending on the number of test cases) by using the `rake acceptance` build command.

Beaker is an example of using Vagrant not only as a development tool within a single virtual environment, but also as a tool to test a Puppet module across several virtual environments and operating systems.

See also

- *Puppet*: `http://puppetlabs.com` (the homepage of Puppet Labs and the Puppet configuration tool)

- *Puppet Labs Documentation*: `http://docs.puppetlabs.com`

- *Beaker*: `https://github.com/puppetlabs/beaker`

- The *puppet-module-skeleton* project: `https://github.com/garethr/puppet-module-skeleton`

C

Using Docker with Vagrant

In this chapter, we will cover the following topics:

- ▶ Running Docker containers with Vagrant
- ▶ Mixed environments – the Docker provisioner

Introduction

The recipes in this book are focused mainly on the management and configuration of *virtual machines* (runtime environments that mimic the operation of entire operating systems). In actual use and operation of a virtual machine, however, there are typically only a few processes running in the machine that are of importance to development and deployment. For example, the deployment of web applications often requires the deployment of a web server (and perhaps some middleware applications), but a virtual machine with a full operating system will also run several processes required to manage the entire operating system of the virtual machine itself. As such, large deployments of virtual machines to service software applications can become more inefficient as computational resources are used for virtual environment operating systems rather than the computational needs of web applications.

While these problems are an issue for hypervisor applications, there have been other attempts to virtualize environments that do not require hypervisors. In fact, the isolation of processes into separate runtime environments and operating systems have been how most multiuser environments have operated since the beginning of the shared environment (from mainframe process isolation to technologies, such as **Solaris Zones** and **BSD chroot jails**). The Linux project (as of version 2.6.24 of the Linux kernel) introduced a similar technology called **Linux Containers** (**LXC**) to run separate processes in isolation from others without requiring hypervisor applications and separate operating systems.

An open source project was started by **dotCloud** (a cloud hosting company) to help manage the complexity of dealing with containers into simple build and deployment processes. This project was named **Docker** and has now grown to become the focus and the name of the company itself. Docker is focused on the use of containers on the Linux operating system. A single host operating system can host containers running software from databases to web servers, and even entirely different Linux distributions.

While there are other methods to manage Linux Containers, Docker has been integrated into a large number of vendor offerings that allows developers many choices to deploy applications packaged as Docker containers. In this appendix, we'll take a look at how Vagrant can integrate with Docker development workflows.

Running Docker containers with Vagrant

The first thing we'll investigate is how to run and develop simple Docker containers using Vagrant. In recent versions, Vagrant ships with a Docker *provider* that allows Vagrant users a simple environment to start and run containers.

Before we can start, however, we need to note that Docker builds on top of Linux containers. As such, a Docker container only runs on Linux operating systems. There are two main approaches to run Docker containers on development workstations:

> ▶ **Developing Docker containers natively on a Linux platform**: This is the approach used in a number of development books and guides, including *The Docker Book* by James Turnbull. Developing with Linux requires either a native Linux installation or perhaps a Linux desktop virtual machine, such as a Linux distribution running on a VMware virtual machine.
>
> ▶ **Developing Docker containers using the boot2docker environment** (http:// boot2docker.io). boot2docker is a Linux VM designed to host Docker containers on OS X or Windows operating systems. boot2docker has a package installer that will guide users in the use of the environment.

 We'll take some care to note that there are two projects that we refer to in this appendix. One is the official **boot2docker** project (http://boot2docker. io), and the other is Mitchell Hashimoto's **boot2docker-vagrant-box** (https://github.com/mitchellh/boot2docker-vagrant-box). These environments are only necessary to use Docker on a Windows or OS X machine. As Docker is built on top of Linux Containers, Docker will run natively on Linux desktop or server machines.

The Vagrant Docker provider can support either one of these approaches: managing containers natively on Linux or managing containers through the boot2docker environment. Vagrant can even manage the installation and operation of the boot2docker environment on Windows and OS X, which can make it simpler for users to get started.

This appendix will focus on using Vagrant on OS X (with the aid of the Docker provider) to create a simple Docker development environment. In particular, we'll launch a MySQL database that uses a container provided by the MySQL project, and use a simple Dockerfile to package a simple web application.

How to do it...

In this section, we'll learn how to install a Docker image from a repository and build a Docker image with Vagrant.

Installing a Docker image from a repository

We'll start with a simple case: installing a Docker container from a repository (a MySQL container) and connecting it to an external tool for development (the MySQL Workbench or a client tool of your choice). We'll need to initialize the boot2docker environment and use some Vagrant tools to interact with the environment and the deployed containers.

Before we can start, we'll need to find a suitable Docker image to launch. One of the unique advantages to use Docker as a development environment is its ability to select a *base* Docker image, then add successive build steps on top of the base image. In this simple example, we can find a base MySQL image on the Docker Hub registry (`https://registry.hub.docker.com`). The MySQL project provides an official Docker image that we can build from.

We'll note from the repository the command to use the image: `docker pull mysqlmysql` and note that the image name is `mysql`.

1. Start with a Vagrantfile that defines the Docker:

```ruby
# -*- mode: ruby -*-
# vi: set ft=ruby :

VAGRANTFILE_API_VERSION = "2"
  ENV['VAGRANT_DEFAULT_PROVIDER'] = 'vmware_fusion'
  Vagrant.configure(VAGRANTFILE_API_VERSION) do |config|
  config.vm.define"database" do |db|
    db.vm.provider"docker"do |d|
      d.image="mysql"
    end
  end
end
```

An important thing to note immediately is that when we define the database machine and the provider with the Docker provider, we do not specify a *box* file. The Docker provider will start and launch containers into a boot2docker environment, negating the need for a Vagrant box or virtual machine definition. This will introduce a bit of a complication in interacting with the Vagrant environment in later steps.

Also note the `mysql` image name taken from the Docker Hub registry.

2. We'll need to launch the image with a few basic parameters. Add the following code to the Docker provider block:

```ruby
db.vm.provider "docker" do |d|
  d.image="mysql"
  d.env = {
    :MYSQL_ROOT_PASSWORD => ""root",
    :MYSQL_DATABASE      => ""dockertest",
    :MYSQL_USER          => ""dockertest",
    :MYSQL_PASSWORD      => ""d0cker"
  }
  d.ports =["3306:3306"]
  d.remains_running = "true"
end
```

The environment variables (`d.env`) are taken from the documentation on the MySQL Docker image page (`https://registry.hub.docker.com/_/mysql/`). This is how the image expects to set certain parameters. In this case, our parameters will set the database root password (for the `root` user) and create a database with a new user that has full permissions to this database.

The d.ports parameter is an array of port listings that will be forwarded from the container (the default MySQL port of 3306) to the host operating system, in this case also 3306. The contained application will, thus, behave like a natively installed MySQL installation.

 The port forwarding here is from the container to the operating system that hosts the container (in this case, the container host is our boot2docker image). If we are developing and hosting containers natively with Vagrant on a Linux distribution, the port forwarding will be to localhost, but boot2docker introduces something of a wrinkle in doing Docker development on Windows or OS X. We'll either need to refer to our software installation by the IP of the boot2docker container or configure a second port forwarding configuration that allows a Docker contained application to be available to the host operating system as localhost.

The final parameter (d.remains_running = true) is a flag for Vagrant to note that the Vagrant run should mark as *failed* if the Docker container exits on start. In the case of software that runs as a daemon process (such as the MySQL database), a Docker container that exits immediately is an error condition.

3. Start the container using the vagrant up -provider=docker command. A few things will happen here:

   ❑ If this is the first time you have started the project, you'll see some messages about booting a box named mitchellh/boot2docker. This is a Vagrant-packaged version of the boot2docker project. Once the machine boots, it becomes a host for all Docker containers managed with Vagrant.

 Keep in mind that boot2doocker is necessary only for nonLinux operating systems that are running Docker through a virtual machine. On a Linux system running Docker natively, you will not see information about boot2docker.

❑ After the container is booted (or if it is already running), Vagrant will display notifications about rsyncing a folder (if we are using boot2docker) and launching the image:

```
2. cothomps@cthompson: ~/vagrantbook/vagrantbook-examples/AppendixIII/A3.1 Docker Provider MySQL (zsh)
▶ vagrant up --provider=docker
Bringing machine 'database' up with 'docker' provider...
==> database: Docker host is required. One will be created if necessary...
    database: Docker host VM is already ready.
==> database: Syncing folders to the host VM...
    database: Rsyncing folder: /Volumes/WD HDD/vagrantbook/vagrantbook-examples/AppendixI
II/A3.1 Docker Provider MySQL/ => /var/lib/docker/docker_1420769020_20836
==> database: Warning! When using a remote Docker host, forwarded ports will NOT be
==> database: immediately available on your machine. They will still be forwarded on
==> database: the remote machine, however, so if you have a way to access the remote
==> database: machine, then you should be able to access those ports there. This is
==> database: not an error, it is only an informational message.
==> database: Creating the container...
    database:    Name: A31DockerProviderMySQL_database_1420769021
    database:   Image: mysql
    database:  Volume: /var/lib/docker/docker_1420769020_20836:/vagrant
    database:    Port: 3306:3306
    database:
    database: Container created: dc6625e43663f386
==> database: Starting container...
==> database: Provisioners will not be run since container doesn't support SSH.

vagrantbook-examples/AppendixIII/A3.1 Docker Provider MySQL   master X        54d ✖ ⁂ ◗
▶ ▯
```

Docker generates unique identifiers for containers and notes any port mapping information.

4. Let's take a look at some details on the containers that are running in the Docker host. We'll need to find a way to gain access to the Vagrant boot2docker image (and only if we are using boot2docker and not a native Linux environment), which is not quite as straightforward as a vagrant `ssh`; we'll need to identify the Vagrant container to access.

First, identify the Docker Vagrant machine from the *global* Vagrant status. Vagrant keeps track of running instances that can be accessed from Vagrant itself. In this case, we are only interested in the Vagrant instance named `docker-host`. The instance we're interested in can be found with the `vagrant global-status` command:

```
2. cothomps@cthompson: ~/vagrantbook/vagrantbook-examples/AppendixIII/A3.1 Docker Provider MySQL (zsh)
▶ vagrant global-status | grep docker-host
d381331   default         vmware_fusion running      /Users/cothomps/.vagrant.d/data/docker
-host

vagrantbook-examples/AppendixIII/A3.1 Docker Provider MySQL   master ✗        54d ✖ ▶ ◒
▶ ▮
```

In this case, Vagrant identifies the instance as `d381331` (a unique value for every Vagrant machine launched). We can access this instance with a `vagrant ssh` command:

vagrant ssh d381331

This will display an ASCII-art *boot2docker* logo and a command prompt for the boot2docker instance. Let's take a look at the Docker containers running on the system with the `docker psps` command:

```
2. vagrant ssh d381331 (bash)
docker@boot2docker:~$ docker ps
CONTAINER ID        IMAGE            COMMAND             CREATED         STATUS
                    PORTS            NAMES
dc6625e43663        mysql:latest      "/entrypoint.sh mysq  5 minutes ago     Up 5 m
inutes              0.0.0.0:3306->3306/tcp   A31DockerProviderMySQL_database_1420769021
docker@boot2docker:~$ ▯
```

The `docker psps` command will provide information about the running Docker containers on the system; in this case, the unique ID of the container (output during the Vagrant startup) and other information about the container.

5. Find the IP address of boot2docker (only if we're using boot2docker) to connect to the MySQL instance. In this case, execute the `ifconfig` command:

docker@boot2docker:~$ ifconfig

This will output information about the network interfaces on the machine; we are interested in the eth0 entry. In particular, we can note the IP address of the machine on the eth0 interface:

```
● ○ ●                    2. vagrant ssh d381331 (bash)

eth0      Link encap:Ethernet  HWaddr 00:0C:29:4C:16:4F
          inet addr:192.168.30.129  Bcast:192.168.30.255  Mask:255.255.255.0
          inet6 addr: fe80::20c:29ff:fe4c:164f/64 Scope:Link
          UP BROADCAST RUNNING MULTICAST  MTU:1500  Metric:1
          RX packets:3541 errors:0 dropped:0 overruns:0 frame:0
          TX packets:2039 errors:0 dropped:0 overruns:0 carrier:0
          collisions:0 txqueuelen:1000
          RX bytes:633094 (618.2 KiB)  TX bytes:305605 (298.4 KiB)
```

Make a note of the IP address noted as the inet addraddr; in this case, 192.168.30.129.

6. Connect a MySQL client to the running Docker container. In this case, we'll need to note some information to the connection:

   ❑ The IP address of the boot2docker virtual machine (if using boot2docker). In this case, we'll note 192.168.30.129.

   ❑ The port that the MySQL instance will respond to on the Docker host. In this case, the Docker container is forwarding port 3306 in the container to port 3306 on the host.

   ❑ Information noted in the Vagrantfile for the username or password on the MySQL instance.

   With this information in hand, we can configure a MySQL client. The MySQL project provides a supported GUI client named *MySQL Workbench* (http://www.mysql.com/products/workbench/). With the client installed on our host operating system, we can create a new connection in the Workbench client (consult the documentation for your version of Workbench, or use a MySQL client of your choice).

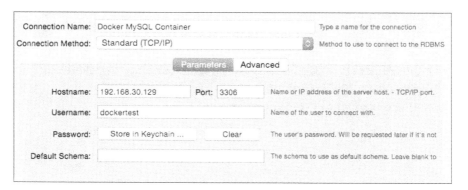

In this case, we're connecting to the boot2docker instance. If you are running Docker natively on a Linux instance, the connection should simply forward to localhost. If the connection is successful, the Workbench client once connected will display an empty database:

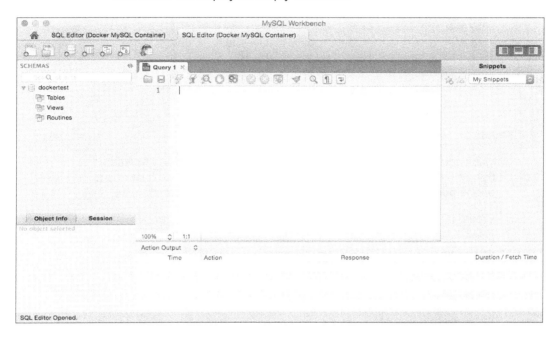

Once we've connected, we can use the MySQL database as we would for any other MySQL instance that is hosted this time in a Docker container without having to install and configure the MySQL package itself.

Building a Docker image with Vagrant

While launching packaged Docker, applications can be useful (particularly in the case where launching a Docker container is simpler than native installation steps), Vagrant becomes even more useful when used to launch containers that are being developed. On OS X and Windows machines, the use of Vagrant can make managing the container deployment somewhat simpler through the boot2docker containers, while on Linux, using the native Docker tools could be somewhat simpler. In this example, we'll use a simple Dockerfile to modify a base image.

1. First, start with a simple Vagrantfile. In this case, we'll specify a build directory rather than a image file:

    ```ruby
    # -*- mode: ruby -*-
    # vi: set ft=ruby :
    ```

```
# Vagrantfile API/syntax version. Don't touch unless you know what
you're doing!
VAGRANTFILE_API_VERSION = "2"
ENV['VAGRANT_DEFAULT_PROVIDER'] = 'vmware_fusion'

Vagrant.configure(VAGRANTFILE_API_VERSION) do |config|
  config.vm.define "nginx" do |nginx|
    nginx.vm.provider "docker" do |d|
      d.build_dir = "build"
      d.ports = ["49153:80"]
    end
  end
end
```

This Vagrantfile specifies a build directory as well as the ports forwarded to the host from the container. In this case, the standard HTTP port (80) forwards to port 49153 on the host machine, which in this case is the boot2docker instance.

2. Create our build directory in the same directory as the Vagrantfile.

3. In the build directory, create a Dockerfile. A Dockerfile is a set of instructions on how to build a Docker container. See `https://docs.docker.com/reference/builder/` or James Turnbull's *The Docker Book* for more information on how to construct a Dockerfile. In this example, we'll use a simple Dockerfile to copy a working HTML directory to a base NGINX image:

```
FROM nginx
COPY content /usr/share/nginx/html
```

4. Create a directory in our build directory named content. In the directory, place a simple `index.html` file that will be served from the new container:

```
<html>
  <body>
    <div style="text-align:center;padding-top:40px;border:dashed
2px;">
      This is an NGINX build.
    </div>
  </body>
</html>
```

Once all the pieces are in place, our working directory will have the following structure:

```
.
├── Vagrantfile
└── build
├── Dockerfile
    └── content
        └── index.html
```

5. Start the container in the working directory with the command:

   ```
   vagrant up nginx --provider=docker
   ```

   This will start the container build and deploy process.

6. Once the container is launched, the web server can be accessed using the IP address of the boot2docker instance (see the previous section for more information on obtaining this address) and the forwarded port.

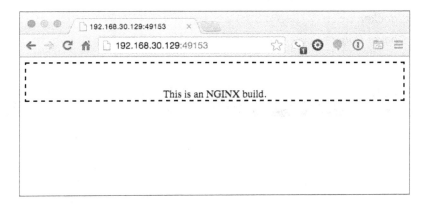

One other item to note, especially, if you have completed both steps in this section without halting or destroying the Vagrant project is that when using the Docker provider, containers are deployed to a single shared virtual machine. If the boot2docker instance is accessed and the `docker ps` command is executed, it can be noted that two separate Vagrant projects deploy containers to a single host.

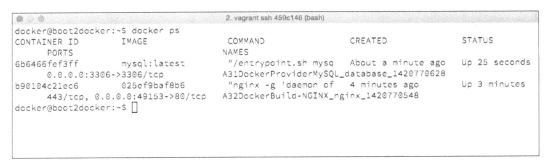

When using the Docker provider, the single instance has a few effects:

► The single virtual machine can use fewer resources on your development workstation

► Deploying and rebuilding containers is a process that is *much* faster than booting and shutting down entire operating systems

Docker development with the Docker provider can be a useful technique to create and test Docker containers, although Vagrant might not be of particular help in packaging and distributing Docker containers. If you wish to publish containers, consult the documentation or *The Docker Book* on getting started with packaging and distributing Docker containers.

See also

▸ *Docker*: http://docker.io

▸ *boot2docker*: http://boot2docker.io

▸ *The Docker Book*: http://www.dockerbook.com

▸ The Docker repository: https://registry.hub.docker.com

Mixed environments – the Docker provisioner

In addition to the Docker *provider*, Vagrant can help manage Docker containers and mixed environments using the Docker *provisioner*. The Docker provisioner can be used to build a virtual machine that hosts Docker containers, or perhaps a host that is provisioned with software with maybe one or two services managed by Docker containers. (For example, a virtual machine can be configured with a database or middleware installation managed in Docker containers, while the machine itself is configured to run a web application *natively*.)

The Docker provisioner will also manage the Docker runtime, which installs Docker on the virtual machine if necessary. In this example, we'll take a look at installing a MySQL database (using the Docker provisioner) and the MySQL image published on Docker Hub.

How to do it...

1. Start with a simple Vagrantfile. This Vagrantfile defines a box (in this case, an Ubuntu image) and a Docker provisioner block:

```
# -*- mode: ruby -*-
# vi: set ft=ruby :
VAGRANTFILE_API_VERSION = "2"

Vagrant.configure(VAGRANTFILE_API_VERSION) do |config|
  config.vm.box = "puppetlabs/ubuntu-14.04-64-nocm"
        config.vm.provision "shell", inline:"apt-get install -y
mysql-client"

  config.vm.provision "docker" do |d|
    d.pull_images "library/mysql"
```

```
    d.run 'library/mysql',
          args: '-e MYSQL_ROOT_PASSWORD=password -p 3306:3306'
  end
end
```

This Vagrantfile also defines the Docker provisioner block. In this case, the block specifies the image to be pulled as well as a run command that will be executed on system startup.

The image being pulled is the `mysql` image from the Docker Hub repository, the `run` command is similar to using Docker's command-line tools. In this case, the `run` command specifies an environment variable (`MYSQL_ROOT_PASSWORD`) and defines a port mapping from the container to the host.

2. Start the Vagrant machine with a `vagrant up` command. When the Docker provisioner starts, the provisioner will install the latest version of the Docker runtime and start containers listed with the Docker `run` command.

3. Verify that the Docker command works by accessing the virtual machine with the `vagrant ssh` command and executing `docker ps`. The process listing will show a running MySQL container:

```
vagrant@localhost:~$ docker ps
CONTAINER ID        IMAGE                   COMMAND              CREATED
STATUS              PORTS                   NAMES
1617686d9a9e        library/mysql:latest    "/entrypoint.sh mysq  About a minute ago
Up About a minute   0.0.0.0:3306->3306/tcp  library-mysql
vagrant@localhost:~$ []
```

While we have an open terminal, obtain the IP address of the virtual machine (if this is not a fixed IP machine) with the `ipconfig` command.

4. From the host operating system, access the MySQL database with the `mysql client` command line, making sure that you have a `mysql` client installed on your host operating system:

```
vagrant@localhost:~$ docker ps
CONTAINER ID        IMAGE                   COMMAND              CREATED
STATUS              PORTS                   NAMES
1617686d9a9e        library/mysql:latest    "/entrypoint.sh mysq  About a minute ago
Up About a minute   0.0.0.0:3306->3306/tcp  library-mysql
vagrant@localhost:~$ []
```

This is a simple example of using the Docker provisioner to install and start software services. The provisioner is designed in a way that allows Vagrant users to bootstrap an entire Vagrant environment that can support Docker and other services effectively, mimicking how a Docker host machine will operate. The provisioner also isolates Docker containers in the virtual machine itself as the provider does not rely on shared services or boot2docker to operate. As such, the use of the Docker provisioner is useful when simulating an entire software stack, where the Docker provider is focused on the container development and interaction.

See also

  ▸ The *Vagrant Docker Provisioner*: `https://docs.vagrantup.com/v2/provisioning/docker.html`

  ▸ The MySQL Docker container distribution: `https://registry.hub.docker.com/_/mysql/`

Index

Thank you for buying
Vagrant Virtual Development Environment Cookbook

About Packt Publishing

Packt, pronounced 'packed', published its first book, *Mastering phpMyAdmin for Effective MySQL Management*, in April 2004, and subsequently continued to specialize in publishing highly focused books on specific technologies and solutions.

Our books and publications share the experiences of your fellow IT professionals in adapting and customizing today's systems, applications, and frameworks. Our solution-based books give you the knowledge and power to customize the software and technologies you're using to get the job done. Packt books are more specific and less general than the IT books you have seen in the past. Our unique business model allows us to bring you more focused information, giving you more of what you need to know, and less of what you don't.

Packt is a modern yet unique publishing company that focuses on producing quality, cutting-edge books for communities of developers, administrators, and newbies alike. For more information, please visit our website at www.packtpub.com.

About Packt Open Source

In 2010, Packt launched two new brands, Packt Open Source and Packt Enterprise, in order to continue its focus on specialization. This book is part of the Packt open source brand, home to books published on software built around open source licenses, and offering information to anybody from advanced developers to budding web designers. The Open Source brand also runs Packt's open source Royalty Scheme, by which Packt gives a royalty to each open source project about whose software a book is sold.

Writing for Packt

We welcome all inquiries from people who are interested in authoring. Book proposals should be sent to author@packtpub.com. If your book idea is still at an early stage and you would like to discuss it first before writing a formal book proposal, then please contact us; one of our commissioning editors will get in touch with you.

We're not just looking for published authors; if you have strong technical skills but no writing experience, our experienced editors can help you develop a writing career, or simply get some additional reward for your expertise.

Mastering Puppet

ISBN: 978-1-78398-218-9   Paperback: 280 pages

Pull the strings of Puppet to configure enterprise-grade environments for performance optimization

1. Implement puppet in a medium to large installation.

2. Deal with issues found in larger deployments, such as scaling, and improving performance.

3. Step by step tutorial to utilize Puppet efficiently to have a fully functioning Puppet infrastructure in an enterprise- level environment.

Managing Windows Servers with Chef

ISBN: 978-1-78398-242-4   Paperback: 110 pages

Harness the power of Chef to automate management of Windows-based systems using hands-on examples

1. Discover how Chef can be used to manage a heterogeneous network of Windows and Linux systems with ease.

2. Configure an entire .NET application stack, deploy it, and scale in the cloud.

3. Employ a step-by-step and practical approach to automate provisioning and configuration of Windows hosts with Chef.

Please check **www.PacktPub.com** for information on our titles

www.ingramcontent.com/pod-product-compliance
Lightning Source LLC
Chambersburg PA
CBHW060542060326
40690CB00017B/3572